SWEET SEASONS

♦ ALSO BY HOWARD SINER ♦

Sports Classics: American Writers Choose Their Best

BASEBALL'S TOP TEAMS

Sweet Seasons

SINCE 1920

HOWARD SINER

With an introduction by
STAN MUSIAL

PHAROS BOOKS
A SCRIPPS HOWARD COMPANY
NEW YORK

The play-by-play commentary in *Sweet Seasons* is reprinted with the expressed permission of the office of the Commissioner of Baseball. Grateful acknowledgment is also made to NBC.

Cover photos: TOP LEFT 1927 New York Yankees; TOP RIGHT 1975 Cincinnati Reds; BOTTOM LEFT 1986 New York Mets; BOTTOM RIGHT 1942 St. Louis Cardinals.

Pharos Books are available at special discounts on bulk purchases for sales promotions, premiums, fundraising or educational use. For details, contact the Special Sales Department, Pharos Books, 200 Park Avenue, New York, NY 10166.

Cover and text design: Nancy Eato

First published in 1988.

Library of Congress Cataloging-in-Publication Data

Siner, Howard.
Sweet seasons.

Includes index.
1. Baseball—United States—Clubs—History.
I. Title.
GV875.A1S56 1988 796.357'64'0973 87-50914

Pharos Books ISBN: 0-88687-332-0
Ballantine Books ISBN: 0-345-35229-7

Printed in the United States of America

Pharos Books
A Scripps Howard Company
200 Park Avenue
New York, NY 10166

10 9 8 7 6 5 4 3 2 1

This Book Is For My Mother

Acknowledgments

First of all, I want to thank David Hendin, the publisher of Pharos Books. His judgment, direction and support were essential.

Hana Umlauf Lane, the editor-in-chief of Pharos, managed the production of *Sweet Seasons* with professionalism and remarkable patience. My thanks go to her and to Tom Aylesworth for their editorial contributions.

Thanks also to Associate Publisher Phyllis Henrici and the entire staff of Pharos Books for everything they contributed to the process.

Diana Drake, Gail Robinson and others at United Media endorsed or encouraged my work. To each of them, I want to express my thanks.

Librarian Tom Heitz and his staff at the Baseball Hall of Fame made vital contributions to the research on *Sweet Seasons.* Key fact-finding assistance was also provided by the news department of Major League Baseball; and by several of the individual teams, especially the New York Yankees.

David Szen of *Yankees Magazine* was particularly helpful.

I also want to thank Marty Hendin of the St. Louis Cardinals. And, of course, thanks to Stan Musial of the Cards for introducing *Sweet Seasons*.

For a variety of reasons, professional or personal, my thanks also go to: Nat Andriani, Brad Bushell, Jane Cassidy, Charles Castillo, Nancy Eato, Richie Filosa, June Foley, Sid Goldberg, John Grabowski, Bill Guilfoile, Mark Hoffman, Heide Lange, Kevin McDonough, Tom McGuire, Susan Reinhard, Gerald Taylor, Tom Tiede, Wendy Wallace, Brad Warner and George Worley.

More personally, I thank Gordon Haight.

Also, Judy Randall.

Finally, I want to thank my two brothers. And my father, who taught us his love of baseball.

H.S.

Contents

Preface

Here are the stories of the 25 most successful major-league baseball teams of the home-run era. The chapters on these world champions are presented in the order of their winning percentages during the regular season.

Sweet Seasons: Baseball's Top Teams Since 1920 describes what happened to the winningest American and National League clubs on the way to their World Series crowns. And dozens of Hall of Famers emerge as the leading characters.

Why are certain ballclubs known as great world champions?

The 1927 New York Yankees are often called the best team ever to play the game. For one thing, no world champion of the home-run era has ever posted a better season record. The '27 Yankees, led by Babe Ruth, went 110-44 on their way to the American League pennant—for a winning percentage of .714.

In 1987, the Minnesota Twins wound up at the bottom of the list. They had the worst winning percentage (.525) ever compiled by any world champion. What they accomplished is indicated by their struggle for recognition.

The yearly major-league standings since 1920 rank more than 1,000 baseball teams. To be considered for *Sweet Seasons*, a club had to have won an unusually high percentage of its games, captured either the AL or NL pennant and become the world champion.

Because of the way baseball has been played for more than half a century, *Sweet Seasons* lists only the top world champions of the home-run era. In the early 1920s, Babe Ruth's homer burst doomed Ty Cobb's old "inside" game of base hits and running. And the livelier ball increased attendance. The "power" game known to today's fans has dominated the sport ever since.

Excluded from *Sweet Seasons* were the World War II

years of 1943, 1944 and 1945—when big-league rosters were heavily depleted. Also excluded was the dismal strike-shortened season of 1981.

Whether one baseball team is better than another has been argued throughout the history of the great American pastime. There is no attempt here to resolve the debate.

Perhaps it's best to keep in mind a baseball adage: "The difference between success and failure is one game in three." The best teams win about two of every three games (.666 percent) they play; the worst teams win about one of every three games (.333 percent).

The margin between the top teams, of course, is much smaller. Yet *Sweet Seasons* offers a valid context for reviewing world champions. It's not likely, for instance, that the 1987 Twins will ever be compared to the 1927 Yankees.

Further, the framework used by *Sweet Seasons* reflects performance rather than potential. The winning percentages aren't based on "maybes" or "what ifs." As Casey Stengel used to say, "You can look it up."

By the way, only one pre-1920 world champion had a better regular-season winning percentage than the '27 Yanks. In 1909, the Pittsburgh Pirates went 110-42 (.724). The 1906 Chicago Cubs were 116-36 (.763), but they lost to the Detroit Tigers in a seven-game World Series.

Finally, there's no reason to simply assume that they played better baseball in the old days. That's what old-timers always claim.

A long time ago, Cap Anson, the Hall of Famer who had played in the 1890s, is said to have taken a dim view of what he saw as "modern" changes in the sport. Looking back, he claimed: "Baseball was a man's game in my day."

Said Cap Anson: "I'd like to see what today's boys would do against the likes of (Old Hoss) Radbourn, (Pud) Galvin, (Tim) Keefe, and (John) Clarkson. I'd like to see Cobb and (Joe) Jackson and Ruth against them . . . why, they probably wouldn't bat .350 between them."

Introduction

BY STAN MUSIAL

The best team I ever played for was the 1942 St. Louis Cardinals. So, it's nice to see them ranked up there along with some of those great New York Yankee teams of the 1920s and 1930s. The Cardinals had a great team, too.

Through the years, the Cards have had a winning tradition in the National League. We've had some outstanding players. And we've been very fortunate in winning nine of the World Series that we played in.

It goes back even before the old Gas House Gang in 1934. There's something in the tradition of a winning team. The only major-league club that's been more successful than the Cards over the years is the Yankees.

You have an advantage from the start with that tradition on your side.

If you play good baseball, without many errors — if your team is competitive — it doesn't matter what the time is. You'll be good in any era. You know, baseball is baseball. I think the 1942 Cardinals could have competed in any era.

The '42 Cardinals were a little bit like the 1986 Mets. The Mets didn't have many great "career" years as individuals — the pitchers had big years. But the Mets relied a lot on teamwork, too.

We didn't make many mistakes in 1942. We had good pitching and a lot of speed. We were hard line drive hitters. And we were daring.

But the best thing we had was that spirit among all of us. We just felt like we were unbeatable. We played together, and we spent a lot of time together. We had a great spirit on that team. I mean, it was just terrific.

For a great baseball team, everything just fits together. Some teams just don't fit properly; our team did. And we were close to one another.

We had a young "veteran" club. We had veterans, we had some guys in between, we had some rookies.

Whitey Kurowski and I were rookies, and so was Johnny Beazley. Kurowski played third base, I was in left field and Beazley pitched. Then we had Marty Marion at shortstop and Enos Slaughter in right field. They were both veterans. And, of course, Terry Moore, the center fielder, was our captain. Walker Cooper, our catcher, and his brother, Mort, one of our top pitchers, were both veterans. So, we had a good mix.

We always looked up to Terry Moore. You see, back in those days we very seldom went to the manager — or to management — with our problems. We always went to Terry. He was our spokesman. He was older than most of us.

Everybody enjoyed the game and loved to play. We took an extra base and we got the job done. A lot of it didn't show up in the record book. It was part of the game, and we didn't make a fuss over it.

We had a manager who was good for this kind of club — Billy Southworth knew how to handle us. He played good fundamental baseball, but daring. We took our chances on the basepaths. First, second, third, and home.

Southworth could get along with the rookies and he handled the veterans very well. We had a set lineup, and we started getting good pitching and defense. At one point in August of '42, we were 10 or 11 games behind. Then, we won 43 out of our final 51 games. It was phenomenal!

And we won a lot of games late. We came from behind in the seventh, eighth, and ninth innings. I guess we were too young to feel the pressure. That's a nice feeling.

We played tough. We battled all of the clubs, especially the Brooklyn Dodgers. They'd knock us down, we'd knock them down. They would take somebody out at second base. It was tit for tat. That was part of the game.

In those days, I don't think the folks out East really knew us. When we were traveling, we had, at the most, two or three sportswriters with us. Now it's different. What we have today is television, writers, radio — everybody has a mike, you know. There are 100 guys around the ballpark and all over.

We really didn't get a lot of press on the road in 1942.

Even after we came from behind and beat the Dodgers, the fans didn't really appreciate our team until we beat the Yankees in the World Series. We had a terrific club. We won 106 games! But they didn't know how good we were until we beat the Yankees. Even today, I think sometimes the '42 Cards are overlooked when people start talking about the great teams. We are in that category.

Not long ago, I was talking to Charlie Keller who was on that '42 Yankee club we faced in the World Series. They knew they had a great club. So they were all surprised that we beat them.

But we had played the Yanks down in spring training. We both trained at St. Petersburg, Florida. We had a five- or six-game series down there, and we beat the Yanks down there in that series. So, we were kind of used to playing against these guys. It was not like a club and saying, "Oh, here we go, we are playing the New York Yankees." We were accustomed to the guys. We played against them. And we felt like we could compete against them.

They did have a great club. When I came up to the Cards, I was in awe of Joe DiMaggio. Of course, he had five years in the big leagues already. He was on those great Yankee clubs in Joe McCarthy's dynasty in the late 1930s. I guess anybody would have admired him, you know.

Nowadays, it's much harder to repeat year after year like those great Yankee teams did. For one thing, the major-league draft is different. The lower clubs get a shot at the best players first.

In 1985, everybody thought Kansas City with Bret Saberhagen was going to be hard to beat for a few years. They didn't do it in 1986. And then the Mets thought they were going to be tough, and they fell off in 1987. It's always hard for a major-league team to stay on top.

Today the championship series in both leagues also makes a big difference. We didn't have to go through that in the old days. You know in a short series, anything can happen. And now there are two of them, not one.

What does it take to come up with a great baseball team?

Well, there are a lot of intangibles. I am a great believer in the right spirit. Love of the game is important. I think that when you are up on top, you want to stay there. But you've got to work hard to stay there. Everybody is shooting at you. Nothing is easy.

To do these things year after year, you have to have courage — and you have got to have talent. And a lot has to do with the intangibles. Like a winning spirit. Of course, *that* comes with confidence. I think pride also plays a great part. You love the game and you want to do your best to keep going and try to repeat the victories.

I think all the great teams have had that pride within themselves. They believe in their team. And as players they know there is nothing better than winning.

To get a group of guys like that together is hard to do. It only happens every once in a while, every 10 or 20 years.

It only happens every once in a while.

Stan "The Man" Musial, an outfielder-first baseman, played for the St. Louis Cardinals throughout his 22-year major-league career (1941-63). He hit 475 home runs and batted .331. Musial won seven National League batting titles and three MVP awards. Also, he played in four World Series. When he retired, Musial was at or near the top of the all-time list in almost every batting category. He was elected to baseball's Hall of Fame in 1969.

1

New York Yankees

1927

110-44

.714

"THE GREATEST TEAM EVER" ♦ BABE RUTH (60 HRS, 164 RBIS, .356 AVG.) DOMINATES "MURDERERS' ROW" WITH LOU GEHRIG (47, 175, .373) ♦ WAITE HOYT (22-7), HERB PENNOCK (19-8) LEAD PITCHERS ♦ YANKEES SWEEP PIRATES IN WORLD SERIES.

Going into the 1927 season, the New York Yankees were led by the biggest star in the history of baseball. They were about to field the best team ever to play the game. Yet, except for Babe Ruth, they weren't quite legends.

"From present indications, the American League race figures as follows: Philadelphia, New York, Washington, Cleveland, Detroit, Chicago, St. Louis, Boston." So wrote Grantland Rice in the *New York Herald-Tribune* two days before the season began. His prediction was typical. Twenty-nine experts polled by the Associated Press picked the Athletics to win the pennant; only nine chose the Yanks.

There were doubts, for example, about how long the 32-year-old Ruth could remain the Sultan of Swat. His prodigious home runs had made him the greatest one-man show on earth, the number one symbol of the emergence in the Roaring '20s of modern-style baseball. But the Bambino was growing older, as were certain Yankee pitchers. Plus there were other worries in the Bronx about the catching, about some of the infielders—and even about the lack of a strong bench.

"All in all, we look forward to a contest this year that should make its mark in the annals of the national game," declared American League president Ban Johnson, who foresaw a historic five-way battle in 1927.

As it was, it was no contest. G.H. Ruth, H.L. Gehrig & Co. proceeded to rewrite the record book. The Yankees, developing quickly from flesh-and-blood contenders into historic champions, simply left all of the competition behind. The '27 Yanks began to slug, pitch and field with a relentless skill that once and for all set them apart. On Murderers' Row, these were their finest afternoons. The Bronx Bombers became the first team in the history of baseball to spend the entire season in first place. Their Opening Day lineup held the winning combination, after all—Earle Combs, cf; Mark Koenig, ss; Babe Ruth, rf; Lou Gehrig, 1b; Bob Meusel, lf; Tony Lazzeri, 2b; Joe Dugan, 3b; Johnny Grabowski, c; and Waite Hoyt, p.

By June, the rising New York Yankees were being called the greatest baseball team of all time. All of the Yankee stars were having the best years of their careers, or nearly the best. The Yanks finished 19 games ahead of the runner-up Athletics. New York won a record 110 games and lost only 44 for a winning percentage of .714—which is still the highest regular-season mark by any world champion since 1920.

"It was murder," Ruth once boasted. "We never even worried five or six runs behind. Wham! Wham! Wham! Wham! And wham! No matter who was pitching."

Nothing had prepared old-fashioned baseball fans for the unprecedented, season-long homer duel between two Yankee teammates: Babe Ruth vs. 24-year-old Lou Gehrig. In his most storied performance, Ruth hit 60 home runs, setting the major-league one-season record for his fourth (and last) time. Bursting into prominence, young Gehrig belted 47 homers. That was more than anybody but Ruth had ever hit before in one year. Batting in the number three spot, Ruth alone clubbed more homers than any other American League team in 1927. In the number four spot, Gehrig belted more homers than four of those AL clubs. By the way, Ruth hit .356, and Gehrig .373. Deep into the summer of '27 the Yankee duo traded heroics, making up to some degree for the lack of excitement in the pennant race. When it was over, Ruth and Gehrig finished 1-2 in the AL, respectively, in homers, slugging (.772, .765), runs (158, 149) and bases on balls (138, 109). Gehrig and Ruth finished one-two in the AL, respectively, in runs batted in (175, 164) and total bases (447, 417).

Not only did the Yankees have the top two batters in most of the American League categories in 1927, but often the number three man as well. "Poosh 'em up" Tony Lazzeri, for instance, hit 18 homers—the third highest AL total. It's the only time in the twentieth century that one team has claimed the top three HR champs. (Like Gehrig who was six months older, Lazzeri, 23, suddenly became a big-league star.) Third in the AL behind Ruth and Gehrig in runs (137) and total bases (331) came Earle Combs, the first great Yankee center fielder. Combs, who hit .356, was the best leadoff man in baseball. He and Gehrig finished 1-2 in the American League, respectively, in hits (231, 218) and triples (23, 18). Combs led the league in singles (166); Gehrig led in doubles (52).

Along with Ruth and Gehrig, Lazzeri and Silent Bob Meusel each drove in more than 100 runs. Lazzeri (a .309 hitter) had 102 RBIs; Meusel (a .337 hitter) had 103. And those two right-handed batters hit behind two left-handed Yankee sluggers whose home runs alone combined to empty the bases 107 times. Meusel ranked number two in the American League in stolen bases (with 24); Lazzeri tied for number three (with 22). And so on.

"When we got to the ballpark," recalled Yankee hurler George Pipgras, "we knew we were going to win. That's all there was to it. We weren't cocky. I wouldn't call it confidence either. We just *knew*. Like when you go to sleep you know the sun is going to come up in the morning."

Part of the reason was that the '27 Yankees pitched

almost as well as they hit, which is what has confirmed their billing down through the years as "The Greatest Team Ever." Naturally, the memory of Murderers' Row has overshadowed the pitching. But no team in the history of baseball ever displayed quite so much skill at bat *and* on the mound. As well as posting the highest AL batting average (.307), the Yankees of '27 delivered the lowest earned run average (3.20)—it took 15 years before any staff in the league did better. Though ERAs went up elsewhere in 1927, they went down for all of the key New York pitchers. The Yanks claimed *four* of the top seven AL hurlers with ERAs of 3.00 or less. And Yankee pitchers led the league with 11 shutouts. The Yanks also had the four best won-lost percentages in the AL: Waite Hoyt (22-7, .759), Urban Shocker (18-6, .750), Wilcy Moore (19-7, .731) and Herb Pennock (19-8, .704). Pipgras (10-3, .769), a rookie, was their fifth pitcher with a winning percentage above .700. He combined with veteran Dutch Ruether (13-6, .684) for a 23-9 total. Hoyt and Shocker were also 1-2 in the AL in ERA (2.63, 2.84 respectively). Actually, Moore, the first great Yankee reliever, did even better (2.28), but he didn't pitch quite enough innings to qualify for the title.

On defense, the Yankees tied for third in the American League in 1927 with a fielding percentage of .969. No team could play the outfield better. Meusel had the best arm in baseball; Combs ranged wide enough to lead AL outfielders in putouts (411); and spindle-legged Ruth, deceptively, could still run, catch and throw like a big-league star. Plus the infield more than got the job done. "It was a team that didn't often beat itself," said Hoyt. "The 1927 Yankees probably beat themselves less than any ballcub that ever lived."

It was all a far cry from the outlook during spring training in St. Petersburg, Florida. Manager Miller Huggins—known for his brainpower as the holder of a law degree—had been particularly skeptical about his aging hurlers. "The Yankee pitching staff," he guessed, "has reached the stage where I must gamble." Faded ace Bob Shawkey was 36, and so was Shocker. Both Pennock (whom Huggins called "the greatest left-hander of all time") and Reuther were 33. And nobody knew what to expect from Moore, a rookie about to turn 30.

"He's too old," a scout had warned Ed Barrow before the Yankee business manager bought the part-time Oklahoma dirt farmer sight unseen. The purchase of Moore from the weak Piedmont League was based on his outstanding totals at one point in 1926. "Anyone who has a 20-1 record anywhere is worth taking a look at," claimed Barrow. He was right. Moore came out of nowhere—his wicked sinker was the result of an old wrist injury—to become a star in 1927. He was 13-3 in relief alone. It was just one of the developments that Huggins wouldn't dare to count on.

A scrappy National League second baseman for 13 seasons, Huggins had been player-manager of the St. Louis Cardinals before switching to the Yankee dugout in 1918. He guided the Yanks to the first three pennants in the history of the franchise (1921, 1922 and 1923), and to their first world championship (1923). But the "Mite Manager"—he was 5-foot-4 and weighed only 140 pounds—then watched his team come away empty-handed two seasons in a row. So, Huggins, 48, knew nothing was certain. His official line in Florida in 1927 was, sure, the Yankees were once again the defending AL champs, but they were facing "a closer race this time."

In 1926, New York had made the biggest jump in American League history by winning the pennant after finishing seventh the year before. But the Yanks had to outlast Cleveland, Philadelphia and Washington to grab the flag. New York finally edged the Indians by only three games. Then the Yankees were upset in the World Series by the St. Louis Cardinals, or, to be exact, by Grover Cleveland Alexander. Just four months before his 40th birthday, "Old Pete" twice evened the Series by going the distance to win the second and sixth games. In Game 7, Alex, fighting a hangover, was called on to relieve with St. Louis leading 3-2 in the seventh inning at Yankee Stadium. With two outs and the bases loaded, he struck out Lazzeri to end the threat. It was one of the most exciting moments in World Series history. Alex stayed on to shut the door on the Yankees. The Series ended when Ruth—who had hit three home runs in game four—was thrown out while trying to steal second base.

As usual, it was the Babe who was being counted on to

bring the Bronx Bombers back in 1927. His salary was proof enough. After a brief pre-season holdout, Ruth signed a three-year pact with Col. Jacob Ruppert, the beer baron who owned the Yankees, for $70,000 a year. Ruth had just returned from Hollywood were he earned a tidy $25,000 in 17 days of filming "Babe Comes Home." Excluding Ruth, the rest of the Yankees received an average of about $8,000 each to play ball in 1927. That's just what Gehrig earned. Among the better-paid, at $12,000, was Hoyt, their Opening Day pitcher.

On April 12, 1927, more than 70,000 fans—still the biggest Opening Day crowd in New York history—flocked to see the Yanks. On Broadway, Helen Hayes was starring in *Coquette,* Ethel Barrymore was appearing in *The Constant Wife* and Jeanne Eagels was playing in *Her Cardboard Lover.* And spectators flocked to the love-triangle murder trial of Ruth Snyder and Judd Gray at the Queens County Courthouse in Long Island City. But the number one show in New York was opening at Yankee Stadium. Game time: 3:30 p.m., on a cool, sunny day. Gentleman Jimmy Walker, the snappy mayor-about-town during the Prohibition era, threw out the first ball to batboy Eddie Bennett, the Yankees' hunchbacked mascot. Facing arch rival Philadelphia, the Yanks won 8-3, as Hoyt scattered eight hits and bested Lefty Grove. The only disappointment was the Babe, who had a head cold and a slight fever. He struck out twice and hit only an infield pop before leaving for a pinch hitter in the sixth inning. But three days later Ruth belted his first homer of 1927. It sparked New York to a 6-3 victory and a three-game sweep of Connie Mack's Athletics. Ruth hit a first-inning solo blast to right field off Howard Ehmke. The Babe's shot landed a few dozen rows back in the bleachers, which stretched from foul line to foul line in the days before the upper tiers of the Stadium extended into the outfield.

Oddly, Ruth preferred to come to bat on the road. Asked a few weeks later about hitting, the Babe condemned the House that Ruth Built: "All the parks are good except the Stadium. There is no background there at all. But the best of them all is the Polo Grounds. Boy, how I used to sock 'em there. I cried when they took me out of the Polo Grounds." In particular, Ruth pined for his previous record of 59 homers in 1921 when the Yanks were still the guests of the New York Giants. In 1927, the Bambino socked 28 HRs at Yankee Stadium—and a major-league record 32 away from home. And, no, he didn't call those shots. "I don't suppose I'll ever break that 1921 record," said Ruth in April. "To do that, you've got to start early, and the pitchers have got to pitch to you. I don't start early, and the pitchers haven't really pitched to me in four seasons. I get more bad balls to hit than any other six men—and fewer good ones." That changed with the rise of the '27 Yankee powerhouse.

On Easter Sunday, April 17, Lou Gehrig led the parade of pin-striped hitters at Yankee Stadium before 35,000 fans (including speakeasy queen Texas Guinan, who flaunted her broad-brimmed yellow hat). As New York trampled Boston, 14-2, Gehrig drove in six runs—three with his first homer of the season, two with his second and another with a sacrifice fly. Word spread, of course. "I'd rather see Ruth than Gehrig in a tight place," said St. Louis Browns manager Dan Howley in mid-May when the Yanks came to town. "Sometimes you can figure what the Babe is going to do, but you never can tell about Gehrig. He is likely to hit any kind of a ball to any field." So, too: Combs, Lazzeri and Meusel. Take Milt Gaston's word for it. "I would rather pitch a double-header against any other club," the Browns hurler vowed, "than one game against the Yanks. There isn't a moment's rest for a pitcher in that batting order. I was so tired when I got through pitching to them the other day that I could hardly drag myself to my hotel." After winning four straight games in St. Louis, the Bronx Bombers were 18-8. On May 15, every other AL club was still within nine games of the front-running New York Yankees; by July 4, none of them would be.

The Indians edged the Yanks, 5-4, in 12 innings in Cleveland on Saturday, May 21. But it was impossible to concentrate on the game alone. It was announced in the first inning that Charles Lindbergh was approaching France on his historic trans-Atlantic solo flight. News of the landing in Paris was received in the bottom of the seventh inning—so, 15,000 fans inside tiny Dunn Field stood while a band played "The Star Spangled Banner."

It took less than a month for the hero of '27, welcomed home with a commission as an army colonel from President Coolidge, to pay a courtesy call on the heroes of '27. "Lindy's coming!" That was the talk of Yankee Stadium on June 16. While 20,000 fans waited, New York beat St. Louis, 8-1, as Ruth hit homer No. 22 and Gehrig hit No. 15. The game had just ended when Lindbergh—fresh from his tumultuous greeting a few days earlier by four million New Yorkers—was driven into the ballpark, smiling and waving, for a belated motor tour. That other American idol, Babe Ruth, missed the whole thing. He was taking a shower.

Perhaps the Bambino, for good reason, was keeping his mind on baseball. His high-flying team was on its way to going 21-6 in June. One of their glory days came a week later in Boston: Gehrig hit three homers (Nos. 19, 20 and 21) in an 11-4 Yankee victory. It was the first time in modern history that two players from one team—Lazzeri had done it on June 8—each had three-homer games in the same season.

Enough was enough, according to Wilbert Robinson, Brooklyn's 64-year-old manager. In late June, he officially dubbed the cross-town Bronx Bombers "the greatest club ever got together." Were the New York Yankees of 1927 even better than the Baltimore Orioles of the 1890s? Yes, admitted "Uncle Robbie," who had caught for the legendary National League team. Claimed Robbie: "Our pitchers never would have stopped Hug's crew."

Independence Day began with Ruth and Gehrig tied at 26 homers apiece. At Yankee Stadium, the Bronx Bombers celebrated the Fourth of July by sweeping a double-header before more than 74,000 fans. New York pounded the Washington Senators, 12-1 and, even more unmercifully, 21-1. Gehrig homered in each game to go two up on Ruth. But the Bambino wasn't easy to top. On July 8, in Detroit, Ruth collected three RBIs on an inside-the-park homer—his only one of 1927—as the Yankees beat the Tigers, 10-8, to gain a split in a double-header. The next day, the Babe hit Nos. 28 and 29 while the Yanks thrashed Detroit, 19-7. On July 24, Ruth ended a 12-day HR drought by hitting No. 31 in Chicago during a 3-2 Yankee victory in newly renovated Comiskey Park. He had now homered at least once in 1927 in every AL ballpark. And by now the pennant race was only a distant memory. New York led number two Washington by 13 games, number three Detroit by 15½ games, number four Philadelphia by 18 games, etc. It was the winningest month of the season for the Yanks. In July, they were 24-7.

What kept fans guessing, though, was the two-man Yankee homer race. As late as August 15, Gehrig led Ruth, 38-36. But the Sultan of Swat went on to blast 24 homers in his final 42 games while his young rival hit only nine more. Ruth's 40th homer during a 9-4 loss in Cleveland was reported in the New York daily newspapers on the morning of August 23. (It happened to be the day accused anarchists Nicola Sacco and Bartolomeo Vanzetti were executed in Massachusetts).

On September 2, the Yanks beat the A's 12-2 in Philadelphia. In the game, Ruth hit homer No. 44—his 400th career home run—to stay in front of Gehrig, who hit Nos. 42 and 43. The Babe's shot was the first of a record of 17 that he clouted in September. Looking back, he recalled: "Pitchers began pitching to me because if they passed me they still had Lou to contend with." But Gehrig's power was failing. A devoted son, he became distracted when his ailing mother underwent a major operation in September. Day after day, he would rush to the hospital immediately following games at Yankee Stadium. "I'm so worried about Mom that I can't see straight," he admitted. The World Series was nearly over before Mrs. Gehrig was taken off the critical list.

Nothing stood in Ruth's way, though. On September 6, he whacked three homers in Fenway Park while the Yanks split a double-header in Boston—a 14-2 win and a 3-2 loss. (After he beat his old HR mark, Ruth admitted: "The first time I believed I had a chance to make it was at Boston early this month, when I socked three in those two games.") The next day, September 7, the Babe hit Nos. 48 and 49—for a total of five HRs in two days—as the Yanks beat Boston, 12-10. Back in the Stadium to close out the season, the Yanks clinched the pennant on September 13 after sweeping a twin bill against Cleveland by identical 5-3 scores. Game 2, the clincher, was Hoyt's 21st victory. In each game, Ruth homered: Nos. 51 and 52. He collected No. 56 in an 8-7 Yankee win against the Tigers on September 22—the day Jack Dempsey failed to regain his heavyweight boxing title from Gene Tunney in Chicago after t-h-e l-o-n-g c-o-u-n-t. ("I've stuck with Dempsey in all his fights," Ruth had declared beforehand, "and I'm sticking with him now.") Finally, the Bambino caught up to his own 1921 home-run record. On September 29, Ruth hit two homers—Nos. 58 and 59—in a 15-4 victory against the Senators. No. 59 was a grand slam, his second in two games.

But just two more games remained to be played. On Friday, September 30, the Babe faced Washington lefty Tom Zachary before a crowd of about 10,000 in Yankee Stadium. Ruth drew a walk in the first inning. "I had made up my mind," Zachary recalled, "that I wasn't going to give him a good pitch all afternoon." Even so, Ruth singled and scored in both the fourth and sixth innings. With the game knotted 2-2, the Babe came to bat in the bottom of the eighth following Koenig's one-out triple. The Senators decided not to walk Ruth to set up a double play because Lou Gehrig was the on-deck hitter in a tie game. And, Zachary claimed: "I was pitching my best." Eyeing the pitcher from the batter's box, Ruth took a fastball for strike one. The next pitch was high for ball one. Zachary later recalled: "I wanted to get the Babe away from the plate." So, the pitcher hooked one inside and knee-high. "I don't say it was the best curve anybody ever threw," said Zachary, "but it was as good as any I ever threw." What did Ruth do? "Instead of stepping back," Zachary said, "he waded right into the ball. He lunged for it before it ever got over the plate and pulled it around into the stands. I don't see yet how he did it. He never hit a worse ball in his life." Homer No. 60 sailed past the right-field foul pole only about 10 feet fair and curved halfway back up into the bleachers. It was the third homer that Zachary had given up to Ruth in 1927.

Tossing down his glove, the Senator pitcher yelled: "Foul ball! Foul ball!" But the Yankees went on to win, 4-2, on Ruth's historic shot. Next day, the Yanks beat Washington, 4-3, with the help of Gehrig's 47th homer. The Bambino went 0 for 3 as New York earned its 110th victory. In his final at bat of the regular regular season, the mighty Ruth struck out.

Now that the Bronx Bombers had devastated the American League—the A's finished a distant second with a 91-63 record— the time was ripe for myths. One hackneyed tale is that the Pittsburgh Pirates (94-60, .610), the National League champs, lost the World Series before it even began. Supposedly, the Pirates became intimidated while watching the Yankees belt home runs during batting practice at spacious Forbes Field the day before game one. "We really put on a show," Ruth was to claim later on. "Lou and I banged ball after ball into the right-field stands, and I finally knocked one out of the park in right-center. Bob Meusel and Tony Lazzeri kept hammering balls into the left-field seats." Rookie Lloyd Waner of the Pirates was reported to have gazed at Ruth and Gehrig, turned to his older brother Paul, and said, "Gee! They're big guys!"

New York swept Pittsburgh in the World Series, winning 5-4, 6-2, 8-1 and 4-3. Had the Pirates been intimidated? "Every time I hear that story," said Lloyd Waner, "I tell people it's not so. But it just keeps on going." Still, he added: "This is not to say we weren't impressed by those Yankees during that Series. We sure were." Yet Ruth alone did the heavy hitting. The Babe hit .400, drove in seven runs and whacked the only two homers of the World Series.

It was Ruth, of course, who was the one larger-than-life hero who could dominate the 1927 New York Yankees. Thus, his name always comes first on the list of their Hall of Famers—Babe Ruth, Lou Gehrig, Earle Combs, Waite Hoyt, Herb Pennock and Miller Huggins. The Babe now played for a club that had echoed his feats, a club that had generated his brand of power and excitement, a club that had joined him forever in the record book. After hitting home run No. 60, Ruth bellowed a personal challenge that might just as well have come from "The Greatest Team Ever." Inside the Yankee clubhouse, the Babe shouted: "Let's see some other son of a bitch match that!"

›››››››››››››› 2 ››››››››››››››

New York Yankees 1939

106-45

.702

McCarthy's Dynasty Takes Record Fourth Straight World Series (Sweeping Reds) ♦ Lou Gehrig Retires In May With All-Time Streak: 2,130 Games ♦ Joe DiMaggio (30, 126 .381) Is Batting Champ, MVP ♦ Ace Red Ruffing Is 21-7.

Nobody realized on May 2, 1939, that the greatest personal tragedy in the history of baseball was unfolding. Even Lou Gehrig was unaware of his actual plight. He knew, though, that he was 35 years old—and that he was struggling physically day after day. He was the last and strongest of the legendary New York Yankees of 1927; he hadn't missed appearing in a single game since two seasons before that great year. Now all of a sudden his baseball skills had vanished. It was cruelest that April. By the end of the month, Gehrig was hitting just .143 through the first eight games of 1939. He had only four singles and one RBI in 28 at bats. Even worse, his slump had left him exhausted with the new baseball season just barely underway. So the captain of the Yankees, the leader who had embodied their perennial brilliance in the late

1930s, benched himself. Gehrig finally took his name out of the lineup when the Yanks arrived in Detroit to open their first road trip of the year. Not yet knowing why, The Iron Horse was forced to halt his record 14-year playing streak after 2,130 consecutive games.

"Maybe that Yankee dynasty is beginning to crumble," guessed Tiger slugger Hank Greenberg. His guess was wrong, of course.

The Yanks in 1939 became the first baseball team ever to win four straight world championships. Manager Joe McCarthy's club did the same thing it had done in 1936, 1937 and 1938: New York pulled away from the rest of the American League by mid-season and cruised to the pennant. Since the birth of modern-style baseball, only one world champion has ever performed at a hotter pace during the regular season—the New York Yankees of 1927. The '39 Yanks went 106-45 (including a phenomenal 54-20 on the road) to finish 17 games in front of runner-up Boston, the last team to put up a struggle. Then New York swept the Cincinnati Reds (97-57, .630) in the World Series.

With his favorite Yankee confined to the dugout for the first time since the mid 1920s, McCarthy could rely on the winning ways of an experienced, business-like club. The best work was done by his rising young center fielder. Twenty-four-year-old Joe DiMaggio—once again displaying Gehrig-like class, dignity and professionalism—earned his first MVP award in 1939. Soft-spoken and graceful, DiMaggio belted 30 homers, drove in 126 runs and hit a career-best .381 to win the AL batting title. He was the first (and only) player ever to break into the majors as a regular on four consecutive world champions.

Several of New York's starting players had big years in 1939. DiMaggio was one of five Yankee regulars to hit .300, and one of four to belt more than 20 homers and more than 100 RBIs. He played in the middle of a .300-hitting outfield: in left, veteran George "Twinkletoes" Selkirk (known for his distinctive gait) hit .306 with 21 homers and 101 RBIs; in right, rookie Charlie "King Kong" Keller (named for his bushy eyebrows and bulging biceps) hit .334 with 11 homers and 83 RBIs. Third baseman Red Rolfe, who batted .329, led the American League in hits (213) and runs (139). At second, Joe Gordon socked 28 homers and drove in 111 runs. And behind the plate, Bill Dickey was sensational: 24 homers, 105 RBIs and a .302 batting average. With all their firepower, the '39 Yanks led the league in a number of hitting categories, including, for the fourth year in a row, runs scored.

The pitchers, meanwhile, led the AL in ERA for the sixth straight year. They were also number one in winning percentage, complete games, saves and shutouts. It was a tribute to McCarthy, who had to juggle his pitching staff all season. The so-called "push-button manager" lacked a solid number two starter in 1939 and he didn't have the luxury of a set rotation. Eight different hurlers made at least 11 starts. New York's ace, 35-year-old Red Ruffing, went 21-7 with an ERA of 2.94—it was his fourth 20-win season in a row. But Lefty Gomez, bothered by a sore arm, slipped to 12-8. Swampy Donald (13-3) set an AL rookie record by winning 12 straight games; and Steve Sundra (11-1) didn't lose until the last game of the year. Other top contributors were Monte Pearson (12-5), Bump Hadley (12-6) and Oral Hildebrand (10-4). Johnny "Fireman" Murphy, one of the first to earn fame as a relief pitcher, topped the American League with 19 saves.

And the hurlers got plenty of support: New York also led the league in fielding. Like both Dickey and Selkirk, Yankee shortstop Frankie Crosetti was the best fielder in the American League at his position. Crosetti, with 118 double plays and Gordon, with 116, formed the AL's top combo. They anchored the strength up the middle completed in center field by DiMaggio and behind the plate by Dickey, who caught at least 100 games for his 11th straight year.

Off the field, the man who built the 1936-39 Yankee dynasty, longtime general manager Ed Barrow, was now president of the team. He had succeeded Col. Jake Ruppert, the brewery tycoon who had owned the New York Yankees for 24 years. Ruppert, 71, died on January 13, 1939. Ownership of the club passed to the Ruppert estate: his two nieces and a woman friend of the family. But Barrow, 71, remained in command of the franchise. "Business will go along as usual," he declared. "We will miss the Colonel, of course. But we will try to carry on the way we know he would want us to carry on." That reflected Barrow's single-minded dedication to baseball. While he was managing Boston in 1918, Barrow turned star pitcher Babe Ruth into an outfielder who could hit every day; then Red Sox owner Harry Frazee sold Ruth to New York to raise cash. Barrow, who was furious, looked for a way out of Boston, too. He became business manager of the Yankees in 1921. The franchise rose to power in the 1920s with Miller Huggins in the dugout and Ruth and Gehrig at bat. Under Barrow, Joe McCarthy was appointed to manage New York in 1931; and George Weiss was also brought in to build up a farm system.

Strict, humorless and hard-working, Barrow always kept New York's owners out of the clubhouse; and he also completely supported the manager. Barrow didn't think "gimmicks," such as night baseball, fit the dignified Yankee image fostered so well by McCarthy. But the front office finally relented when it came to radio. Fearing the impact on attendance, the Yankees, Dodgers and Giants had agreed not to broadcast their games regularly in New York. It was virtually the only big-league city still without local radio broadcasts. When the Dodgers finally decided to go on the air in 1939, the other two teams reluctantly dropped their blackouts. The Yanks were to be heard on WOR with the play-by-play sponsored by Wheaties. One of the original Yankee announcers was a young law school grad from Alabama: Mel Allen. And the first regularly scheduled radio broadcast from Yankee Stadium was Opening Day.

Heading into the season, the big question was: "What's wrong with Lou?" It was obvious that he, coming off what for him was a weak year, hadn't returned to normal in spring training. In 1938, he hit 29 home runs, collected 114 RBIs and batted .295. But not since 1928 had he hit fewer home runs; and not since 1925 had he driven in fewer runs or posted a lower batting average. For Gehrig, time was running out.

"The trouble started in 1938 when his batting average slipped 56 points," recalled Gehrig's wife, Eleanor. "Nobody touched off any skyrockets. He was in a 'slump,' so they just looked the other way.

"Then, that winter, there were times when he stumbled over curbstones, and maybe I looked the other way. When we went skating, Lou started to fall down more than usual, too. And at home, he began to drop things, as though he'd lost some of his reflexes. He was in a slump?"

During spring training in St. Petersburg, Florida, Gehrig, who always had kept himself in good shape, was the first to report in the morning and the last to leave in the afternoon. Yet his performance remained dull and sluggish. His teammates told him not to drive himself; they reasoned that his playing streak was a record that would never be challenged. But Gehrig kept laboring.

"He was down there three weeks in spring training and he wasn't even fouling the ball," DiMaggio was to recall. "The balls that he finally did hit were just little weak grounders toward second. He just couldn't break a piece of glass. It was that bad.

"It was pretty depressing for all the ballplayers to see this man who used to hit balls harder than any man I ever saw. He'd hit balls to left center as hard as I could hit 'em—and he was a left-hander. He hit the most devastating line drives that would tear the gloves off the infielders. Then to see this man weakly hit ground balls was awful."

For most of the Yankees, though, Opening Day couldn't arrive soon enough. After all, they had just won three straight world championships. Things finally got underway in New York on April 20 following three consecutive days of rain postponements. In Yankee Stadium, New York beat Boston, 2-0, on Ruffing's seven hitter. As usual, Gehrig was stationed at first base. The game marked the major-league debut of Ted Williams, who struck out in his first two times at bat. Next time up, Williams got the first of his 2,654 career hits—a double off the 407-foot sign in right-center. In the game,

DiMaggio went one for two: it was the first time he had played for the Yankees on Opening Day. Nine days later the injury jinx stopped him again. DiMaggio caught his spikes in the muddy outfield at the Stadium while chasing a line drive by Washington's Bobby Estalella. The New Yorker was to be sidelined for about five weeks with torn leg muscles. DiMaggio fell injured on April 29, the day before Gehrig played his last game. No wonder Greenberg was tempted to speculate about the possible decline of the Yankee dynasty.

Bearing the right to decide for himself when to interrupt his playing streak, Gehrig was, in effect, his own manager. The slumping Iron Horse had to balance his determination and pride against the obligation to produce on McCarthy's pennant-minded team. Reluctantly, Gehrig decided he had no choice but to take himself out of the lineup. He made up his mind after a 3-2 loss to the Senators in Yankee Stadium on Sunday, April 30. At bat, he stranded five runners; in the field, he did little. "I made a routine play on a ground ball," Gehrig later explained, "and Murph, Gordon and Dickey all gathered around me and patted me on the back. 'Great stop,' they all said. . . . Then I knew I was washed up. They meant to be kind. But if I was getting wholesale congratulations for making an ordinary stop, I knew it was time to fold."

In Detroit, Gehrig went up to McCarthy's hotel room just before the team was to leave for the ballpark on Tuesday. It was a visit the manager had been hoping for. He knew full well that his first baseman's reflexes were shot; and he didn't want him to be struck and hurt by a baseball.

This is how McCarthy remembered what Gehrig had to say: " 'Joe,' he said, 'how much longer do you think I should stay in this game? When do you think I should get out?'

" 'Right now, Lou,' I said.

"He didn't say anything right away, just sat there. Then he said, 'Well, that's what I wanted to know.'

" 'That's what I think,' I said.

" 'That's the way I feel too,' he said. 'I'm not doing the ballclub any good.'"

Gehrig hadn't missed a day's work for 15 seasons. He had

played through different stretches with colds, viruses, bruises, aching bones, sore muscles, lumbago, spike wounds and broken fingers. He was beaned twice during the streak. In mid 1934, Gehrig once had to limp out of a road game due to back pain. Listed in the following day's batting order at shortstop, he led off the contest with a single and immediately left for a pinch runner. Thus, his streak reached 1,427 games. But that happened when Gehrig was in his prime as a hitter. Now it was a different story. Unable to produce, he hesitantly told the press before the Tiger game: "Maybe a rest will do me some good. Maybe it won't. Who knows? Who can tell? I'm just hoping."

At Briggs Stadium, Gehrig, performing his duty as captain, took the Yankee line-up card up to home plate. The stunned Detroit crowd gave him a thunderous ovation when it was announced that he wouldn't be playing. Back in the dugout, the Iron Horse stood by the water fountain and cried. It took club wit Lefty Gomez to break the tension. "Hell, Lou," he joked, "It took 15 years to get you out of the game. Sometimes I'm out in 15 minutes." Coming off the bench, Babe Dahlgren, 27, replaced Gehrig at first base—with a bang! The substitute homered and doubled while New York pounded the Tigers, 22-2. "Lou, you had better get in there now and keep that streak going," urged Dahlgren in the seventh inning. Gehrig smiled: "You guys are doing fine without me." And so they did, the rest of the way.

Until mid May, New York bounced up and down between first and second place. Then they broke out of the AL pack with a 12-game winning streak. New York went into first place on May 11 and stayed there for the rest of the season. By the end of the month, the Yanks were a 34-10—even without DiMaggio. He returned a week later, rapping a homer, a double and a single during a 7-2 win in Chicago.

On June 12, the major leagues took a break to dedicate the Hall of Fame in Cooperstown, New York, marking what was determined to be the official "Centennial of Baseball." The first to be inducted were Ty Cobb, Babe Ruth, Honus Wagner, Christy Mathewson and Walter Johnson. "They started something here," Ruth told the small-town crowd of 15,000. "And the kids are keeping the ball rolling. I hope some of you kids will be in the Hall of Fame."

The next day, Lou Gehrig, still hoping to revive his own Hall of Fame career, checked into the Mayo Clinic in Rochester, Minnesota, for a week-long exam. The diagnosis was shocking. He was found to have amyotrophic lateral sclerosis, a chronic form of polio. "The nature of this trouble makes it such that Mr. Gehrig will be unable to continue his active participation as a baseball player," said the Mayo announcement a day after his 36th birthday. "Don't worry, Ellie," Gehrig told his wife by telephone, "I have a 50-50 chance to live." He rejoined the Yankees and remained in uniform for the rest of the season despite everything. The Iron Horse had less than two years left.

Though stunned, the Yanks kept rolling on the field. They finished June at 50-14, one of baseball's best starts ever. A visit to Philadelphia late in the month was notable: on June 26, the Yanks lost 3-2 in Shibe Park while playing under the lights for the first time in their history. After a day off, New York swept the Athletics in a double-header, winning 23-2 and 10-0. The Bronx Bombers hit 13 homers in the twin bill—eight of them in the opener when they made 53 total bases. On that day, DiMaggio, Dahlgren and Gordon each belted three home runs; Dickey, Selkirk, Crosetti and Tommy Henrich each homered once. In all, the Yankees collected 43 hits and 33 runs. Amid the slugging, Gomez blanked the A's in game two.

On Tuesday, July 4, "Lou Gehrig Appreciation Day" drew 61,808 fans to Yankee Stadium for what turned into the greatest tribute in the history of baseball. Thirteen members of the 1927 Yankees, the first of Gehrig's six world championship teams, marched out to begin the holiday program. The ceremony was held between the games of an Independence Day double-header against the Washington Senators. (New York lost the opener, 3-2, but won the nightcap, 11-1.) Leading the '27 delegation was Babe Ruth, who before long embraced Gehrig in a friendly bear hug to end their five-year old private feud. Among the other former Yanks on hand were Everett Scott, the ex-shortstop whose endurance mark the Iron Horse had surpassed; and Wally Pipp, the ex-first baseman who had lost his job when Gehrig took over his spot. Gehrig's wife and parents were also on hand.

At home plate, the Yankee captain swayed on wobbly legs—old Ed Barrow had to steady him at one point—as he accepted gifts and listened to speeches by McCarthy, Mayor Fiorello LaGuardia and Postmaster General James Farley. Finally, the applause faded into absolute silence in the vast stadium. Tearful and shaken, Gehrig momentarily seemed unable to speak. But, with memorable courage, he rose to the occasion: "Fans, for the past two weeks you have been reading about a bad break I got. Yet today I consider myself the luckiest man on the face of the earth. . . ." Thanking his baseball colleagues along with his family, Gehrig repeated, "Sure, I'm lucky." And he concluded: "I might have had a tough break, but I have an awful lot to live for!"

Three days later, the Yankees—perhaps suffering an emotional letdown that contributed to a 16-12 record in July—began an untimely five-game homestand against the surging Boston Red Sox. New York lost each contest, all of them close: 4-3, 3-1, 3-2, 4-3 and 5-3. Joe Cronin's homer in the final game helped the Bosox to sweep a double-header in Yankee Stadium for the second time in two days. That extended Boston's winning streak to 12 games. And it put the Red Sox back into the pennant race on the eve of the All-Star break.

The seventh annual All-Star Game was the first to be held at Yankee Stadium. American League manager Joe McCarthy started six Yankee players, including Red Ruffing who opened on the mound with three strong innings. The New York regulars in the AL starting lineup were: Joe DiMaggio, George Selkirk, Red Rolfe, Joe Gordon and Bill Dickey. Lefty Gomez, Johnny Murphy and Frankie Crosetti were also All-Stars. They sat on the bench along with Lou Gehrig, who was named an honorary member of the AL team. DiMag delighted most of the 62,892 fans in Yankee Stadium by capping the day's scoring with a 450-foot solo blast into the left-field bleachers; it was to be his only home run in 11 All-Star Games. The American Leaguers of '39 defeated the National Leaguers, 3-1. Complained an NL backer: "They ought to make Joe McCarthy play an All-Star American League team. We can beat them—but we can't beat the Yankees."

New York City was made the host of baseball's mid-summer classic because it was also staging the World's Fair in 1939. When "The World of Tomorrow" exposition opened at Flushing Meadow in April, NBC began regular U.S. television service with a pioneering broadcast seen by 1,000 metropolitan area viewers. (On August 26, NBC also staged major-league baseball's TV debut: Two "radio cameras" showed the Brooklyn Dodgers-Cincinnati Reds double-header at Ebbets Field.) Despite such glimpses of progress, the summer of '39 turned gloomy: Hitler's Germany began World War II in Europe by invading Poland on September 1. For the moment, though, America under President Roosevelt was more concerned with working itself even farther out of the Depression. And doing so to the Big Band beat of musicians such as Benny Goodman, Glenn Miller and Harry James. By 1939, more than 27 million U.S. families owned radios. Many of those sets also tuned in to big-league baseball.

Coming off the All-Star break, the Yankees dropped a 10-6 contest in Detroit to push their losing streak to six games. The footsteps the Yanks heard in back of them belonged to the Red Sox. But the Bronx Bombers suddenly got hot on the road. They won their next eight games: two in Detroit, three in Cleveland and three in St. Louis. The Yanks finished out the month at a 13-3 clip, which ended the pennant race in the American League once and for all. The burst by New York peaked on July 26 in Yankee Stadium. Bill Dickey hit three consecutive homers to lead the Bombers to a 14-1 victory over the Browns. (St. Louis was on its way to finishing an AL record 64½ games behind the Yankees.) In the game, New York banged 20 hits and scored in every inning. Ruffing, meanwhile, limited the Browns to just three hits. By the end of July, the Yankees had improved their record to 66-26.

It was more of the same in August while the Bombers pounded out another 21 victories. On August 12, Babe Dahlgren, toiling at the thankless job of succeeding a legend, had a day worthy of the great Gehrig. Their new first baseman led the Yanks to an 18-4 win in Philadelphia. His grand slam homer paced a four-for-six performance during which he scored four times and collected eight RBIs. Babe D. belted a pair of home runs the next day in game two of a double-header as New York beat the A's, 21-0, the most lopsided shutout in AL history. DiMaggio also hit two home runs to hike the scoring. It might have been worse: the nightcap (the A's had won the opener 12-9) was called after eight innings. Backing up his shutout, Ruffing, who batted .307 in 1939, contributed four hits. New York's other Red, meanwhile, was just as hot in August. Rolfe, hitting in the number two spot, scored at least one run in 18 consecutive games.

But nobody did it like DiMaggio—at bat or in the field. On August 2, the Yankee Clipper made what is often called the greatest catch in the history of Yankee Stadium. It happened during a 7-2 loss to Detroit before 12,341 fans. Getting a jump on Hank Greenberg's blast to deep center, DiMaggio, who was known for his ability to play shallow, instinctively ran with his back to the plate all the way out to the 461-foot sign. Next to the famed monuments, he reached up and grabbed the ball without looking back. And DiMag did some heavy hitting of his own while the Bronx Bombers went 21-10 in August. The Clipper belted a grand slam, a three-run homer and a run-scoring single on August 28 in Detroit to lead the Yanks to an 18-2 win. That brought his batting average close to .400.

DiMaggio drove in another six runs on two triples and a single in Cleveland on September 1—the Yankees triumphed 11-8. It extended his batting streak to 17 straight games and left him with 27 hits in his last 53 at bats. He raised his average to .408 on September 8, threatening to become the first major-leaguer to hit .400 since Bill Terry in 1930. On September 16, New York clinched the American League pennant by defeating Detroit, 8-5, in Yankee Stadium. DiMaggio's bat cooled during the final weeks of the season: He fell to .381, but easily won the AL title. Never since in the major leagues has a right-handed hitter topped .380.

"I was batting more than .400," DiMaggio recalled, "then I got this terrible allergy in my left eye, my batting eye, and I could hardly see out of it. Joe McCarthy didn't believe in cheese champions, so he made me play every day. I went into a terrible slump.

"McCarthy had to know the agony I was going through, but I'll never understand why he didn't give me a couple of days off. I guess it was the rule of the day—you played with anything short of a broken leg."

Dedication by the Yankees to cool, machine-like efficiency resulted in a sweep of the 1939 World Series. Beating the NL champion Cincinnati Reds, the Yanks ran their winning streak in the Fall Classic to nine games in a row. New York went 16-3 in World Series games on its way to four consecutive world titles. Going back to 1927, it was the 28th Yankee win in their past 31 Series games. Asked years later about the World Series of '39, Reds first baseman Frank McCormick responded: "What World Series?"

For the third consecutive time, New York's pitching in October was sensational. Posting a 1.22 ERA, the Yankees bested the Reds 2-1, 4-0, 7-3 and 7-4. Monte Pearson even no-hit Cincinnati for the first seven innings of game two. Ironically, some experts had predicted the Yanks might have trouble with Cincinnati's hurlers. Reds ace Bucky Walters, the NL MVP, had a 27-11 record; and Paul Derringer had a 25-7 mark. But New York was overpowering.

The Series ended in Cincinnati with a legendary incident in game four. With the scored tied 4-4 in the top of the 10th, Crosetti was at third and Charlie Keller at first. DiMaggio singled to right to score Crosetti—and when right fielder Ival Goodman bobbled the ball Keller dashed for home. In the collision at the plate, Keller accidentally kicked catcher Ernie Lombardi in the groin. That knocked the ball loose and scored the run. Then while Lombardi lay stunned in his infamous "snooze," DiMaggio scored, too. Unfairly, the Reds catcher became the goat of the Series.

The hero was "King Kong" Keller. The 23-year-old Yankee rookie wielded a monstrous bat. In four games, he hit .438 with three homers, a triple, a double and six RBIs. Which symbolized New York's dominance on the way to its fourth straight world title. To the cry "Break up the Yankees," a Reds fan vowed: "Yankees, hell! Just break up Keller!"

On the train back to New York, some Yanks understandably began to celebrate their unprecedented success by parading through the Pullman cars. This drew a proud reproof from Joe McCarthy. "Cut that out," he ordered. "What are you? Amateurs? I thought I was managing a professional club." He was. The New York Yankees, under trying circumstances in 1939, had become one of the finest teams in the history of baseball. During the World Series, their heroic benchridden captain wore pinstripes in October for the last time.

3

New York Yankees 1932

107-47

.695

FIRST WORLD CHAMPIONSHIP FOR JOE MCCARTHY ♦ YANKS SWEEP CUBS IN WORLD SERIES AS BABE RUTH "CALLS" HR ♦ AT AGE 37, THE BABE (41, 137, .341) THRIVES ♦ SO DOES LOU GEHRIG (34, 151, .349) ♦ GOMEZ IS 24-7; RUFFING, 18-7; ALLEN, 17-4.

This was Babe Ruth's last hurrah. The 37-year-old Babe, wielding Ruthian power for the final time, led the New York Yankees to their seventh pennant in 12 seasons and to their fourth world championship. Running the 1932 Yankees—occasionally called the best team ever—was manager Joe McCarthy, who had the job Ruth wanted. Steady, colorless Lou Gehrig, 29, was great that season; he even belted an unprecedented four home runs in one game. And the Yankee pitching was sensational all year long. But the Sultan of Swat ultimately prevailed. He bid farewell to the World Series by "calling" his shot before hitting the most controversial home run in major-league history.

Opening the '32 season, the Bronx Bombers got off to a fast start. They took advantage of a schedule that, for the most part, called for them to play the better American League teams (particularly Philadelphia and Washington) in the first half. The Yanks captured first place for good by mid May and just kept winning. By July, they were cruising toward the AL pennant. On the way, New York brushed by the weaker western teams. The '32 Yankees went 107-47 (a winning percentage of .695) to finish 13 games in front of the second-place Athletics and 14 ahead of the third-place Senators. In Yankee Stadium, the Bronx Bombers were 62-15. They swept the National League champion Chicago Cubs (90-64, .584) in the World Series. To some, it was a season that measured up to the legendary performance of the 1927 New York Yankees.

"It's a tossup as to which club was better, '27 or '32," Hall of Famer Joe Sewell once claimed while looking back to the old days. He was the third baseman on the 1932 Yankee team; and he played for Cleveland against the '27 New York club. "The more I think about it," he decided, "the more I feel the 1932 Yankees would have beaten the '27 Yankees."

To doubters, Sewell urged, "Look at the records and decide for yourself, but for me, I've seen every good team in the last 60 years, and I never saw a better one than the '32 Yanks."

Sewell explained: "We won the pennant easily in '32 and just slaughtered the Cubs in the World Series. I'd have to think we had to beat out a better Athletics team in '32 than the one the '27 club beat for the pennant.

"The '32 A's were coming off three straight pennants. Jimmie Foxx won the home run (58) and RBI (169) titles. Jimmie Dykes was playing third instead of first. And Lefty Grove had one of his best years, winning the ERA title (2.84).

"If you ask me, the only edge the '27 Yankees had over the '32 Yankees was possibly in left field (where Bob Meusel preceded Ben Chapman)—and the fact that Ruth and Gehrig had their greatest seasons in '27."

By the way, Sewell set a modern major-league record in 1932: he fanned just three times in 503 at bats. Sewell batted .272 with 11 homers and 68 RBIs.

"We were as good as a defensive club as '27, too," claimed Sewell. "And we had better pitching. We had Lefty

Gomez (24-7), Red Ruffing (18-7), Johnny Allen (17-4)—plus Herb Pennock (9-5) and George Pipgras (16-9) from the '27 club were still around.

"Gomez was almost as good as Lefty Grove, in my opinion.

"Frankie Crosetti (at shortstop in '32) didn't hit much (.241), but he was just a rookie. And we had five .300 hitters and a .299 hitter (Ben Chapman) in our starting lineup without him."

The big five Bronx Bombers in 1932 were: right fielder Babe Ruth (41 homers, 137 RBIs, .341), first baseman Lou Gehrig (34, 151, .349), center fielder Earle Combs (9, 65, .321), catcher Bill Dickey (15, 84, .310) and second baseman Tony Lazzeri (15, 113, .300).

On the mound, though, New York was even better. Yankee pitchers led the AL in ERA (3.98), strikeouts (770) and shutouts (11). They tied the A's for the lead in complete games (95). Finishing 1-2-3 in the AL in winning percentage were Allen (.810), Gomez (.774) and Ruffing (.720). Plus Ruffing became the first Yankee to lead the league in strikeouts (190).

They got plenty of support at the plate, even though the Yankees failed for the first time in ten years to hit the most home runs in the American League. In a power duel with the A's, the Bombers hit 160 homers, just 13 fewer than their league-leading rivals. But New York topped the AL by scoring 1,002 runs (including a AL high of 955 RBIs). The Yanks weren't even shut out once in 1932 by opposing pitchers. No Yankee batter finished number one in any major hitting category. However, Chapman, rugged, aggressive and fast, led the league with 38 stolen bases. And New York's explosive lineup drew a total of 766 walks, topping the AL and setting a club record. The Bambino, of course, walked more than anybody else in the league—130 times.

For his aging legs, it was a relief. The mighty Ruth, growing fatter and slower, had begun to bear the weight of time. In 1932, the Babe lost forever the homer title he virtually had owned since 1918 (except for gaps in 1922 and 1925). Before the '32 season, Ruth was forced to take a $5,000 salary cut to

$75,000 in deference to the times—America was hitting bottom in the Great Depression. "I haven't noticed the Yankees in any depression," he complained.

It was to be the summer of the "Bonus Army" in Washington, D.C. Hoping to keep his job, President Hoover would mount a losing re-election campaign against Gov. Roosevelt of New York. Furor erupted over the fatal kidnapping of infant Charles Lindbergh Jr. A political scandal forced Mayor Jimmy Walker of New York to resign. And sports fans kept up with the '32 Olympics in Los Angeles—as well as with baseball. And, with Babe Ruth.

As it turned out, Ruth's labors paid off in 1932. Not that he could still play day in and day out. The tiring Bambino began to leave games more often in the late innings, stepping aside for his his young outfield "caddies," Sammy Byrd or Myril Hoag. Benched twice during the season by aches and pains, the Babe played in only 133 games. His once superb fielding had diminished. Yet Ruth's bat could still boom.

"I always had three ambitions," the Babe explained after he retired. "I wanted to play 20 years in the big leagues. I wanted to play in ten World Series, and I wanted to hit 700 home runs. Well, '32 was one away from my 20th year, and that Series with the Cubs was number ten; and I finally wound up with 729 home runs, countin' World Series games. So, I can't kick."

What Ruth used to kick about, though, was Joe McCarthy. The Bambino had hoped to become a player-manager like Chicago's Rogers Hornsby, who was promoted when McCarthy was ousted by the Cubs in 1930. Ruth felt he had earned the opportunity. But the Yankee brass—owner Jake Ruppert and general manager Ed Barrow—believed the profligate Babe couldn't handle himself, let alone a baseball team. So, when they fired Bob Shawkey, the unsuccessful manager who had succeeded Miller Huggins, McCarthy was signed for 1931. McCarthy treated ballplayers as individuals. He learned to handle the sulking Ruth, the dominant figure in the game, by leaving him alone. For his part, the Babe resented McCarthy and tried to undermine his authority from time to time. No wonder the quiet, professional Gehrig was the new manager's favorite. In fact, McCarthy became popular with most of Ruth's teammates. He coaxed the runner-up Yanks to a classy 94-59 finish in 1931, but that left them 13½ games behind the pennant-winning A's.

On April 12, 1932, Opening Day, the Yanks slammed five home runs—including a shot by Ruth—to beat the A's, 12-6, in Philadelphia. It started a record AL streak by the Bombers. They hit at least one home run (20 in all) in the first eight games of the season. From the start, their powerful intentions were fully apparent. The Yankees went 10-3 in April; and 18-8 in May. On May 30, New York closed out the month by sweeping Boston, 7-5 and 13-3, in a double-header at Yankee Stadium. That afternoon the Yanks dedicated the first of three historic monuments in deep center field. Their late manager, Miller Huggins, was honored as "a splendid character who made priceless contributions to baseball and on this field brought glory to the New York club of the America League."

More glory was supplied by Lou Gehrig on June 3. He became the first AL batter ever to hit four home runs in one game. It happened while the Bombers pounded the A's 20-13 in Philadelphia during a Shibe Park marathon.

In the game, New York, which came from behind twice, belted a total of seven homers—including one each by Ruth, Combs and Lazzeri (who hit for the cycle). The two teams combined for an American League record of 77 total bases; New York alone had 23 hits and 50 total bases.

Gehrig hit home runs in each of his first four times up. In the first and the fifth innings, he hit balls into the seats in left-center; in the fourth and seventh, he hit shots over the right-field wall.

Eventually, George Earnshaw, who was 19-13 for the A's in 1932, was able to joke about it: "Do I remember the day Gehrig hit four homers off me? No, I don't. Because he only hit three off me. The other he hit off Roy Mahaffey.

"Connie Mack always liked Mahaffey, so after Gehrig hit his third off me, he brought in Roy to cool 'em off. Boy, he sure did cool 'em off. Scored twenty runs that day—and they only got me for seven of them. Roy came in for one inning and he gave up something like six straight hits.

"The funny part, though, was I was ready to head into the shower after Connie took me out, only Gehrig was coming up again. And Connie says, 'Wait a second. I want you to see how Mahaffey pitches to Gehrig.' So Gehrig steps up and kills Roy's first pitch—a real screamer, right out of the park. 'I see what you mean,' I said. 'May I go now?'"

In his last at bat in the ninth, Gehrig hit his longest shot of the day—a blast that descended near the flagpole in deep center. His old roommate, Bill Dickey, recalled: "Al Simmons boosted himself up on the fence and made the greatest one-handed catch you ever saw on it. Lou very easily could've had five homers in one game."

Typically, the biggest headlines on the sports pages the following morning didn't go to Lou Gehrig, who had just played the greatest game of his career. His four consecutive home runs were hit on the day John McGraw announced plans to retire after 31 years of managing the New York Giants. For Gehrig, of course, being upstaged by a legend was familiar and bittersweet.

The Yankees split that early June series of six games with the A's in Philadelphia. But New York lost only five games all month. Going into July, the Bombers had a record of 48-19. And hopes were fading for the rest of the American League. On July 4, though, the Senators swept a double-header from the Yanks, 5-3 and 12-6, in Washington. Even worse, a punch thrown at home plate by usually mild-mannered Bill Dickey led to his suspension for 30 days. After they collided, the Yankee catcher sent outfielder Carl Reynolds to the bench for six weeks with a broken jaw.

As it turned out, the Yanks barely noticed Dickey's absence. Five days later, for instance, New York swept Detroit, 7-6 and 14-9, in a a twin bill at Yankee Stadium. The Bombers won the opener on homers by Ruth, Gehrig and Sewell; they won the nightcap on Chapman's three homers, two of them inside-the-park shots. Not even the loss of Ruth for nearly two weeks in mid July—the Bambino tore leg muscles while chasing a fly ball—sidetracked the Yanks. On July 23, the Yankees pleased Bronx fans by beating the A's 9-3 behind 22-year-old Lefty Gomez. Tall and lanky, the young ace was 7-1 vs. Philadelphia in 1932.

One of New York's other pitching heroes, Red Ruffing, 28, did it all on August 13 during a 1-0 victory in Washington. He shut out the Senators for ten innings and won his own game with a home run. Besting Washington's Tommy Thomas, the Yankee right-hander struck out ten and allowed only three hits.

"Ruffing was a less-than-.500 pitcher when the Red Sox had him," Ben Chapman said years later. "Then he came over to the Yankees (in 1930) and he had the good fastball and he was a hell of a competitor. . . .But it wasn't until he got to the Yanks that he became great. He got a good team behind him and he couldn't lose."

Coming off their hottest month (New York was 23-5 in August), the Bombers had all but wrapped things up. They hiked their AL lead to 12½ games by defeating the second-place A's, 8-6 and 6-3, on September 5 in a doubleheader at Yankee Stadium. Two days later, old man Ruth, troubled by shooting pains in his right side, left the Yanks in Detroit and rushed back to New York to see the team doctor. The Babe was sure he had appendicitis. But there was no operation. With a low fever, Ruth was packed in ice and kept in bed. In Cleveland, the Yankees clinched the pennant on September 13, beating the Indians, 9-3. Would Ruth be ready for the World Series? A few days later, the Sultan of Swat worked out at Stadium while the club was still on the road: he failed to hit even one pitch into the stands. "I'm so weak," Ruth declared, "I don't think I could break a pane of glass. But I'll be OK in a few days." Back in the lineup for the last five games of the season, he went just 3 for 16 at the plate.

In the World Series, the Babe rose again. It was perhaps the most heated and bitter Fall Classic ever played. But what's remembered best is how Ruth single-handedly foiled the Chicago Cubs with one dramatic home run.

Revenge was on the minds of the Yankees in the 1932

World Series. They knew how sweet victory would be to Joe McCarthy. He had been dumped by the Cubs for finishing only second in 1930 after having captured the NL flag the year before. Now McCarthy, who had just become the first manager to win pennants in both major leagues, wanted to prove he could also win a world championship.

The Yankees also resented the way Chicago had treated its new shortstop, Mark Koenig, one of their old boys of '27. The Cubs had voted the ex-New Yorker (who played in 33 regular-season games for them) only half a World Series share even though he hit .353 after being called up from the minors. So, the Yanks—especially Ruth, who hated tightfistedness—loudly branded their National League foes as cheapskates. No share at all was set aside by Chicago for Rogers Hornsby. The Rajah, tactless and blunt, had been fired as manager on August 2, 1932, following a dispute with owner William Wrigley. First baseman Charlie Grimm was the new Cub skipper. So, McCarthy had to settle for beating his old team, but not his replacement.

For their part, the Cubs, underdogs in a natural rivalry between the two greatest U.S. cities, didn't hesitate to trade crude taunts with the Yanks. Particularly with Ruth, their biggest target. Chicago's bench jockeys ran wild throughout the World Series. On the day of the Babe's historic clout in game three, even Cubs trainer Andy Lotshaw joined the Wrigley Field banter. He yelled to Ruth: "If I had you, I'd hitch you to a wagon, you potbelly." That upset the great Bambino, even though he always relished being the center of attention. "I didn't mind no ballplayers yelling at me," explained Ruth, "but the trainer cutting in—that made me sore."

Invading Yankee Stadium to open the World Series, Chicago was led by left fielder Riggs Stephenson, right fielder Kiki Cuyler, catcher Gabby Hartnett—and four right-handed starters: Guy Bush, Lon Warneke, Charlie Root and Pat Malone. The Yankees won 12-6 in game one (Ruffing over Bush), and 5-2 in game two (Gomez over Warneke). Cubs pitchers walked ten New York batters in the first two games and nine of them scored. So, the rivalry grew even fouler.

Nearly 50,000 fans—including Democratic presidential candidate Franklin D. Roosevelt—jammed into Wrigley Field for game three (Pipgras vs. Root). With a strong wind blowing toward right field, the Yanks put on a show in batting practice: Ruth hit nine pitches into the seats, Gehrig seven.

As Ruth waited to hit in the first inning, reported Richards Vidmer in *The New York Herald Tribune*, "He paused to jest with the raging Cubs, pointed to the right field bleachers and grinned." The Babe promptly delivered a homer to right with two men on base, giving the Yanks a 3-0 lead. In the third, Gehrig made it 4-0 with a solo bast. But the Cubs tied the game 4-4 in the fourth.

Thus, the stage was set. Babe Ruth walked up to the plate in the fifth inning with one out and the bases empty. This is how play-by-play announcer Tom Manning of NBC Radio recounted the action:

"Babe Ruth steps into the batter's box. Now Charlie Root gets the sign from his catcher, Gabby Hartnett. Here's the first pitch. And it's a strike—right down the middle! And the fans are certainly giving it to Babe Ruth now. Looking over at the Cubs' bench, the Cubs are all up on the top step. And they're yelling 'flatfoot' and throwing liniment and everything else at Babe Ruth! But he steps out of the batter's box. He takes a hitch in his trousers, knocks the dust off his shoes. And now he's back in there again.

"And Root winds up again and here it comes! And it's outside—and it's evened up on Babe Ruth. Boy, what a powerful figure he is at that plate! And once again, Root gets the signal, winds up, and here it comes. And it's called strike two! And the fans are giving it to him from all corners of this Wrigley Field. The Cubs are up on the bench—they're all hoping that Babe Ruth will strike out. Again Charlie Root winds up. And here's that pitch and it's high inside, and it drove Babe Ruth out of the batter's box! And the count is ball two and strike two. And, boy, the Cubs are giving it to Babe now!

"Oh, oh, Babe Ruth has stepped out of the batter's box. And he steps about two feet away from home plate. Now he steps towards the Cubs' dugout! We thought for a moment that he was going over and toss his bat at them or something. No, he's smiling at them. He takes off his hat, he holds up his two fingers with his right hand. Now he drops his bat and he's indicating that the count is ball two and strike two. He gets back into the batter's box. The umpire again warns the Cubs. Charlie Root gets his signal.

"And Babe Ruth steps out of the batter's box again! He's holding up his two and two. Oh, oh, and now Babe Ruth is pointing out to center field. And he's yelling at the Cubs that the next pitch over is going into center field! Someone just tossed a lemon down there. Babe Ruth has picked up the lemon and now he tosses it over to the Cub's bench. He didn't throw anything, he sort of kicked it over there. After he turns, he points again to center field! And here's the pitch. It's going! Babe Ruth connects and here it goes! And it's a home run! It's gone! Whoopee! Listen to that crowd!"

Nothing about Babe Ruth ever became more legendary—or subject to more dispute. Did he really call his shot? The eye-witness account of Tom Manning is confirmed by old movie film shot at Wrigley Field during the game. It displays Ruth standing at home plate with his bat resting on his left shoulder and pointing, with his right arm extended shoulder-high, straight out in the direction of the mound. Or beyond.

From the on-deck circle, Gehrig had a perfect view of the finger-pointing. Known always as fair and honest, he saidthat Ruth, responding to the jeers of the Cubs, had warned Root: "I'm going to knock the next pitch right down your goddamn throat." Which, of course, "called" the swing—if not the home run itself. Ruth's gesture defied the pitcher and indicated something was going to happen. It turned out to be a home run. In the clubhouse after the game, the Babe yelled: "Did Mr. Ruth chase those guys back into the dugout? Mr. Ruth sure did!" That night, Gehrig asked sportswriter Fred Lieb, a close friend, "What do you think of the nerve of that big monkey, calling his shot and getting away with it?"

Over the years, Ruth thrived on the epic controversy over his gesturing. Variously, he either claimed he had predicted a home run, or only hinted that he had done so, or indicated he hadn't, or actually said he hadn't or ducked the question. Perhaps his truest remark was: "I didn't exactly point to any spot. All I wanted to do was to give the thing a ride out of the park." He left no doubt, though, about how he felt when he connected for the last World Series home run of his career. "As I hit the ball," the Babe said, "every muscle in my system, every sense I had, told me that I had never hit a better one, that as long as I lived nothing would ever feel as good as this."

Little noted was the fact that Lou Gehrig, the forgotten man, immediately followed Ruth's blast with a home run of his own. It was also his second of the day. New York won 7-5 in Game 3 and 13-6 in Game 4. As the Yankees pushed their World Series win streak to 12 games in a row, Gehrig excelled. His hitting performance in the '32 Fall Classic remains unequalled. In four games, he hit .549 with nine hits—including three home runs. Gehrig also drove in eight runs and scored nine times. But who remembers?

It was Babe Ruth's triumph. And the tired Bambino, who hit .333 in the Series with two homers and six RBIs, was overjoyed. So were the Yankees. After the final game, coach Art Fletcher led one of the greatest baseball teams ever in singing "The Sidewalks of New York." For Joe McCarthy, it was the first and most satisfying of what would be seven Yankee world championships in a span of 12 years. Even the Babe found a way to praise him. Despite his grudge, Ruth went over and shook hands with the manger. "What a victory!" he said. "My hat is off to you, Mac."

›››››››››››››› 4 ››››››››››››››

Philadelphia Athletics

1929

104-46

.693

CONNIE MACK STARTS NEW A'S DYNASTY ♦ POWERED BY AL SIMMONS (34, 157, .365), JIMMIE FOXX (33, 117, .354) ♦ FOUR MORE A'S, INCLUDING MICKEY COCHRANE, TOP .310 ♦ GEORGE EARNSHAW IS 24-8, LEFTY GROVE IS 20-6 ♦ A'S DEFEAT CUBS IN FIVE-GAME WORLD SERIES.

Joe DiMaggio hit safely in 56 straight games. Lou Gehrig played in 2,130 consecutive games during 15 seasons. Cy Young won 511 games in his 22 years in baseball. But Cornelius A. McGillicuddy holds a more durable record.

Connie Mack managed the Philadelphia Athletics for 50 seasons in a row.

The "Tall Tactician" led the Athletics through 7,590 games from 1901, when he was 38 years old, until 1950, when he was 87. For half a century, the 6-foot-1, 150-pound manager was a distinctive sight in the A's dugout. He invariably wore a dark business suit, a stiff white collar and either a derby or a straw hat. During games, Mack positioned his fielders by signaling with a rolled up scorecard.

Mr. Mack, as he was known throughout baseball, guided the Athletics to nine American League pennants and five world championships, all of them prior to his election to the Hall of Fame in 1937. A founding owner of the team, he built two Philadelphia dynasties—one beginning in 1910 and the other later in 1929.

The world champion '29 A's were the most successful team Connie Mack ever fielded. Early the following year, the *Spalding Official Base Ball Guide* reported: "Whether the Athletics were the greatest team to win an American League pennant is a question subject to debate." Thus, the club was immediately compared to the New York Yankees of 1927.

Not only did the '29 Athletics have a pair of sluggers—Al Simmons and Jimmie Foxx—who rivaled Bronx Bombers Babe Ruth and Lou Gehrig, they also had perhaps the top battery in baseball history: Mickey Cochrane and Lefty Grove. Each of those four Philadelphia stars were future Hall of Famers. Now it's argued that perhaps no manager ever had four better major leaguers playing for him in their prime at the same time. And the revival of the A's, who finished 18 games in front of second-place New York in 1929, was seen back in those days as a tribute to the 66-year-old Mack near the end of his long career.

In the early 1880s, Cornelius Alexander "Slats" McGillicuddy of East Brookfield, Massachusetts, was already playing pro baseball. His bulky Irish name was shortened to fit minor-league box scores in New England newspapers. He was one of the first catchers to work close to the batter, and he helped to promote overhand pitching. Then Mack became a popular figure in the National League (1886-1896) as the "talking catcher" who disrupted hitters with his high-pitched chatter. He also batted .247 through 11 big-league seasons, the last three of them as a player-manager for the Pittsburgh Pirates.

At that point, Mack accepted an offer from his friend Ban Johnson, who ran the Western League, to manage the Milwaukee club. In 1901, Johnson turned the circuit into the American League, awarding the Philadelphia franchise to Mack.

Holding a one-quarter share of the team, Mack obtained most of his financing from Ben Shibe of the Reach Sporting Goods Company.

Mack, a master builder and a keen judge of talent, quickly won pennants in Philadelphia in 1902 and 1905. In the early days, he raided the National League for underpaid stars. Angered, John McGraw of the New York Giants belittled the A's as "white elephants." So, Philadelphia adopted the nickname and it became the team symbol. Mack's original dynasty and first three world titles came in 1910, 1911 and 1913. Those A's featured Frank "Home Run" Baker and Eddie Collins (both members of the "$100,000 infield"), along with pitchers Chief Bender and Eddie Plank. Philadelphia won the AL pennant again in 1914. But Bender and Plank jumped to a rival circuit; and Mack had to sell Baker and Collins. "I tore the club apart," said Mack, "because Federal League teams were offering them far more than I could, and I wanted them to stay in the American League. I decided to sell off and start over again almost from scratch."

And so he did. Philadelphia finished last for seven years in a row, losing 100 or more games five times. Attendance at Shibe Park during those lean years averaged only about 1,500 per game. And there were complaints that Mack, never among the wealthiest of owners, ought to sell the club to somebody else and leave town. In 1925, though, the A's climbed back into to the first division and finished second. Mack had begun to rebuild. In 1926, Philadelphia wound up in third place, only six games behind the Yankees. For a time, Mack boosted the gate by bringing in old-timers such as Ty Cobb, Eddie Collins, Zack Wheat and Tris Speaker. But he was finding younger talent, too. This was to be the last baseball dynasty built on purchases from unaffiliated minor-league clubs. The Mackmen finished second in 1927 at 91-63, and found themselves 19 games behind the greatest New York team ever. In 1928, Philadelphia trailed the Yanks by 17 games at one point. But the A's swept into first place in early September before finishing as the runner-up at 98-55, just 2½ games behind New York.

As the Roaring '20s faded, the power-packed rivalry between New York and Philadelphia was the talk of the American League. "With those two monsters in the league, the rest of us started the season fighting for third place," explained Roger Peckinpaugh, who managed Cleveland in those days.

The Athletics reached the top in 1929 mostly on the strength of great performances by their four leading stars:

• Left fielder Al Simmons, 27 years old. He hit 34 homers, drove in 157 runs and batted .365 for Philadelphia in 1929. He led the league in RBIs and total bases (373); placed second in hitting, and slugging (.642); and finished third in homers, and hits (212). Born Aloysius Harry Szymanski, he was a Polish-American from Milwaukee. Before the 1924 season, Mack purchased Simmons from the Milwaukee Brewers of the American Association for about $50,000. The young right-handed hitter was called "Bucketfoot Al" because he always strode toward third base as he swung at a pitch. At 5-foot-11 and 190 pounds, Simmons still had more than enough power to become an immediate star in the American League. He was a fierce competitor who always faced pitchers with an intimidating glare. He was also a solid outfielder with a strong arm.

• First baseman Jimmie Foxx, 21 years old. He hit 33 homers, drove in 117 runs and batted .354 for Philadelphia in 1929. He was third in the AL in slugging (.642); fourth in homers; and fifth in batting, and total bases (323). "Double X" was the son of an Irish farmer from Sudlersville, Maryland. At age 16, the boy was a catcher at Easton in the Eastern Shore League. When both the A's and the Yanks expressed interest in him, Home Run Baker, who was managing Easton, steered Foxx to Connie Mack, as a favor to his old skipper. Ironically, the muscular slugger eventually was called "The Right-handed Babe Ruth." He had a demeanor and outlook much like the Babe's. As a teen-ager, Foxx broke in slowly with Philadelphia, starting in 1925. But the A's didn't need him behind the plate.

• Catcher Mickey Cochrane, 26 years old. He hit seven homers, drove in 95 runs and batted .333 for Philadelphia in

1929. He usually batted third, in front of Simmons and Foxx. It was an odd spot for a catcher, but Cochrane, the fiery team leader, was quick. He was also the top fielder at his position in the American League. No wonder "Black Mike" is often described as the best catcher in the history of baseball. A career .320 hitter, he was one of the nimblest men ever to crouch behind the plate. He joined the Athletics in 1925 and turned into their spark plug. Years later, Mack wrote: "Mickey Cochrane became a foundation stone upon whom I started to rebuild." Cochrane had worked his way through Boston University partly as a semipro ballplayer, using the assumed name "Frank King" to protect his amateur status. He turned pro with Dover in the Eastern Shore League. In a $200,000 deal, Mack bought control of both Cochrane and Portland of the Pacific Coast League, where the young catcher was assigned in 1924. The following year, his boundless energy and skill immediately made him the A's regular catcher.

• Pitcher Lefty Grove, 29 years old. He was 20-6 with an earned run average of 2.81 for Philadelphia in 1929. He led the league in ERA, winning percentage (.769) and strikeouts (170). He was third in wins, and innings (275); and tied for fifth in complete games (21). Robert Moses Grove was named in a 1969 poll of legendary ballplayers as the greatest living left-handed pitcher. His career totals: 300-140, 3.06. Grove, who stood 6-foot-3 and weighed 190 pounds, threw hard, inning after inning. His fastball sometimes "looked like a flash of white sewing thread coming up at you," according to Hall of Famer Joe Sewell. "Sure we knew what was coming," Sewell added. "So what?" Grove was dour, mean-tempered and enormously self-confident. Out of the coal mines in western Maryland, he didn't reach the majors until he was 25. Despite wildness, Grove pitched Baltimore of the International League to five straight flags (1920-24). Then Mack agreed to pay Baltimore owner Jack Dunn, the man who had developed young George Ruth, who played his first season with Baltimore, a total of $100,600 for Grove. Dunn insisted on charging $600 more than he did for the Babe. By 1927, "Old Mose" had recorded the first of seven 20-win seasons in a row.

Between them, Cochrane and Grove typified the hard-nosed competitiveness of the A's, despite Connie Mack's gentlemanly image. Mack, a family man who didn't drink, smoke or curse, quietly got the best out of players no matter their nature. His number one battery, for example. Mack was the only one who called Lefty Grove "Robert." He used to refer to him as "Groofs," and to his catcher as "Corcoran." But he knew enough to tolerate their tempestuous behavior. "Lose a 1-to-0 game and you didn't want to get into the clubhouse with Grove and Cochrane," recalled Doc Cramer, an ex-Philadelphia outfielder. "You'd be ducking stools and gloves and bats and whatever else would fly."

On the other hand, the New York Yankees, by 1929, had lost their old desire. On May 14, the day Philadelphia moved into first place to stay, Yankee manager Miller Huggins offered a prophetic assessment. Said Huggins: "I don't think the Yanks are going to catch the Athletics. I don't think these Yanks are going to win any more pennants, or at least, not this one. They're getting older and they're becoming glutted with success. They've been in three World Series in a row, remember, and they've won the last two Series in four straight. They've been getting fairly high salaries and they've taken a lot of money out of baseball, a whole lot of money. They have stock market investments and these investments are giving them excellent returns at the moment. When they pick up a newspaper now, they turn to the financial page first and the sports page later. Those things aren't good for a club, not a club which is trying to beat a club like the one Mr. Mack has."

Sure, the A's were hungry. For all his virtues, Mack was never particularly generous with salaries. Actually, the franchise was in chronic financial trouble, so he had to be a skinflint. For instance, Foxx never was paid as much as the other top big-league hitters. In 1929, as the youngest Philadelphia regular, he earned just $5,000. Thus, the winning World Series share—$5,620—was a big incentive for him. And for the other A's, too.

To go with their four top stars, the '29 Athletics had a balanced array of hitters, pitchers and fielders. They were number two in the AL in runs (901), homers (122), slugging (.451) and batting (.296). But they led the league with the lowest ERA (3.44), least runs allowed (615), least errors (146) and best fielding average (.975). One oddity was the fact that Philadelphia finished last in the American League in double plays. Perhaps it was because the A's pitchers were tops in strikeouts. Catching and the outfield were their strongest fielding positions.

Six key A's batted .300. Besides Simmons, Foxx and Cochrane, they included: right fielder Bing Miller (8, 93, .335), infielder Jimmy Dykes (13, 79, .327); and center fielder Mule Haas (16, 82, .313). Miller, a speedster, was third in the league in both triples (16) and stolen bases (24). Topping the AL in walks (128) was A's second baseman Max "Camera Eye" Bishop (3, 36, .232), the club's leadoff hitter. He seldom drew an intentional walk, but he was simply a hard man to pitch to, and he was a table-setter for the Philly sluggers.

On the mound, Mack had a hard-throwing righty to go with Lefty Grove. George Earnshaw (24-8, 3.29), led the league in wins and was second in games pitched (44). A graduate of Swarthmore, Earnshaw, 29, had the first of three 20-win seasons for Connie Mack's new dynasty. Like Grove, the 6-foot-4, 210-pound ace had been purchased from Baltimore. Mack paid $80,000 for him. The other top starter in 1929 was Rube Walberg (18-11, 3.59), a 32-year-old left-hander. "We'd pitch Grove, Earnshaw and Walberg the first three games," said Doc Cramer, "and we didn't care who they pitched. We had 'em wore out." Finally, right-hander Eddie Rommel (12-2, 2.85) was the top reliever in the AL.

By '29, only Rommel, 31, and Jimmy Dykes, 32, the man who eventually would replace Mack as manager of the Athletics, could remember back to the leanest years at Shibe Park. Two 32-year-old regulars—third baseman Sammy Hale (1, 40, .277) and shortstop Joe Boley (2, 47, .251)—were later arrivals. But the resurgent A's were looking ahead, not back.

The Mackmen opened the 1929 season on April 17 in Washington, blasting the Senators, 13-4, as Rommel picked up the win. President Hoover, enjoying his lull before the

Great Depression, threw out the first ball. A few days later, the president warned in New York that law and order was America's chief worry, but he said most real crime had nothing to do with Prohibition. Hoover didn't point out that one-third of all the personal income in the United States was held by the richest five percent of the people, or that wages hadn't been keeping pace with rising corporate profits and soaring prices on Wall Street.

That summer, well-to-do theater-goers on Broadway were buying front-row seats to such attractions as *Show Girl* at the Ziegfeld Theater. It featured Jimmy Durante along with the music of George Gershwin (including *An American in Paris*) played by Duke Ellington and his Orchestra. From the audience, Al Jolson sang the song "Liza" to his wife, Ruby Keeler, on stage. Over at the Hudson Theater, Louis Armstrong starred in an all-black revue that included songs such as Fats Waller's "Ain't Misbehavin'." But attendance in the American League didn't break any records in 1929. For the first time in years, the Yankees stumbled. And Philadelphia destroyed the pennant race.

In their first showdown of the year, the A's split a pair of games with New York at Yankee Stadium. After losing 2-1 to Yankee ace Waite Hoyt on April 19, Philadelphia triumphed, 7-4, behind Lefty Grove two days later.

On April 23, the Mackmen lost their home opener. Repaying the favor, Washington beat Philadelphia, 4-3, at Shibe Park in 11 innings as Walberg took the loss. Next day, Foxx went four-for-four, including a homer and two doubles, as the A's ripped the Senators, 9-4.

Then the Yankees came to town for three big games: old Jack Quinn, 44, beat the New Yorkers in the first contest, 5-2. But Yankee hurler Wilcy Moore picked up the victory in the second game—New York won, 9-7. In the final contest, the Athletics crushed the defending AL champs, 10-1. Walberg got the win and Yankee hurler Henry Johnson picked up the loss.

Despite their failure that season, the Yankees didn't go quietly. For example, one of the younger stars, Bill Dickey, who is sometimes ranked above Mickey Cochrane as baseball's best catcher ever, was an intense rival of the A's. Much later, Dickey, a mild-mannered type off the field, recalled: "I think the maddest I've ever been in my life was in 1929. We were playing the Philadelphia Athletics. I don't remember what inning it was, but the bases were loaded and there wer-etwo outs. The ump was Bill Dinneen, who was a good ump, and a good guy. Cochrane was the hitter. He hit a swinging bunt down the third-base line, and Henry Johnson, our pitcher that day, made a great play and threw the ball to me. I looked around at Dinneen, and he said, 'Safe!'

"I said, 'Why was he safe?' He said, 'You didn't tag him.' I said, 'Bill I didn't have to tag him! The bases were loaded!' Then he said, 'You weren't on the base.' I was so mad, I couldn't see! I had the ball in my hand and I threw it, but I didn't mean to let it go. But I was so mad, and I threw it so hard, that it slipped away from me and rolled toward the A's dugout. Well, I took out after it, and the men were running the bases. When I got back, another runner had scored, and I was crying. Well, of course, Dinneen put me out of the ballgame, and they suspended me for three days.

"But here's the funny part. I was so mad that I stayed mad all night. I got up early 'cause I couldn't sleep and went down to eat breakfast. Got me a newspaper and I opened it up. There I was in a cartoon throwing off my mask, my chest protector—everything's up in the air—and there was a little old lady in the front row of the grandstand with her hands over her eyes, pleading, 'Please, don't take off any more!'

On May 1, the A's put on a display in Boston. Philadelphia won, 24-6, at Fenway Park while collecting 29 hits. Facing four Red Sox pitchers, Simmons went five-for-six, including a homer and a double. He drove in six runs and scored four times. Jimmie Foxx also belted a pair of homers. Lefty Grove won the game; and he followed up the next day with a 5-1 victory. On May 5, Walberg tossed a one-hitter in St. Louis as Philadelphia trimphed, 2-0.

The Browns and the Yankees had been taking turns in first and second place in the American League since the season began. But the heavy-hitting Mackmen moved on top to stay on May 14 when they won, 10-8, in Detroit.

Three days later, Grove triumphed, 4-1, in Washington as the A's began an 11-game winning streak, their longest of the season. In 1929, Philadelphia also won six games in a row three times during the season, five in a row three times, and the A's won four straight on five occasions.

On May 24, the Athletics beat Washington, 10-3 (Earnshaw over Bump Hadley) in Philadelphia, as Cochrane went four-for-four with a home run. The next day, they edged the Senators, 5-4, in 12 innings. On May 26, in Washington, the A's won their fifth straight game in four days against the Senators. Rommel was the winner, 4-3.

In all, Philadelphia went 16-4 against Washington in ln 1929. Against their two strongest rivals during the season, the A's were: 14-8 vs. New York, who finished second; and 14-7 vs. Cleveland, who finished third.

On Memorial Day, Mack's White Elephants swept a double-header in Boston, which turned out to be the last-place team in 1929. Philadelphia won, 9-2 and 9-3, as Bing Miller started a 28-game hitting streak, the longest of the season in the American League. The front-running A's, in the midst of a six-game winning streak, finished May with a 29-9 record for the year.

Not until June 17, when the Chicago White Sox triumphed, 6-4, at Shibe Park, did Philadelphia lose two games in a row in 1929.

Four days later, the A's returned to New York for another key series with the Yanks. It began with a double-header on June 21 at Yankee Stadium. In the opener, the Mackmen won, 11-1, behind Lefty Grove while Al Simmons turned into a one-man gang. He went five-for-five and accounted for eight runs against three New York hurlers—Herb Pennock, Roy Sherid and Wilcey Moore. Simmons, who blasted two homers in the game, scored five runs and drove in three more. In game two, the Yanks won, 8-2. The next day, the two teams split another twin-bill. Walberg of the A's triumphed, 7-3; then Quinn picked up a loss, 4-3, in a 14-inning game. Behind veteran

Howard Ehmke, Philadelphia beat the Yankees, 7-4, on June 23 to end the series.

When the Athletics swept a double-header against Boston at Shibe Park on June 25, they opened up a 10-game lead in the AL race. Then they split a pair of ball games when New York came to town again. By the end of June, Philadelphia had a record of 48-17 for the season.

The Mackmen virtually wrapped up the pennant race by going 24-9 in July, their winningest month of the year. On the Fourth of July, the A's took morning and afternoon games against Boston, 3-1 and 8-1, at Shibe Park. Winning the opener, Lefty Grove fanned 11. On July 20, he beat the Tigers, 6-2, in Detroit to win his 16th game. Back in Philadelphia, Earnshaw beat the Tigers, 5-4, in 10 innings on July 30; Simmons singled home the winning run. The next day, the A's scored nine runs in the fifth inning and went on to a 10-1 victory against Detroit. On a seven-game winning streak, Philadelphia ended the month at 72-26.

In August, the A's slumped to 15-14, but they were never in danger of losing the pennant from late in the month until the end of the season. In the middle of the month, Philadelphia notched a key win: On August 14, the Athletics triumphed, 5-3, in Cleveland as Grove pitched 17 innings to earn his 18th victory.

Soon thereafter, Miller Huggins told Yankee owner Jacob Ruppert that it was all over. The brewery tycoon protested that, with six weeks to go, New York could still catch up. "Not this bunch," said Huggins. "I've been talking to them for 20 minutes. I bawled them out. I called them everything I could think of, even accusing them of quitting, which I know they haven't. And nothing happened. I might as well have been talking to myself."

On Labor Day, September 2, the Macks swept the tired New York Yankees in a twin bill at Shibe Park. Philadelphia won, 10-3 and 6-5. The next day, Earnshaw finished off the Yanks with a 10-2 victory. (The untimely death later in the month of Miller Huggins, 49, deepened the gloom in New York.)

On September 14, Moose Earnshaw blanked the Chicago White Sox, 5-0, to give the Mackmen the American League pennant.

Now they could look forward to playing the heavy-hitting Chicago Cubs in the World Series. Managed by Joe McCarthy, the Cubs (98-54, .645) finished 10½ games ahead of Pittsburgh. Chicago had Rogers Hornsby (40, 149, .380), Hack Wilson (39, 159, .345), Riggs Stephenson (17, 110, .362) and Kiki Cuyler (15, 102, .360). But Connie Mack was planning to foil those right-handed batters.

After his retirement, Mack wrote: "The Chicago Cubs . . . feared Grove, Earnshaw and Walberg. . . .I knew if they could lick one of these star pitchers they could break the spell and ride on to victory. A major surprise at the offset would break their spirit, so my strategy was to nullify the Chicago plan . . . at the start."

Privately, Mack told 35-year-old Howard Ehmke before the end of the regular season that he was going to release him—even though he was 7-2 on the year with a 3.27 ERA. "I've got one more good game in me," said Ehmke, "and I'd like to give it to you in October." That was just what the Tall Tactician wanted to hear. So Mack ordered Ehmke to stay in Philadelphia during the club's final Western trip, to work out quietly, and secretly to scout the Cubs when they came to town to play the Phillies.

On October 8, Connie Mack unveiled his surprise. Howard Ehmke started game one of the World Series in Chicago. It was a risky move that stunned even Mack's own players. "Is he going to work?" asked Simmons. "Yes," said Mack, "have you any objections?" "Nope," Simmons replied. "If you think he can win, it's good enough for me."

In those days, Wrigley Field didn't yet have its ivy-clad outfield wall. So Mack was counting on Ehmke's side-arm curves to be obscured by the white shirts in the center field bleachers. And the manager felt his pitcher's off-speed deliveries would upset Chicago.

That's exactly what happened.

Philadelphia beat the Cubs, 3-1, as Ehmke went the

distance. Prepared to match their big hitters against one of Mack's fastball aces, Chicago was just unable to deal with Ehmke's off-speed deliveries. The wily veteran set a World Series record by striking out 13 batters. Ironically, during the regular season, Ehmke had only fanned 20 American Leaguers in 55 innings.

In game two, the A's defeated Chicago, 9-3. Earnshaw, started for Philadelphia, pitched half a game and earned the victory with relief help from Lefty Grove. Together, they struck out another 13 Cubs. Foxx whacked a three-run homer, and Simmons added a two-run shot.

Back in Philadelphia, Earnshaw went the distance in game three, but the Cubs triumphed, 3-1. Cuyler's two-run single was the game-winner in Shibe Park.

In game four, the Mackmen put together the biggest rally in World Series history to win a slugfest, 10-8. Going into the bottom of the seventh, Chicago was leading, 8-0, after working over Quinn, Walberg and Rommell. Then Philadelphia got to Cubs starter Charlie Root. And center fielder Hack Wilson became the goat on defense.

For the home team, Simmons opened the seventh by hitting a homer onto the roof of the left-field stands. Then consecutive singles by Foxx, Bing Miller (as Wilson lost the ball in the sun), Jimmy Dykes and Joe Boley cut the deficit to 8-3. After an infield out, Max Bishop's run-scoring single cut the lead in half. In came Art Nehf to relieve Root. But Mule Haas hit a fly ball to center and Wilson again was bothered by the sun. Behind Dykes and Boley, Haas circled the bases for an inside-the-park three-run homer that cut Chicago's lead to 8-7. Next, Cochrane walked. Sheriff Blake replaced Nehf on the mound. After Simmons singled, Foxx's base hit tied the game, 8-8. Pat Malone came on in relief. He hit Miller to load the bases. Then Dykes doubled to the left-field wall, driving in the two runs that won the ballgame. The record-setting rally ended when the next two batters fanned.

In game five, Philadelphia trailed 2-0 going into the bottom of the ninth inning. Ehmke, the starter again, had given up both runs in the fourth inning before Walberg relieved him. In the last turn at bat for the A's, Bishop hit a one-out single off Malone, the Chicago starter, and Haas drilled a homer over the right-field wall to tie the game. Then Cochrane grounded out. But Simmons doubled and Foxx drew an intentional walk. Bing Miller's double to the scoreboard won the game, 3-2, for Philadelphia. And it made Connie Mack the first big-league manager to win four world championships.

Despite the stirring comebacks by the A's, what gave Connie Mack the most pleasure was Howard Ehmke's big victory in game one. Looking back on that game following 66 years in the big-leagues, Mack wrote: "It was one of the greatest thrills in my life."

Ten days after the World Series, the stock market crashed.

Eventually, the Great Depression ruined the second A's dynasty, which added another world championship in 1930 and another American League pennant in 1931. Thereafter, Connie Mack, caught again in a financial squeeze, had to sell his star players for the second time in his career.

And the old man's glory days were over for good.

5

St. Louis Cardinals 1942

106-48

.688

GREATEST STRETCH DRIVE EVER ♦ CARDS WIN 43 OF LAST 51 GAMES TO GAIN N.L. FLAG ♦ UPSET YANKS IN FIVE-GAME WORLD SERIES ♦ GENERAL MANAGER BRANCH RICKEY REAPS YOUNG TALENT ♦ STAN MUSIAL HITS .315; ENOS SLAUGHTER .318; ♦ MORT COOPER (22-7, 1.77) IS NL MVP.

It was the St. Louis Cardinals of 1942, who staged the greatest pennant drive of all time. On the way to the National League flag, St. Louis, steady and relentless, won 43 of its last 51 games. Nearly all of the Cardinals, who glided through the stretch at a winning rate of .843, were youthful products of Branch Rickey's innovative farm system. But the Redbirds overtook the veteran Brooklyn Dodgers in mid-September and clinched the pennant on the final day of the season.

In '42, St. Louis was 106-48 (.688); Brooklyn, the front-runner for most of the year, was 104-50 (.675). To squeeze by, the Cards, managed by Billy Southworth, beat the Dodgers, under Leo Durocher, in five of the last six games between the clubs. Not since the old dead-ball era had a pennant winner and the number two team each won more than 100 games. Never during the modern years since have two stronger clubs battled so fiercely all season long.

Moreover, the surprising Cards were the youngest team to capture a flag since the pre-1920 days. Averaging only 26 years of age, they even upset the powerful New York Yankees in the 1942 World Series, winning four of the five games. And the boys from St. Louis did it the old-fashioned way, like they did everything else that season—with speed, defense and great pitching.

Ex-center fielder Terry Moore, who was St. Louis' captain and oldest regular (at age 30) in 1942, recently pointed out: "Connie Mack saw the Series and said, 'I have to take my hat off to the Cardinals. They played the game the way it ought to be played. They took advantage of everything and didn't give anything. I think that's the greatest club I've ever seen.'"

"The St. Louis Swifties," as they were dubbed by New York cartoonist Willard Mullin, formed a brash gang that specialized in winning tight, low-scoring games. "Too much energy, entirely too much," complained Cubs manager Jimmy Wilson. "No team can keep charging around a park the way they do and stay in one piece. The Cardinals knock you out of the way just for fun."

Throughout 1942, they did stay in one piece—with style and grace, actually. The Redbirds backed up flashy pitching with some of the smoothest fielding ever seen. They held their opponents to only 3.1 runs per game, fewest in the National League.

Tall and rangy, Marty "Slats" Marion, 24, was one of the best defensive shortstops in the history the game. Behind him was an outfield just as good. In the middle of the outfield, Moore, the team leader, covered the most ground. He could also scoop up balls like an infielder and throw accurately. Flanking him were two future Hall of Famers. In right field, Enos "Country" Slaughter, 26, was a tough go-getter who hustled his way to greatness. In left rookie Stan Musial, 21, was just beginning an even more brilliant career. In those days, Stan the Man was called "The Donora [Pennsylvania] Greyhound."

The St. Louis trio of Musial, Moore and Slaughter became famous in 1942 for suddenly closing gaps in the outfield—often with acrobatics. Recalling one of their key late-season visits to Ebbets Field, Brooklyn's Billy Herman said: "I don't know how many extra-base hits they took away from us that day. We just couldn't believe what they were doing out there. It got to the point where it just didn't pay to belt one into the outfield."

Not that the Dodgers were used to belting Cardinal pitchers. Nobody was. The St. Louis hurlers—tops in the NL in strikeouts (651) and shutouts (18)—finished the '42 season with an earned run average of just 2.55. That was to be the lowest ERA by any pitching staff during the home-run age until 1967.

The Cardinal ace was Mort Cooper, who became the NL's MVP. He went 22-7 with a sizzling 1.77 ERA. The 29-year-old right-hander led the league in wins, ERA, starts (35) and shutouts (10). Cooper, at 6-foot-2 and 210 pounds, threw a baffling variety of overhand fastballs and forkballs. Against the Dodgers, he was 5-1. Next on the Card staff came Johnny Beazley, the best first-year hurler in the National League since Grover Cleveland Alexander in 1911. Beazley even beat out Musial for Rookie of the Year honors. The righty went 21-6 with an ERA of 2.14. He had the top winnning percentage (.778) among NL hurlers with at least ten complete games. A hard thrower with a sharp curve and good control, Beazley, 24, began the year in the bullpen. By mid-season, though, he was a starter. And he matched wins with Cooper down the stretch. Helping out when it counted most was lefty Max Lanier (13-8, 2.96), who went 5-2 against Brooklyn.

On the attack, the '42 Cards topped the National League in batting (.268), slugging (.379), runs (755), total bases (2,054), doubles (282) and triples (69). And they stole 71 bases, just eight fewer than NL leader Brooklyn. So, the Redbirds weren't hindered by their lack of impressive power (only 60 HRs).

The timeliest hitting for St. Louis was done by the two greatest batters: Slaughter (13, 98, .318) and Musial (10, 72, .315). Slaughter led the league in hits (188), total bases (292), singles (127) and triples (17). Marty Marion (0, 54, .276) led in doubles (38). Another key batter was Terry Moore (6, 49, .288). And catcher Walker Cooper (7, 65, .281) did his share of hitting, too.

"Big Coop," Mort's 6-foot-3, 210-pound younger brother, typified the rugged, versatility of the Cards. The 27-year-old knew how to call the right signals, hit—and even run. He was also a bruiser who kept the opposition honest. Behind the plate, he liked to distract hitters by squirting tobacco juice at their spikes. "The guy would step out and glare down at Coop," recalled Enos Slaughter. "Coop would look up at him and say, 'Well, what are you going to do about it?' Here's this giant crouching there, tough as an oak and wearing a mask and chest protector to boot. I'll tell you what they did about it. They did nothing."

For all their vigor, the young '42 Cardinals weren't replicas of Frankie Frisch's rowdy, old Gas House Gang. Nobody remained from the 1934 St. Louis club, the franchise's most recent world champion. Ironically, Leo Durocher had carried that brawling, hell-bent style to Brooklyn. The Cards of '34 were the last previous big-leaguers to win the pennant on the final day of the season. But Billy Southworth's youngsters belonged to a new breed.

Groomed like their manager in Branch Rickey's pioneering farm system, they knew precisely what to do on the field. The brilliant St. Louis general manager had built the first minor-league empire in baseball. It stretched from New Iberia, Louisiana, Daytona Beach, Florida, and Greenville, Mississippi, up to the top teams in Rochester, New York, Columbus, Ohio, and elsewhere. Major-league clubs were used to bidding openly for the best talent from independent minor-league teams throughout the country. But Rickey changed things. He signed raw, promising ballplayers to $75-a-month contracts and stocked his own farm network with several hundred prospects at a time. His bold idea paid off.

In 1941, an injury-plagued St. Louis team had enough young depth to win 97 games and finish second, just 2½ games behind Durocher's Dodgers. That season the Redbirds lost 283 player days on sick call. Among other things, Terry Moore was beaned and suffered a brain concussion. Enos Slaughter fractured his collar bone. Mort Cooper underwent surgery for elbow chips. Walker Cooper broke his shoulder blade. And Johnny Mize (who was accused of malingering and sold during the off-season) also had shoulder aches. All this, despite owner Sam Breadon's training-camp orders to his Cards to join America's newest craze—vitamins. Ultimately, their peppy second-place finish in the face of injury was seen, if nothing else, as an endorsement of vitamins. On the bright side, Stan Musial, called up from the minors to stay, hit .426 in 12 games late in the year. And the youthful Redbirds learned how to play in a pennant race.

No wonder baseball experts predicted St. Louis would be a healthy favorite in 1942—if there was going to be a season. In the wake of Pearl Harbor, doubts were raised about the future of baseball during World War II. But President Franklin Roosevelt decided the game was vital to U.S. morale. So, the major leagues carried on. The season of '42 unfolded while the U.S. Navy halted the Japanese tide in the Pacific at the Battle of Midway; while American B-17 bombers began raids on Nazi Europe; and while folks at home rationed gasoline and sugar. On the radio, Artie Shaw's "I Don't Want to Walk Without You" was the first big emotional song of WWII. Nightclub attendance doubled from coast to coast. Daylight-saving time (renamed "war time") was adopted throughout the nation. And, there was baseball.

This would be the final season largely unhindered by either World War II enlistments or the military draft. After 1942, more and more of the best major leaguers were lost for the duration. Left behind, for the most part, were faded old-timers and draft-rejected journeymen. Not until 1946 would big-league baseball return to its normal level.

During the star-short war years, Branch Rickey's farm chain helped St. Louis to survive—and even thrive. The

Cards won the NL pennant again in 1943, and the World Series again in 1944. But both achievements were tarnished by the lowered quality of major-league play. And they occurred after the departure of Rickey himself. The old Mahatma jumped to Brooklyn to take over when Dodger boss Larry MacPhail, caught in a stockholder dispute, resigned and joined the service.

Those events were yet to come. In the meantime, baseball was preparing in 1942 for one more authentic big-league battle. And the frustrated Cardinals were eager to take another shot at Brooklyn. There was bad blood between the two teams. It began in 1940 shortly after St. Louis traded ex-Gas House Ganger Joe Medwick to the Dodgers. Before a game at Ebbets Field, Medwick argued in a New York elevator with former teammate Bob Bowman. That night, Bowman fired a pitch that hit Ducky in the head. The beaning ignited a furor, but threats of legal action were dropped. Medwick, who had to be hospitalized, was never again quite as strong a hitter as he once was in St. Louis. Now, two seasons later, the feud lingered even though Bowman was no longer a Cardinal.

While touring the spring camps, New York sportswriter Grantland Rice reported from St. Petersburg, Florida, that the Redbird pitching staff displayed "exceptional depth." Throwing along with Cooper, Beazley and Lanier were, among others, Howie Krist, Harry Gumbert, Ernie White and Howie Pollett.

As it turned out, the biggest task for Billy Southworth, who had been managing St. Louis since 1940, was selecting the best infielders. He was a 49-year-old veteran. Southworth had managed the Cards for some of 1929 at the end of his 13-year career as a big-league outfielder. After becoming a minor-league manager and major-league coach, he returned to the Cardinal chain in 1935. Southworth managed for Rickey in dugouts from Asheville, North Carolina, to Columbus to Rochester. So he knew the talent well.

In 1942, just one St. Louis infielder—Marion, the shortstop—wound up keeping the same job all season long. Coming out of spring training, Southworth had Jimmy Brown at third base; Frank "Creepy" Crespi (named for his ability to move sideways) at second; and Ray Sanders, a defensive improvement over Mize, at first. But it took until late June to find the winning combination. That was: Whitey Kurowski (9, 42, .254), at third base; Brown (1, 71, .256), at second; and Johnny "Hippity" Hopp (3, 37, .258) at first. In particular, it was a tiring opportunity for Kurowski, 24. The "miracle" athlete, who lacked three inches of bone in his right forearm due to childhood surgery for osteomyelitis, had never learned how to sleep on trains.

In 1942, the favored Cardinals got off to a slow start. On Opening Day, St. Louis disappointed its fans at Sportsman's Park (capacity: 34,000) by losing, 5-4, to the Cubs. Lefty reliever Johnny Schmitz of Chicago blanked the Redbirds for three innings. For a while thereafter, the Cards had a bit more than their usual trouble with left-handers. And with right-handers, too. St. Louis was shut out in five of its first two dozen games. The team looked sloppy. It was back in the NL pack and lucky to be 15-15 on the verge of greeting the front-running Dodgers for the first time.

"I'm cracking down on everybody, myself included," Southworth vowed before the showdown at Sportsman's Park. "We're not going all-out—but we will from now on, I assure you. You'll see a change in this ballclub."

In the game that day, the Cardinals beat Brooklyn, 1-0, behind Mort Cooper's pitching. Thus, Cooper paid back Dodger starter Whit Wyatt, who had beaten him 1-0 the previous September to virtually clinch the '41 pennant. This time around, Mort's brother, Walker, scored the only run by coming home on a fly ball after hitting a triple. The Cards also swept a bitter double-header from Brooklyn. Stan Musial, who used his tradmark corkscrew stance to unwind perfect left-handed swings, got five hits. Game two went into the books after it was called because of darkness. In the game, players from each side were ejected following long, hot arguments. The two teams had spilled onto the field when Ducky Medwick stepped on Ray Sanders' ankle during a play at first. After four wins in a row, St. Louis was still 6½ games in back.

Brooklyn, which had led the league from the first day of the season, kept rolling on the way to one of the best starts in NL history.

By late May, the Cardinals had climbed past Pittsburgh and Boston to move into second place, six games in back of Brooklyn. St. Louis won four straight games at the end of the month; and six in a row in early June. This, even though young Musial stumbled. He nearly broke his ankle on Memorial Day in Chicago when his spikes caught home plate as he tried to score from first on a short double. After sitting out a week, Musial "slumped" to .298 in mid-June. But the Redbirds, for the most part, eluded major injuries in 1942. The key exception among the regulars was Johnny Hopp, who missed the first several weeks of the season with a broken thumb. In June, the first baseman struggled at the plate. But St. Louis was already established in second place. It was locked for good in the two-team NL race (eventually, the New York Giants finished third, 20 games from the top.) The Cards never looked back—except for a brief unsuccessful threat by Cincinnati late in June when the Redbirds stumbled in Brooklyn.

At Ebbets Field, the Bums won four of five games in another hard-fought series against the Cards. In the only game the Cards won, Musial, destined to earn his "Stan the Man" title in Brooklyn, hit a homer and a triple. His batting average climbed to .315.

Ending the first half of its schedule, St. Louis posted an excellent 47-30 record. But the Cards had fallen eight games behind. The Dodgers won 55 of their first 77 games, the best first-half NL record since before 1920.

"They've got a fine ballclub," admitted Southworth. "In fact, they have two fine ballclubs. That's what makes them so tough to beat. When one man goes out of the lineup, another comes in who is just as strong. They reminded me of Notre Dame when Knute Rockne had two teams—shock troops who soften you up and then a first team to polish you off."

Five Cardinals played in the 1942 All-Star Game as the American League won, 3-1, at the Polo Grounds in New York on July 6. Joining starter (and loser) Mort Cooper were: cf Terry Moore, 2b Jimmy Brown, lf Enos Slaughter and c Walker Cooper. It was reported by the Associated Press that NL managers had "overlooked" Stan Musial when they selected the All-Star team.

Could St. Louis still catch Brooklyn? Some of the Cardinals began to wonder in early July when veteran pitcher Lon Warneke was waived to the Cubs. But owner Sam Breadon denied he was merely unloading Warneke's $15,000 salary, the team's highest. He claimed: "We've sold Lon to make room on the starting staff for young blood—like Jimmy Beazley." Next day Beazley got his ninth victory, shutting out the Giants.

The Dodgers literally ran into trouble on July 19 when they were swept by St. Louis, 8-5 and 7-6, in a double-header at Sportsman's Park. Pete Reiser of Brooklyn dashed head first into the concrete wall in center field on the play that ended game two. He caught and then dropped Country Slaughter's game-winning inside-the-park homer off Johnny Allen. Reiser, who in 1941 had been the first rookie ever to win a major-league batting title, suffered a slight concussion. He missed only a few games, but his batting average plunged due to recurrent dizzy spells. It was a severe blow to the Dodgers, who were now just six games ahead. For a while thereafter, the Cardinals struggled; but they came on strong in August and September. The day he was hurt, Reiser was leading the National League at .350. "Pistol Pete" batted only .244 the rest of the way.

Going beyond aggressiveness, Brooklyn's unusually rough play had begun to anger virtually everybody in the National League. During the July 19 twin-bill in St. Louis, for example, Stan Musial, always known as a gentleman, rushed the mound for the only time in his career. He had been knocked down on two straight pitches by Les Webber, a mediocre right-hander. Only intervention by Redbird coaches Mike Gonzales and Buzzy Wares prevented a fight. Such hard-nosed tactics helped Durocher's Bums win 71 of their first 100 games, the hottest pace since the dead-ball era. But "Leo the Lip" was making too many enemies. Brooklyn's lead peaked on August 5 at 10½ games.

On August 8, Boston manager Casey Stengel had blasted the Dodgers after his lowly Braves won, 2-0, when Manny Salvo bested Whitt Wyatt in an unprecedented beanball war. To the press, Stengel growled: "If I had a ballclub as good as Durocher's, I wouldn't throw at a ballclub as bad as mine. We're going to battle these guys all the harder from now on, and I've talked to Frisch [of Pittsburgh], Wilson and other managers who feel the same. Sure, they've got a big lead. But they're not in yet. In case you guys didn't notice it, St. Louis is winning steadily." The Boston and New York writers smiled. "I mean it," said Stengel. "Those jack-rabbits from St. Louis are coming."

Larry MacPhail of Brooklyn felt the same way. He called a team meeting in front of the writers at Ebbets Field and harangued his players for being smug. They weren't hustling, scolded the boss. Then he warned they were about to blow the pennant despite their big lead. The Dodgers just ignored him.

Meanwhile, there was joy in St. Louis. The Cards, who only once lost two games in a row during the second half of the season, won eight straight games in mid August. The Redbirds had begun their record drive. They won three of the four games during Brooklyn's final trip to Sportsman's Park in late August. St. Louis triumphed, 7-1, behind Lanier in the opener. The next night, the Cards won, 2-1, in a 14-inning game (Cooper vs. Wyatt). Walker Cooper had tied that contest in the bottom of the 13th with a run-scoring single. St. Louis notched another 2-1 victory the following day in a 10-inning game. It was Johnny Beazley's 16th triumph. But after the Dodgers bounced back to win, 4-1, on August 27, St. Louis still trailed by 5½ games with only 30 left to play.

"Never mind what Brooklyn does," Southworth told his Cards. "It's what we do that counts." They paid attention and kept on winning. To defuse the pressure, the close-knit young ballplayers—led by their colorful trainer, Doc Weaver—liked to sing in the clubhouse. The amateur musicians turned one of Spike Jones' novelty recordings, "Pass the Biscuits,

Mirandy," into the team's fight song. Meanwhile, Mort Cooper, who previously defied superstition by wearing 13 on his back, was borrowing uniforms from teammates to bring him luck at whichever number victory he sought. On the field, the Cardinals rose because of teamwork.

This wasn't the biggest gap a pennant winner ever closed late in the season. But never has any team come from behind with so high a winning rate through so much of the stretch.

It all came down to a two-game series in Brooklyn on Friday, September 11, and Saturday, September 12. Arriving for the showdown, St. Louis was just two games back. Finally, the Cardinals seemed tense. Even veteran Jimmy Brown shook while moving under a pop up in the first game before the hostile Brooklyn fans. But the Cards got by the early innings and won, 3-0. Beating Wyatt, Mort Cooper collected his 20th win on a three-hit shutout. The next day, Max Lanier topped the Dodgers, 2-1, on Whitey Kurowski's two-run homer. Now St. Louis, having just won 29 of its last 34 games, was tied for the lead with just 14 games left to play.

On Sunday, September 13, the Cardinals, once and for all, had first place to themselves. While the Dodgers lost a pair of games to Cincinnati, the Cards split a doube-header in Philadelphia by identical 2-1 scores. Right-hander Beazley, with a knife wound in his pitching thumb, nearly won the opener in Shibe Park. He had been cut slightly the night before during a train-station dispute with a local redcap. In game two, Terry Moore's homer broke the tie.

To gain the pennant, St. Louis won 11 of its final 12 games, including the last seven in a row. But the Dodgers never folded. Brooklyn won 10 of its final 12 games, finishing with eight straight wins. The Cards clinched the NL flag on the final day when they beat the Cubs, 9-2, behind Ernie White in the first game of a twin bill at home. And Beazley tuned up for the Series with a 4-1 victory in the nightcap.

Thrilled for his team, Southworth declared: "We won this one the hard way, and no one won it for us. We went out and won it ourselves. And we'll go out and beat the Yankees the same way." GM Branch Rickey felt so, too. "Usually with a team so young, both in years and baseball experience," he said later, "you see three or four men go to pot under stress. That has not happened with Southworth's team, which is a great tribute to him. If the Cardinals keep their feet on the ground and play the kind of ball they have been playing, they can win."

New York (103-51, .669), the American League pennant winner in 1942, was coming off five world championships in six years. They were made better than 2-1 favorites in the World Series. The New Yorkers were led by Joe DiMaggio, Charlie Keller and Joe Gordon, who beat Triple Crown winner Ted Williams of Boston for the AL MVP title in '42.

But St. Louis simply wasn't frightened by the reputation of the New York Yankees, a team they were used to playing in spring training. "They'll have to beat us out on the field, not in the newspaper columns," said Southworth. "And I don't think they will beat us on the field. When I played on the Cardinals in 1926, we weren't overawed [by the Yanks in the World Series], and Landis paid us the bigger checks."

The young Redbirds, badly underpaid, were driven, of course, by the chance to earn big money in the World Series. "We flat out needed it," explained Mort Cooper. Rookie Stan Musial, for instance, earned just $4,250 during the regular season; his winner's share in the Fall Classic was $6,192.50.

Bound for St. Louis (where they usually played the weak AL Browns), the high-paid Yankees took it all for granted. "Somehow, I can't seem to get it through my head that we are going out there to play the Series," said catcher Bill Dickey. "It seems just like any other trip to St. Louis."

Things began that way. Red Ruffing of New York pitched a no-hitter until the eighth inning of game one at Sportsman's Park. In the ninth, he was one pitch away from a two-hit shutout. But the Yanks had to settle for a 7-4 victory after surviving a two-out St. Louis rally. Marion hit a two-run triple before Ken O'Dea and Moore hit run-scoring singles. Even though the game ended on Musial's bases-loaded grounder to first, the Cards had regained their confidence. Also, they had worried the mighty New Yorkers. Rightly so.

St. Louis won the next four games—the last three of them at Yankee Stadium. The Cards triumphed, 4-3, behind Beazley in game two. Country Slaughter, who scored the winning run on Musial's single in the eighth inning, fired a great throw in the ninth to choke a Yankee runner at third base. In game three, the Yankees were blanked in the World Series for the first time since playing the Redbirds in 1926. Ernie White allowed just five singles as St. Louis whitewashed New York, 2-0. Three great catches by Moore, Musial and Slaughter late in the game were later said by Southworth to be the turning points of the Series. The Cards won, 9-6, in game five, as the two sides combined for 22 hits. To become world champions, St. Louis beat the Yankees, 4-2, in game five in the Bronx. Whitey Kurowski hit a tie-breaking two-run homer in the top of the ninth inning. Then Beazley picked up his second win of the World Series—while Doc Weaver and the Card benchwarmers cast a double-whammy on the Yanks.

In the visitor's clubhouse, the "St. Louis Swifties" jumped for joy. They hoisted old Judge Landis up to the ceiling. Then Branch Rickey got the same treatment. So did Kurowski, whose uniform was ripped to shreds. And the Cards charged into their rendition of "Pass the Biscuits, Mirandy."

6

New York Yankees 1961

109-53

.673

ROGER MARIS HITS 61 HRs TO TOP BABE RUTH'S MARK ♦ MICKEY MANTLE HITS 54 ♦ N.Y. BELTS RECORD 240 HRs WITH SIX 20-PLUS MEN ♦ WHITEY FORD IS 25-4 ♦ MANAGER RALPH HOUK LEADS YANKS IN FIVE-GAME WORLD SERIES VS. REDS.

Six sluggers on the most powerful team in the history of baseball each hit more than 20 home runs. Two of them hit more than 50 homers apiece. And one hit more than 60—setting, by far, the greatest of those records.

". . . Hit deep to right," yelled broadcaster Phil Rizzuto. "This could do it! Holy Cow! He did it! Sixty-one home runs!"

Roger Maris beat the calendar on October 1, 1961. After a grueling, six-month campaign, the New York Yankees hitter broke the record of 60 homers that Babe Ruth had set in 1927, more than three decades before. The home-run mark fell on the final day of the most remarkable season the Yankees ever played.

That historic shot by Maris gave New York its 109th win—just one fewer than Ruth's 1927 Yankees, who are known as the best team ever to play the game. Paced by

Maris, the Bronx Bombers won the 1961 American League pennant by hitting a total of 240 home runs, which was an unprecedented number. It was also 82 more than their Murderers' Row ancestors had belted in 1927.

On his big Sunday afternoon, Maris' 61st homer was the only run in an uncharacteristic 1-0 New York victory. He delivered his fourth-inning solo clout off Boston's Tracy Stallard before just 23,154 spectators in cavernous Yankee Stadium. The stands in The House That Ruth Built were two-thirds empty chiefly because it was Maris who already had tied the Babe's record—not Mickey Mantle, the designated Yankee heir. Mantle had hit 54 homers, the most ever by a switch hitter, before a late-season hip injury forced him out of the race. He had to watch the final blow on TV from a hospital bed.

Dour and aloof, Maris long since had been harried beyond despair by the pressure of chasing Ruth's legend. Maris wasn't a homegrown Yankee like Mantle; it was only his second year in New York. Privately, Maris had earned the confidence and respect of his teammates. But he was still a virtual outsider in the eyes of many traditional Yankee fans, and some of the press, too. Under the working scrutiny of the New York-based media, Maris was questioned tediously and compared to Ruth over and over again. Sometimes, Maris, a small-town North Dakotan, began to appear somewhat ungrateful—or downright surly. "Anybody can be nice when they're going good," he jousted. It got no better when less-experienced journalists caught up to the bandwagon. Exhausted by the rising tension, Maris, 27, even began to shed clumps of his crew-cut hair. The distant Yankee front office, meanwhile, did little to help its young iconoclast face the relentless publicity, an icy fact never lost on Maris, of course. Nor did the powerful Yankee bosses intervene when commissioner Ford Frick—an ex-sports reporter who had been Ruth's buddy and ghostwriter—threatened to pin an asterisk on Maris. It was supposed to diminish any new homer record set beyond the Babe's old 154-game limit. But the traditionalist Yankee front office hoped the extra deadline and further controversy would sell even more tickets during that season.

Not that a tiny asterisk could stop anything.

Finally, Maris stood by himself at home plate. Alone. This was his moment. Swinging with a graceful, left-handed uppercut, he popped a waist-high 0-2 fastball about ten rows back into the lower deck near the Yankee bullpen. It was homer No. 61. Against all odds, Maris did it.

"It was a fastball low and away," Maris was to recall. "I went with the pitch because there was no way I could have pulled it. I knew it was gone when I hit it, but for the first time I realized what number it was—61 flashed through my mind. I had never thought of a number on any other homer.

"I heard the roar of the crowd, but my mind went blank. I was dazed, in a complete fog, and don't even remember running the bases. I started to come out of the fog as I reached the dugout and started down the steps.

"But then I felt my teammates holding me up on the steps and out of the dugout. They were all yelling and congratulating me, but insisting I stand out in front of the dugout for the fans. I stood and waved my cap. It was the greatest thrill of my life."

Years later, Mantle, who had traded homers with him until late September, testified: "The single greatest feat I ever saw was Roger Maris hitting his 61 home runs to break Babe Ruth's record."

The "M&M boys," combining for 115 homers, went into the books as the top slugging duo ever to play on one club in the same year; Ruth and Lou Gehrig, with 47, hit eight fewer together in 1927. Despite ludicrous newspaper gossip, Roger and Mickey were friendly rivals. In fact, they shared an apartment that summer in Queens along with teammate Bob Cerv. Every once in a while, Mantle, relaxing at home, would lower his sports pages, stare over at Maris and swear: "I hate your guts."

Kidding aside, both knew their batting duel—Maris hit .269 and drove in 142 runs, Mantle hit .317 and drove in 128—was good for them. And for the club. Maris and Mantle were only the body and soul of a strong baseball team. They staged their home-run derby—knocking the fear of Ruth into American League pitchers—from the middle of a uniquely potent lineup. Other '61 Yankees wore solid pinstripes: Moose Skowron hit 28 homers; Yogi Berra hit 22; Elston Howard hit 21, and so did Johnny Blanchard, a pinch-hitter and reserve catcher who couldn't even find a regular job.

Their year hadn't begun with overwhelming promise. It was a time of change for New York, coming off its upsetting loss to Pittsburgh in the 1960 World Series. Rookie manager Ralph Houk inherited the Yankee squad: Casey Stengel had been fired soon after winning his tenth pennant in 12 seasons in the Bronx. "I'll never make the mistake of being 70 again," Stengel had vowed. Yet the Ole Perfessor remained sharp that winter. He was asked if Maris—who had used his natural Yankee Stadium swing to hit 39 homers in 1960 and win the first of two straight AL MVP titles—was bound to surpass Ruth's record. "Why shouldn't he break it?" responded Casey. "He's got more power than Stal-een."

The director of the coming assault, "Major" Houk, 42, was an ex-Yankee player and coach who had been a U.S. Army combat officer during World War II. It was Houk who junked the old Yankee strategy. Where hard-to-please Stengel platooned regulars and juggled hurlers, Houk turned in a set lineup and stuck to a pitching rotation. He also named oft-booed Mantle, 29, who had outgrown Stengel's critical fathering, to be the new team leader—and unofficial captain. Immediately, Mantle thrived. Whitey Ford emerged as "The Chairman of the Board" under the Houk regime—as fiery new pitching coach Johnny Sain stepped up to help. Known as New York's "money" hurler, Ford, who Stengel had kept rested for the big starts, worked every fourth day for the first time. Amid the Yankee home-run frenzy, the little lefty posted his first 20-win season. "I went 25-4 and nobody noticed," he joked. But Ford won the Cy Young Award in '61. During the season, he completed only 11 games. His frequent relief partner was Louis Arroyo, the unlikely new bullpen ace who became the darling of Houk's reconstructed pitching staff. The dumpy Cuban screwballer saved 29 Yankee games. Arroyo also won 15 more, backed by the late-inning Yankee power long ago dubbed "5 o'clock lightning." Other key winners: Ralph Terry, 16-3, and two fresh young starters, Bill Stafford, 14-9, and Rollie Sheldon, 11-5.

In spring training, Houk propped up an unsettled mound squad by ordering Ellie Howard to call the signals every day behind the plate. Which became Howard's specialty. He also hit a career-high .348 in 1961. Aging backstop Yogi Berra, 36, shared left field with unpredictable Hector Lopez. But fleet-footed Mantle, in center, and rifle-armed Maris, in right, helped the Yanks lead the A.L. in fielding. Anchored by Skowron at first base, they also put together the best infield in baseball. Houk assigned three young Yankees—Clete Boyer, 3b; Tony Kubek, ss; and Bobby Richardson, 2b—to play their positions full-time. What happened? Diving left and right, Boyer simply wowed everybody with his glove. Kubek and Richardson, meanwhile, became the league's best double-play combo. At bat, those two also set the table for the power hitters: Kubek scored 84 runs; Richardson, 80. And Blanchard, once an unsung bench warmer, made the most of his 243 at bats. He stroked 21 homers, eight of which either tied the game or put New York in front. In one sensational stretch, Blanchard hit four homers—the first two were pinch-hits—in consecutive trips to the plate over three games.

"There were no loners on the club," Blanchard said much later. "Everyone took care of everyone else and stuck up for each other. I think part of the reason so many guys had such good years was that all the pressure was on Roger and Mickey. With all the talk about home runs, they were under the gun and the rest of us were free to play and not worry. It was a team with so much pride, we couldn't lose."

It took a while, though, for everything to come together.

After the first 30 games of the season, New York had only a 16-14 record—despite Mantle's ten homers. Except for Ford (at 4-1), the starting rotation had failed. And Maris, with only four homers, was batting in the low .200s. (He had gone homerless in the first 11 games of the season before hitting No. 1 on April 25 off Paul Foytack in Detroit.) By May 20, the Yankees had drifted five games behind the first-place Tigers. Suddenly, however, Maris was booming. He had been advised by Roy Hamey, the new Yankee general manager, that the front office wanted him to forget his batting average and go for home runs. Maris hit nine in the last 12 games in May. On Memorial Day, the Yanks topped Boston, 12-3, in Fenway Park while belting seven homers—two by Maris (Nos. 10 and 11); two by Mantle (Nos. 12 and 13); two by Skowron; and one by Berra. It was only the beginning.

Soon people began wondering if the Yankees' heavy hitting was caused by some kind of light new "rabbit" baseball. But tests reported by *The New York Times* during the summer were inconclusive. Day after day, the Bombers kept pounding extra-base hits (and the pitching came around, too). Hefted by the big shots of Maris and Mantle, the Yanks won nearly three out of every four of their games from late May through mid September—for a spectacular rate of .730 percent.

It all happened while Americans were humming "Moon River," heaping glory on pioneer astronauts Alan Shepard and John Glenn, and flocking to the movies to see *The Guns of Navarone*. The front pages that summer reported about President Kennedy and the Berlin Wall crisis; the "Freedom Riders" defying segregation in the South; and the suicide of Ernest Hemingway. But the sports pages belonged to the Yankees.

Their 13-4 rout of Washington on July 2 at Yankee Stadium was a typical explosion. Completing a three-game sweep of the Senators, New York hit five home runs in the one-sided contest—two by Maris, one by Mantle, one by Howard and one by Skowron. Maris went eight games up Babe Ruth's pace by hitting Nos. 29 (high on the right-field foul screen) and 30 (into the upper deck in right). Mantle hit No. 28 (into the upper deck in right) after drawing four walks, and scoring on two of them. It was The Mick's fourth homer in three games against Washington. On June 30, Mantle scored standing up on a 455-foot inside-the-park homer as New York triumphed, 5-1. It raised Whitey Ford's record to 14-2. On July 1, Mantle hit a 470-foot home-run blast into the center-field bleachers to collect his 1,000th career RBI; he also hit another 400-foot home run in the game. But Washington led 6-5 in the bottom of the ninth until Maris finally won that game with a two-run homer down the right-field line.

In just three games against Washington, Maris and Mantle combined for seven HRs and 17 RBIs. They went 13 for 21 (.619) and crossed the plate 12 times. Senator manager Mickey Vernon complained: "Those two beat us by themselves."

On July 4, a holiday double-header vs. Detroit drew 74,246 customers to Yankee Stadium—the largest Stadium crowd since 1947. New York was fighting the Tigers for possession of first place. The Yanks won the first game, 6-2; but Detroit won the nightcap, 4-3, in 10 innings. So the Tigers (50-28) kept a slight edge over New York (48-28) in the American League pennant race. On that day, Maris hit No. 31.

With the excitement rising, Commissioner Frick decided to issue a ruling. He announced: "Any player who may hit more than 60 home runs during his club's first 154 games would be recognized as having established a new record. However, if the player does not hit more than 60 homers until after his club has played 154 games, there would have to be a distinctive mark in the record books to show that Babe Ruth's record was set under a 154-game schedule and the total of more than 60 was compiled while a 162-game schedule was in effect." What did Maris think about that? "A season's a season," he said.

For four months in a row, the Bronx Bombers won at least 20 games—in June, they were 22-10; in July, 20-9; in August, 22-9; in September, 21-8. And they were nearly unstoppable at Yankee Stadium all season long—setting a major-league record (65-16, .802) for winning games at home.

That's exactly what it took to fend off powerful Detroit. The '61 Tigers eventually won 101 games—only to wind up eight games back in second place. They were led by hard hitters Al Kaline, Norm Cash and Rocky Colavito, along with two "Yankee killers" of the mound, Frank Lary and Don Mossi.

Coming home to Yankee Stadium to begin a three-game showdown on September 1, first-place New York led Detroit by just one game. In the opener, Ford, Bud Daley and Arroyo combined to blank the Tigers for nine full innings; and Mossi did the same thing to New York into the bottom of the ninth. Then he retired Maris and Mantle, but singles by Howard, Berra and "Moo-oose" Skowron won it.

For a long time to come, Maris was to savor their 1-0 triumph. He later recalled: "Mickey and I really enjoyed that one. We had been insisting all season that winning the pennant was a job shared by all 25 men on the ballclub, not just a couple of home-run hitters. Here, in the biggest game of the year, we had won, and neither Mickey nor I did a thing to help. It was a night that made me proud to be a Yankee."

Next day: Maris homered twice (Nos. 52 and 53) in New York's 7-2 victory over Detroit. In the last game, Mantle homered twice (No. 49 and 50); his second blast, a 450-foot shot, tied it 5-5 in the bottom of the ninth before Howard's three-run clout, later in the inning, skinned the Tigers, who couldn't depart fast enough. The 8-5 win gave the Yanks a 4½-game lead over Detroit.

The Bronx Bombers went on to win each of their 12 games during that home stand in Yankee Stadium. So much for Detroit, which simply faded.

So did the Maris-Mantle home-run battle. The Mick suddenly developed a serious hip infection after getting a shot for a cold. That knocked him off his feet during the final weeks of the season. And Maris went on by himself.

Tony Kubek recalled that the Yankee players never really took sides in the race between the M&M boys to beat Ruth's homer record. "There may have been some feeling early that if anybody was going to do it," said Kubek, "it would be nice if it was Mickey. He had succeeded Joe DiMaggio, he was the heart of the Yankees for a long time, and he was just about at his peak as a player. He wouldn't have many more chances. By the middle of the season, I think the feeling was maybe both of them could do it. When Mickey got sick at the end and dropped out, we really pulled hard for Roger to make it."

On September 20, the Yanks were in Baltimore, getting set to clinch the pennant in their 154th official game. This was the last chance for Maris—who by now had 58 homers—

to ward off the asterisk. With Mantle absent from the fourth spot in the batting order, Maris, who hit third, had been seeing fewer and fewer good pitches. And his deadline had kept nearing.

Hours before the start of Game No. 154, Maris faltered. He was in tears and shaking when he burst into Houk's office. "I need help," cried Maris. "I can't stand it any more. All those goddamn questions. I'm at the end of my rope. I just can't take it any more." Not so. Maris calmed down.

In the game, he hit No. 59 off Milt Pappas to help the Yanks capture the A.L. flag with a 4-2 win. For the moment, though, Ruth's record was intact.

Remembering how close Maris had come, Bob Cerv said: "He came up later in the game and hit one even better than he hit No. 59. But the wind had changed and it hung up there, and they caught it against the wall. I used to kid Roger, 'That was the ghost of Ruth that blew that ball back in.' Actually, it really was Ruth's ghost that stopped Roger. See, Ford Frick was against him. I used to tell him, 'Ah, don't worry. Frick was Babe's ghostwriter.'"

On September 26, Maris hit No. 60 in Yankee Stadium during a 3-2 victory against Baltimore. This is how he remembered the record-tying homer:

"Jack Fisher was pitching for Baltimore. I got a single in the first inning. In the third, Fisher started bearing down, trying to get me out. Then I saw it coming, it was a high curve. I swung, connected, and heard the roar of the crowd. I stood at the plate watching. It hit the upper deck about four feet in fair territory and then bounced back onto the field. . . .

"I came off the field and found myself on television. I was surprised to see Mrs. [Claire] Ruth [Babe's widow] there. She had said all along that she hoped the record wouldn't be tied or broken. I knew how she felt. I admired her for being honest. Mrs. Ruth took my hand, and I think I kissed her on the cheek. . . . 'You had a great year,' she said. 'I want to congratulate you, and I mean that, Roger, sincerely. I know that if Babe were here, he would have wanted to congratulate you too.' I told her, 'I'm glad I didn't tie the Babe's record in 154 games. This is enough for me.' I meant it then. I mean it now."

Finally, Maris also hit No. 61.

It was the only time Maris ever won a 1-0 game with a home run. And it left him with 142 RBIs, enough to win that 1961 title (over Baltimore's Jim Gentile) by just one run. Maris hit No. 61 at a point when he had walked up to the plate just four more times than Ruth did in 1927. "I have nothing to be ashamed of," said Stallard. "He hit 60 others didn't he?"

Actually, it wasn't the final home run of 1961 by Maris.

In the World Series, New York and Cincinnati split their first games at Yankee Stadium. Moving to Crosley Field, they were tied 2-2 going into the last inning of game three. Maris, wearing an 0-for-10 Series collar, led off the top of the ninth against Bob Purkey with one more homer—the game-winning shot sailed 20 rows deep into the right-field seats. Reds manager Fred Hutchinson labeled it "the most damaging blow of the Series."

While Maris hit a tired .105 and Mantle limped heroically, the Bombers called up the reserves. And they got the job done: the Yankees won four out of five World Series games.

It made Major Houk only the third rookie to manage a world champion. Houk, whose big-league experience stretched from the 1940s to the 1980s, recalled: "When I think about it, the '61 club was the greatest team I ever saw."

Ironically, the highlight of the World Series wasn't the Yankee hitting. Pitcher Whitey Ford extended his World Series shutout skein to 32 consecutive innings, erasing a prize record of 29⅔ scoreless innings established long before by a young American League hurler named George H. Ruth.

Said Ford: "This sure wasn't a good year for the Babe."

7

New York Mets 1986

108-54

.667

"TEAM" SUCCESS FOR MANAGER DAVEY JOHNSON ♦ METS LEAD NL EAST BY 21½ GAMES WITHOUT GREAT PERSONAL STATS ♦ TOP HOUSTON IN PLAYOFFS, BOSTON IN WORLD SERIES ON HISTORIC COMEBACKS ♦ CATCHER GARY CARTER GUIDES METS STAFF: SIX WINNERS IN DOUBLE FIGURES.

"Baseball like it oughta be!"

—N.Y. METS ADVERTISEMENT (1986)

All season long, the New York Mets, rejoicing constantly with high fives and curtain calls, celebrated their success. It was a lopsided year. The upstart Mets, without preeminent individual totals, dominated in 1986 like no team ever had during the home-run era. Mostly, the National League witnessed the ostentatious rout first with awe, then anger and, finally, certain respect.

It started in April in St. Louis when the Mets, already in first place to stay, swept the defending NL champions in a four-game series. New York ended the month with 11 straight victories, its longest winning streak of the season. In May, the Mets won another seven in a row; then another six. "When they had the NL East seemingly sewed up by Memorial Day," reported *Sports Illustrated,* "comparisons with the Yankees of the '20s, '30s and '50s began."

The Mets, jubilant over their early surge, responded eagerly to the give-'em-hell encouragement of manager Davey Johnson. "We don't want to just win," he had vowed in Florida, "we want to dominate." In mid-June, New York won seven games in a row. On July 4, it completed an eight-game win streak. At the All-Star break, the Mets (59-14) were on top by 13 games—the biggest mid-season NL edge since the start of division play in 1969. Gary Carter, leading New York's hitters with 16 homers and 65 RBIs, was calling signals behind the plate for the hottest pitching staff in baseball. Sid Fernandez had 12 wins, Dwight "Dr. K" Gooden ten, Bob Ojeda ten and Ron Darling nine. It underlined what St. Louis manager Whitey Herzog had conceded weeks before. Nobody in the NL East was going to stop the Mets.

"The way it turned out, it looked like we were worrying about nothing," said Wally Backman, the Mets' scrappy number two hitter. "But it wasn't that easy. We didn't have to worry, but nobody rolled over and played dead for us.

"We were pretty intense all year. We had to be after a while. People were gunning for us. They didn't like the way we acted (during celebrations on the field). They came at us pretty good. Some of them wanted to fight us because they knew they couldn't beat us playing baseball."

During the season, the Mets—a few of whom even battled off-duty police at a nightclub in Houston—were involved in four bench-clearing brawls. The last fight took place on July 22 during the wildest game of the year. In Cincinnati, the Mets outpaced the Reds, 6-3, in a musical-chairs contest that took 14 innings and lasted five hours.

Foes grumbled more and more that the cake-walking New Yorkers were being arrogant, insensitive and unprofessional. But the Mets, flaunting their enthusiasm, defied NL critics by winning all summer. The bear-hugging, hand-slapping and cap-tipping continued. And so did out-of-town resentment of the Madison Avenue hype (books, rock videos, TV commercials, magazine covers) for baseball's winningest team in America's media capital. In 1986, it wasn't "Damn Yankees!" It was "Damn Mets!"

Not in Shea Stadium, of course. More than 2.7 million fans turned out during the regular season to watch the home team at Flushing Meadow in Queens. Never before had so many paid to see any New York club, no matter how great. On September 17, the Mets clinched the NL East title at home before 47,823 customers. The 4-2 victory against Chicago marked the earliest finish ever of a race in the division. When the regular season ended, New York led number two Philadelphia by 21½ games. It was the biggest winning margin in major-league baseball since the pre-1920 period.

In October, the Mets ran out of teams to beat. They defeated Houston, four games to two, to win the National League pennant, and Boston, four games to three, to win the World Series. The two Game 6 showdowns were historic: New York won them both on dramatic late-inning rallies. "I've never played against a team like the Mets," said Houston's Billy Hatcher. "They keep coming at you—I mean from all directions." The front-runners of 1986 could also fight back with everything they had. Which was how they got to be world champions.

For the Mets, the spectacular had been routine since April. Perhaps the biggest surprise was that their winning chemistry lacked main ingredients. No player on the club wound up with towering personal statistics. Despite the runaway, there weren't any individual feats reminiscent of Babe Ruth or Joe DiMaggio or Mickey Mantle. "Most of the players have had good years, but not a lot of great years," said Davey Johnson, looking back at '86. He led the Mets to victory by alternating players at as many as four positions. "It's really not my philosophy to platoon as much as I do," Johnson claimed. "Ideally, I would like to have a set lineup." His contributions weren't fully recognized. Johnson finished second to Hal Lanier of the Astros as the NL Manager of the Year. Actually, none of the Mets won any of the major awards in 1986—even though the club overwhelmed baseball.

How did the Mets do it?

"The way to dominate is not to rely on one aspect of the game," said Johnson. "If you do, you're susceptible to slumps. The best pitching staffs can slump. The best hitting team can slump. Our hitters slumped and our starters slumped—not very much, though. But we got through it because we could win in a lot of ways. We could beat you 1-0, 2-1, 7-4, or 10-8. We could win early, we could win late. It didn't make any difference to us how we did it. We could win on a shutout, a home run, a stolen base, or two doubles and a sacrifice fly. Good teams have more ways than one to win."

The Mets were 75-19 when scoring first—plus 88-5 when leading after six innings; 90-3 when leading after seven innings; and 94-2 when leading after eight innings. But they also had 39 come-from-behind victories. New York scored four or more runs in an inning 36 times. Yet no NL club was as good as the Mets (29-20, .592) in one-run games. They also won 11 shutouts while losing only four. New York went 62-32 vs. right-handed pitchers and 46-22 vs. left-handers. The Mets were 77-37 on grass (the surface they played on at Shea); and 31-17 on artificial turf. Also they went 66-35 at night, and 42-19 during the day. And finally, New York was 55-26 at home, and 53-28 away—which tied an NL record for road wins in a 162-game season.

From start to finish, it was a balanced team effort. Said Mets coach Bill Robinson: "The strongest thing about this team is the absence of weaknesses." New York led the National League in batting (.263), slugging (.401), on-base percentage (.339), runs (783), hits (1,462), total bases (2,229), runs batted in (730) and walks (631). They were third in home runs (148). On the mound, the Mets also led the NL in earned run average (3.11). They were second in strikeouts (1,083), complete games (27) and total runs allowed (578); and third in hits (1,304), walks (509), shutouts (11) and saves (46). In fact, virtually the only thing ordinary about the '86 Mets that season was their fielding.

At one point, Johnson explained: "I always felt that, if it wasn't a total liability, you should go with the best offense you can put out there, and go with defense later. It never made much sense to me to start with a defensive team, get behind, and then have to pinch hit for it."

Reflecting on the success of the Mets in '86, Roger Craig, manager of San Francisco, said: "They don't have that many weaknesses. It's unusual to see a team that leads the league in hitting and pitching. But regardless of what they do offensively, it's always the pitching that grabs you."

Not since the '27 Yankees had any world champion possessed four pitchers with 15 or more victories each and winning percentages of at least .667. The Mets had the first such staff in baseball since the '71 Orioles and the '54 Indians, both AL pennant winners who didn't go on to win the Series.

The four young Mets starters had combined record of 66-23. Right-handers Dwight Gooden (17-6, 2.84) and Ron Darling (15-6, 2.81) were joined by lefties Bob Ojeda (18-5, 2.57) and Sid Fernandez (16-6, 3.52). They each had winning percentages of .700-plus, a level reached by no other NL starter in '86.

Even so, Gooden, 21, who was New York's $1.3 million ace, had a worrisome year. He became the only major-leaguer ever to fan 200 batters in each of his first three seasons. But there was talk that—coming off a Cy Young Award effort (24-4, 1.53) in 1985—his fastball had lost some of its heat. Gooden also struggled with his curve in some games. And he got into a couple off-the-field scrapes. Then he went 0-2 with an 8.00 ERA in the World Series. Eventually, Gooden underwent drug rehabilitation treatment; and cocaine was cited as a possible factor in what had happened to him in 1986.

Meanwhile, New York's other starters each had the best years of their careers. Darling, 26, who earned more than his share of no-decisions, tossed junk compared to Gooden's heat. "The strength of our staff is in our differences, our variety," said Darling. His own variety was impressive; he threw sliders, curves, fastballs, forkballs and changeups. A Yale man, Darling was one of the few Mets who had second thoughts about whether the slap-happy club was showing up too many opponents. "I can see why other teams don't like us," he admitted. "I'd hate to pitch against us." Newly acquired from Boston, Ojeda, 28, won with a good fastball and a remarkable change-up. He had been just 44-39 in six years with the Red Sox. Fernandez, 23, a Hawaiian of Portuguese-Irish descent, wore uniform number 50 for the 50th state. He overcame his weight and wildness problems and won big with a hopping fastball and a slow-breaking curve. In one game, he fanned 14 batters in seven innings. Another key contributor was Rick Aguilera (10-7, 3.88), a 25-year-old righty who worked both as a starter and a reliever.

The stars of the bullpen were right-hander Roger McDowell, 26, and lefty Jesse Orosco, 29. They combined for 43 saves and 22 wins—thus playing key roles in 65 of the team's 108 victories. McDowell, tossing the best sinker in the NL, went 14-9 with 22 saves; Orosco, firing a wicked slider, went 8-6 with 21 saves. It was only the second time in NL history that a pair of teammates each had more than 20 saves in the same year. McDowell's earned run average was just 3.02; Orosco's was even better: 2.33.

Thirty-two-year-old Gary Carter had a lot to do with the fact that six Mets won in double figures. Despite throwing problems, he was still the best catcher in the National League. No wonder the pitchers relied so often on his judgment. "Here you've got a staff where the ace is 21 and the oldest is only 28," said Carter. He steadied Gooden, helped Darling mix his pitches, got Ojeda used to NL batters and kept an eye on Fernandez in his first full season. It was the tenth year in a row that Carter had caught at least 100 games. Though he missed 14 games with a late-season thumb injury, Carter belted 24 homers, drove in 105 runs, and hit .255. He scored 81 runs himself and had the most clutch RBIs on the team. Carter, who usually batted in the clean-up position, was tops in the majors with an average of .840 RBI per base hit. His totals included one 7-RBI game; one 5-RBI game; three 4-RBI games; and six 3-RBI games. In one stretch, Carter drove in 39 runs in 36 games. For his efforts, he finished third (behind Mike

Schmidt of Philadelphia and Glenn Davis of Houston) in the National League MVP voting.

Naturally, Carter, still known as "The Kid" for his boyish enthusiasm, was the Met who took the most heat from the rest of the National League. It seemed that he was the guy everybody loved to hate. Some of that went back to his days in Montreal. "He tries too hard to be good," said one old Expo teammate. "He wants to be all things to all people." In New York, Carter acquired an even higher profile. For one thing, he was the best-paid Met, earning more than $2.1 million in 1986. He did the most interviews; and the most ads. In '86, Carter was a spokesman for Polaroid, Ivory soap, Chemical Bank, *New York Newsday* and Northville gas stations. "We'd hate the Mets even if they weren't in first place," said a St. Louis player. "No one can stand Carter."

In a quieter way, Keith Hernandez (13, 83, .310), who batted third, also made his presence felt throughout the league. He was the toughest out in the Mets' lineup. Hernandez, an intense competitor, tied for the NL lead in on-base percentage (.413) in 1986; and he led the NL in walks (94). He scored 91 times, more often than any other Met. Hernandez had a dozen three-hit games. And he extended the Mets' runaway by hitting .368 with 26 RBIs in August. Further, Hernandez, 32, was the conscience of the team. He was a consummate professional who had outlasted drug problems in St. Louis to realize his full potential in New York. For the fourth time in a row, he hit over .300 as a Met. In '86, Hernandez also captured his ninth straight Gold Glove at first base. He finished fourth (right behind Carter) in the National League MVP voting.

Darryl Strawberry, the Mets' 24-year-old right fielder, collected more All-Star votes than any other major leaguer in 1986. He went on to have a fine year. Strawberry hit 27 homers, knocked in 93 runs and batted .259. He led the team in slugging with a percentage of .507, second best (behind only Mike Schmidt) in the National League. Yet Strawberry, whose raw talent created huge expectations, had his troubles from time to time. He had been the Rookie of the Year in 1983.

Now, the New York fans demanded quality and consistency from the moody young player. Strawberry occasionally heard boos in Shea Stadium for hitting or fielding lapses. He drew the wrath of opposing pitchers for lolling around the bases on home runs. And he sulked over a few of his manager's lineup shifts.

Davey Johnson was an expert on the club's growing pains. Before he took over in 1984, New York had finished last in five of the previous seven seasons—and next to last in those other two. It was a long way from the team's world championship in 1969 and its National League pennant in 1973. Johnson, who was brought in by general manager Frank Cashen, knew how to win. The new skipper had played second base on the great Baltimore Orioles in 1970; and he had won two minor-league managerial titles. In 1984, the Mets, under Johnson, went 90-72, as Gooden became a rookie sensation. Still, New York finished second to Chicago. Then Cashen engineered a four-for-one deal with Montreal to land Gary Carter in the off-season. In 1985, the injury-plagued Mets improved to 98-64, but finished second behind St. Louis. However, Cashen had built a strong foundation. In 1986, team chairman Nelson Doubleday claimed: "The reason for the Mets' success is Frank Cashen—no ifs, ands or buts."

Cashen, who had spent ten years with the Orioles, was hired when Doubleday & Co. purchased the New York Mets in 1980. Since then, New York had turned to the free-agent draft for key young players: Stawberry ('80); Lenny Dykstra ('81); Gooden and McDowell ('82); and Aguilera ('83). The Mets had also acquired several big-leaguers in a series of moves: Darling ('82); Hernandez and Fernandez ('83); Carter and Howard Johnson ('84); and Ojeda ('85).

Before spring training of '86, Cashen also obtained second baseman Tim Teufel from Minnesota. Like they had for Ojeda, the Mets gave up only minor leaguers for Teufel, a right-handed hitter. He was to be platooned at second base with Backman, a lefty batter. That left third base as the problem spot—again. More than six dozen players had played third in the 24-year history of the Mets. Now Ray Knight, 33, was being pressed by youngsters Howard "HoJo" Johnson and Kevin Mitchell. So Cashen tried to shop the aging veteran to another club. But he found no takers for a slow player who had hit .218 in 1985. That suited Johnson, who had to argue against cutting Knight before the season began. As it turned out, it was an older Met regular, left fielder George Foster, 37, who was released a few months later.

Another important development involved Mookie Wilson. During a pre-season rundown drill in St. Petersburg, Florida, he was hit in the right eye by a ball thrown by shortstop Rafael Santana. Wilson missed the first six weeks of the season. So, Lenny Dykstra, 23, called "Nails" for his hard-nosed play, opened the year in center field. "I think Dykstra and Backman are the most potent offensive weapon the Mets have," said Philadelphia's Mike Schmidt. In fact, New York's two rally-starters combined to score 144 runs.

For the Mets, ranked as the favorites in the NL East, the season began on April 8 in Pittsburgh. New York won 4-2 on Gooden's six hitter. Dr. K went the distance and Hernandez drove in two runs. On April 14, the Mets fell below .500 for the first and only time. It happened on Opening Day at Shea Stadium: St. Louis triumphed, 6-2, in 13 innings before a sell-out crowd of 47,752. Two runs scored on Howard Johnson's bases-loaded error with no outs; two more scored on Ozzie Smith's double. That left the Mets at 2-3 on the year. Immediately, they began an 11-game winning streak to move on top to stay.

On April 23, New York, which thus far was 7-3, had the day off. But the Mets took sole possession of first place for good in the NL East when the Cubs beat the Cardinals, 6-0.

The next day, the Mets began a four-game sweep in St. Louis. In the first contest, New York triumphed, 5-4, in ten innings. HoJo's two-run homer tied it in the ninth; and Foster's run-scoring single won it. "We play October games in April," said St. Louis skipper Whitey Herzog. "Every game with these guys seems like this." On April 25, Gooden blanked the Cards, 9-0, as Knight hit a pair of home runs. In the next game, New York won, 4-3. The game ended with one of the best defensive plays of the year. Second baseman Wally Backman dove to his right to turn Terry Pendleton's potential game-tying single into a double play. To end the series, the Mets won, 5-3, on Teufel's two-run homer. "It was important for us to establish ourselves early on and prove to ourselves and to the Cardinals that we could beat them," Hernandez was to recall. "There's no question that series did it." And more. The pennant race never really began.

New York, on its way to winning 20 of its first 24 games in 1986, never lost its early-season momentum. The Mets finished April with a record of 13-3. It was a bright opening month for Knight, who batted .306 and hit six homers in the club's first dozen games. Dykstra, who hit safely in 12 of his first 15 games, hit .327 in April. And Gooden went 4-0 for the month. In May, it was more of the same. The Mets went 18-9. Knight, the guy who almost didn't make the team, hit .348 for the month. On May 27, Darling tied a Mets record for starting pitchers by earning his sixth win without a loss. He fanned 12 as New York beat Los Angeles, 8-1, at Shea Stadium. In the game, the Mets became involved in their first bench-clearing brawl of 1986. It erupted after George Foster hit a grand slam off Tom Niedenfuer. On the next pitch, the Dodger reliever hit Knight, who charged the mound and began the free-for-all. Much to the resentment of their opponents, the Mets were riding high. They ended May with a record of 31-12 and a lead of six games.

In June, New York went 19-9, built its season record to 50-21 and opened up a 9½-game lead (over the Expos) in the NL East. Among the highlights: on June 10, Teufel's pinch-hit grand slam in the bottom of the 11th off Tom Hume gave the Mets an 8-4 win over Philadelphia. On June 13, Gooden struck out 13 Pirates during a 6-5 New York win. On June 14, Fernandez three-hit Pittsburgh for a 5-1 Mets triumph and their lead reached double figures (10 games) for the first time. On June 28, McDowell, pitching in relief, became the first Met ever to start a year at 7-0; New York triumphed, 5-2, in Chicago. On June 30, the Mets began a three-game sweep in St. Louis, and the Cards fell 11 games behind.

On July 4, the Mets beat Houston, 2-1, to complete an eight-game winning streak. It was Gooden's tenth victory; Dykstra hit two doubles to raise his average to .312.

Only 28,557 fans showed up for that Independence Day game on Friday afternoon at Shea Stadium. Much of New York was celebrating the 100th birthday of the Statue of Liberty. On ABC-TV, the "Liberty Weekend" show thrilled millions of Americans. Also hits during the summer of '86 were the films *Top Gun, Legal Eagles* and *Ruthless People.* The number one recording was "Invisible Touch" by Genesis. And Judith Krantz was on the best-seller list with *I'll Take Manhattan.* Which the Mets were doing.

They sent five players to Oakland for the July 15 All-Star Game (the American League won 3-2): Strawberry, Carter, Hernandez, Gooden and Fernandez.

A few days later four New York Mets made headlines off the field. After a scuffle at Cooters Executive Games and Burgers, a Houston nightspot, Teufel, Darling, Aguilera and Ojeda spent the night in jail. Eventually, Teufel and Darling were put on probation briefly; but the charges against Aguilera and Ojeda were dropped.

New York ran into an on-the-field battle in Cincinnati on July 22. The Reds led 3-1 with two outs in the ninth when Dave Parker dropped a routine fly to right, letting a pair of runs score to tie the game. In the tenth, Eric Davis slid hard into third base and Ray Knight punched him in the jaw, which cleared both benches. In the extra-inning game, Johnson wound up flip-flopping McDowell and Orosco between the mound and the outfield. Carter also became the 80th third baseman in Met history. Finally, New York won, 6-3, in 14 innings on Howard Johnson's three-run homer off Ted Power. By the end of July, the Mets had a record of 66-32 for the season and a lead of 15½ games.

On August 7, New York announced the release of George Foster, the $2 million outfielder who was batting just .227 with 13 homers and 38 RBIs. Foster had been upset because Johnson decided to platoon Kevin Mitchell and Mookie Wilson in left field. Reportedly, the 17-year veteran of the major leagues complained of racial motives in some of the team's decisions. The controversy led to his departure, which Johnson had sought for some time. But the incident didn't hinder the Mets on the field. They won 21 games in August, their winningest month of the season, despite the fact that Carter was put on the 15-day disabled list when he hurt his hand while playing first base. Hernandez wielded the hottest bat in August. On the mound, McDowell went 4-2 during the month and saved eight games. Now the Mets were 87-43 on the year with a 19-game lead. And the front office began to advertise "a September to remember."

It was. The Mets' lead in the NL East peaked at 22 games on September 10 when they beat Montreal, 6-1, on first-inning homers by Wilson and Hernandez. A week later, rookie Dave Magadan went three-for-four and drove in two runs in the 4-2 divison clincher against the Cubs. On September 25, the Mets triumphed, 6-5, in Chicago. It was their 100th victory, tying the club record set by the "Miracle Mets" of 1969. In the game, Mitchell hit New York's 140th homer of the season, breaking the club record set in 1962—the team's first season. That was the year Casey Stengel's dead-end Mets posted a record of 40 wins and 120 losses and finshed 60½ games behind. 1986 was a different story.

The Mets kept pouring it on until the end of the regular season. "I want to win 105 games," said Davey Johnson. "If we do that, it means we will be 100 games over .500 in my three years here." New York did even better. They won 15 of their last 17 games to finish with 108 victories. The final win was a 9-0 triumph at Shea Stadium against Pittsburgh. Strawberry hit a grand slam to go with homers by Carter and Knight; and Darling and Fernandez combined for the shutout. It was the 17th time New York had beaten the Pirates in their 18 games during the season.

Could the New York Mets win it all when the chips where down?

The answer was yes. They displayed their character and resilience during the National League playoffs and the World Series. In the regular season, the Mets, who were used to having their way, won by a typical score of 5-2. Their most productive innings were the first and the fourth. In post-season games, New York added an extra dimension. The Mets scored more than half of their runs against Houston and Boston after the sixth inning.

It took clutch hitting to get the job done.

In the NL playoffs, New York also relied on tight defense and solid relief pitching. It had to. The Mets batted only .189 against Houston, while striking out 57 times in six games. Mike Scott fanned 14 New Yorkers to win the 1-0 opener in the Astrodome. But Ojeda triumphed, 5-1, in game two. Back at Shea, the Mets won 6-5: Stawberry's three-run homer in the sixth inning helped to erase a 4-0 Houston lead, and Dykstra won it with a two-run shot in the bottom of the ninth. In game four, Scott, ignoring scuff-ball charges, three-hit New York for a 3-1 Houston win that evened the League Championship Series. Then the Mets went one up with a 2-1 victory in 12 innings. Carter, breaking a 1-for-21 slump, won game five with a run-scoring single.

Game six was the most dramatic contest in playoff history. During the 16-inning game in Houston, nine pitchers struggled to gain the victory. It began at 3:06 p.m., EDT, and didn't end until 7:48—by which time millions of Wednesday night commuters in New York had delayed their homeward rush to catch glimpses of the action on TVs throughtout the city. Down 3-0 in the top of the ninth inning, the Mets rallied to tie the game on RBIs by Wilson, Hernandez and Knight. In the 14th, Backman singled home a run, but Billy Hatcher homered to tie the game in the bottom of the inning. Finally, the Mets took a 7-4 lead in the top of the 16th on Knight's one-run single, a run-scoring wild pitch and Dykstra's base hit. In the bottom of the inning, Houston scored a pair of runs on singles by Billy Hatcher and Glenn Davis. That left the potential tying and winning runs on second and first with two outs. But Jesse Orosco, visibly tired after three high-pressure innings, fanned Kevin Bass. And it was over. The relief pitcher got his third and biggest win of the playoffs. Thus, New York won, 7-6, to gain the National League pennant.

The '86 World Series lacked such excitement—until game six. The Boston Red Sox (95-66, .590) were led by ace Roger Clemens, who went on to win the Cy Young and MVP awards for going 24-4 with an ERA of 2.48. But he didn't win a game in the Series. The Red Sox had come within one pitch of being defeated in the American League playoffs by California. Even so, they quieted fans in Shea Stadium by beating the Mets 1-0 (behind Bruce Hurst) and 9-3 in the first two games of the World Series. In Boston, the Mets silenced Red Sox fans for two games. New York won 7-1, as Ojeda beat his ex-teammates; and 6-2 as Carter belted two homers. Then Hurst pitched Boston to a 4-2 victory in game five. It was the first World Series contest of '86 in which the home team had scored first. And it gave the Red Sox a 3-2 edge in games.

Next came another thrilling game six. Back at Shea, Ojeda pitched until the sixth inning, and Clemens pitched until the seventh. The Red Sox broke a 2-2 tie in the seventh inning with the help of Ray Knight's throwing error. The Mets, facing elimination, tied the game, 3-3, in the bottom of the eighth on Carter's sacrifice fly. In the top of the tenth, Dave Henderson homered off Rick Aguilera and Boston added another run for a 5-3 lead. Then came the fireworks. New York staged one of the most memorable comebacks in the history of the World Series. It began with two outs and nobody on base. Carter singled to left on a 2-1 pitch from Calvin Schiraldi. He moved to second when Mitchell singled to center on an 0-1 pitch. Then Knight fell behind 0-2 and the Mets were within one pitch of losing the World Series. But Knight drove in Carter with a single up the middle that moved Mitchell, the potential tying run, to third. In came Bob Stanley, a relief pitcher. The count went 2-2 on Mookie Wilson, who fouled the next two pitches. Then Stanley threw an inside fastball that sailed back to the screen after Wilson leaped to avoid it. Mitchell rushed home on the wild pitch, knotting the score at 3-3, as Knight moved to second base. Back from the brink, New York was in a position to win. Wilson fouled off a pair of 3-2 pitches. Then he hit what looked like an easy bouncer down the first base line. Suddenly, the ball skipped under first baseman

Bill Buckner's glove for an error and Knight scored. "The ball bounced and bounced and then it didn't bounce," said Buckner. The Mets won, 6-5, on the most incredible rally in World Series history. In extra innings, on the verge of losing it all with two outs and nobody on base, they had scored three runs. Now there was one more game to play.

In game seven, the Mets beat Boston, 8-5, to become world champions. It was another come-from-behind victory. New York tied the game, 3-3, on three runs in the bottom of the sixth inning. In the seventh, Knight's home run sparked another three-run inning that was enough for the victory. It also was enough to earn the veteran third baseman the World Series MVP title. In the Fall Classic, Knight hit .391 and drove in five runs.

Ultimately, the turn of events thrilled New Yorkers and broke hearts across New England. It was the fourth time the Red Sox had played in the World Series since last winning it in 1918. Each of those four losses came in the seventh game. Now Buckner's miscue loomed as the biggest frustration of them all.

"That was an error," said Davey Johnson. "Errors are part of the game. We made them. They made them. We didn't win because of luck or an error. We won because we were the best team."

Spoken, perhaps, like a true New Yorker. Yet the 1986 Mets had a right to be proud. The team had nothing left to prove. It had won everything in sight. The Mets gained their World Series crown on their 116th victory of the season.

Said their manager: "This is as good as it gets."

8

Cincinnati Reds 1975

108-54

.667

BIG RED MACHINE WINS BY 20 GAMES ♦ PETE ROSE (.317) MOVES TO 3B ♦ JOE MORGAN (17, 94, .327) IS NL MVP ♦ JOHNNY BENCH COLLECTS 110 RBIs; TONY PEREZ, 109 ♦ DON GULLET IS 15-4 FOR THE SEASON ♦ CINCINNATI TOPS BOSTON IN THRILLING SEVEN-GAME WORLD SERIES.

Sparky Anderson called it the best hunch he ever had. The manager of the Cincinnati Reds felt his team couldn't win the National League pennant in 1975 without a solid third baseman. So, he asked Pete Rose to do the job.

The stopgap move, nearly a month into the season, turned the Big Red Machine into one of major-league baseball's top teams ever. Not only did Rose, 34, fill Cincinnati's persistent gap at third base, but also his switch from left field opened up a regular spot for 26-year-old George Foster. Quickly, the team stopped faltering; and it began to win like never before.

The '75 Reds rolled to victory behind the hitting of NL

MVP Joe Morgan, Johnny Bench and Tony Perez, as well as Rose and Foster. Relying heavily on a strong bullpen, Cincinnati finished 20 games ahead of runner-up Los Angeles in the NL West. The Reds swept Pittsburgh, 3-0, in the League Championship Series. Then Cincinnati, reaching the top for the first time since 1940, beat the Boston Red Sox in a dramatic seven-game World Series. It was the best season in the 99-year history of baseball's oldest franchise.

Going into 1975, the outlook in Cincinnati was cloudy. Anderson was still worrying about third base. He had used eight different players at the hot corner in 1974. The Reds went 98-64 only to wind up four games behind the Los Angeles Dodgers. Under Anderson, Cincinnati had finished first in three of the previous four seasons; but they failed to win the World Series in 1970 and 1972, and failed to win the pennant in 1973. And something was still missing.

On Friday, May 2, 1975, things changed. Opening a home stand at Riverfront Stadium, second-place Cincinnati, with a 12-11 record, trailed Los Angeles, the defending NL champions, by three games. By then, Anderson was back looking for more offense at third after using glove man John Vukovich unsuccessfully early in the year. That night, the manager found the right candidate for the spot.

When he walked out of the clubhouse before the home game with Atlanta, Anderson spotted left fielder Pete Rose fielding grounders at first base. Rose explained that he was breaking in a first-baseman's mitt for his daughter, Fawn.

This is how Anderson recalled what happened next:

"'Pete, you look pretty good around this bag,' I said. 'How do you think you'd do at the other corner?'

"'Are you serious, Sparky?'

"I said I was.

"'I'll do anything to help the ball club,' Pete said. 'I'll sure try.'"

Simple as that. The two Cincinnati veterans agreed privately to make the big switch the following day. And the manager promised not to embarrass his new third baseman by leaving him there for long if the shift didn't work out.

Pete Rose was a second baseman when he broke in with the Reds in 1963. Three years later he was assigned to third for a while in spring training, but he didn't like it. So he returned to his original spot for another year before shifting to the outfield in 1967. Now, eight seasons later, he found that he liked third base—being in the infield kept him more involved in the game. It was the right place for a talkative, fiery guy called "Charley Hustle." At third, Rose found time to talk to pitchers, umpires, baserunners, and coaches. He adjusted to his new spot by fielding 400 ground balls a day and doggedly turned himself into a decent fielder. At bat, Rose (7, 74, .317) thrived. He collected 210 hits and led the National League in runs (112) and doubles (47).

Meanwhile, George Foster (23, 78, .300), beginning to live up to his potential, hit more homers than he ever had before as a pro. Previously, he had been platooning with Ken Griffey in right and Cesar Geronimo in center. But Rose's shift to third settled the outfield. Speedsters Griffey (4, 46, .305) and Geronimo (6, 53, .257) combined with Foster to help give Cincinnati the best all-around outfield in the league.

The Reds' infield in '75 was even better. In fact, Joe Morgan, at 5-foot-7 and 165 pounds, was a one-man team. The little second baseman became the fourth Cincinnati star in six years—Bench did it in 1970 and 1972, and Rose did it in 1973—to win the NL MVP crown. At age 32, Morgan (17, 94, .327) was a six-time All Star. Rose called him "the cog that puts the Big Red Machine in gear." He batted second, behind Rose, or third, behind Griffey. Morgan led the NL in walks (132) and finished second in steals (67). He was versatile enough to post an on-base percentage of .472 and a slugging average of .508.

Next in the batting order came Cincinnati's two big RBI men: catcher Johnny Bench (28, 110, .283) and first baseman Tony Perez (20, 109, .282). Bench, 28, lost his chance for a fourth RBI title because of a late-season foot injury. He also was bothered all season long by a shoulder injury that occurred in April during a home-plate collision. For the ninth straight year, though, Perez, 33, drove in at least 90 runs. His roommate, shortstop Dave Concepcion (5, 49, .274), was no RBI man. But he was the best fielder in the NL at that position in 1975. So were Bench, Morgan and Geronimo. That gave the Reds the kind of defensive strength up the middle that typifies many world champions. The club set a major-league record by playing 15 straight games without an error.

On the mound, Cincinnati was far less imposing. Anderson became known as "Captain Hook" because his starters only completed 22 of 162 games. In fact, they set a record by going 45 straight games without a pitcher having finished what he started. Admitted Captain Hook: "That's one record I'm not too proud of." The ace of the staff, 24-year-old Don Gullett (15-4, 2.42), had eight complete games in 1975, but he contributed nothing to the mid-season runaway by the Reds. A hard-throwing lefty, Gullett missed two months when he was struck by a ball that broke the thumb on his pitching hand. He was 9-3 when he was forced out on June 16 with Cincinnati leading the NL West by just 3½ games. By the time he won again on August 18, the Reds had a 17½-game edge.

Six of Cincinnati's pitchers, including Gullett, won in double figures. The other five were: Gary Nolan (15-9, 3.16), a veteran who had been sidelined for two years with a shoulder injury; Jack Billingham (15-10, 4.11); Fred Norman (12-4, 3.73); Pat Darcy (11-5, 3.57); and Clay Kirby (10-6, 4.70).

But it was Anderson's superb manipulation of his bullpen that turned out to be crucial. The top relievers were right-hander Rawly Eastwick (5-3, 2.60, with 22 saves), a 24-year-old rookie, and left-hander Will McEnaney (5-2, 2.47 with 15 saves), a 23-year old. Recalled from the minors in late May, Eastwick pitched in 58 games; McEnaney, who had two streaks of 25-plus scoreless innings, pitched in 70. They kept National League hitters off-balance all season long.

The summer of '75 was marked by the arrest of Patty Hearst, the disappearance of Jimmy Hoffa and the attempted assassination of President Gerald Ford. Americans watched *Jaws* in the movie theaters, read James Michener's *Centennial*, and listened to "Love Will Keep Us Together," by The Captain & Tennille.

In Cincinnati, Reds fans cheered for a front-runner. But not right away.

The Reds won six of their next seven games after Anderson switched Rose to third base in early May. But then the team dropped six in a row, their longest losing streak of the year. During loss number six, Joe Morgan was spiked in a collision and needed 14 stitches in his shin to close the bloody wound. He was hurt in Montreal during a 4-2 Expos victory on May 16. Next day, he offered to play despite the obvious pain. So Anderson called a clubhouse meeting to shake up the team. "If Joe can play, we all can play," said the manager. That's when the Reds began their winning drive.

Cincinnati won nine of its next 10 games—including seven in a row. By June 7, the Reds moved into first place to stay. They won 43 of the next 53 games (a winning percentage of .811) after that clubhouse session in Montreal. Morgan led the way in June. During the month, he hit .388, with seven homers and 27 RBIs. On June 13, he had company: the Big Red Machine collected 24 hits during an 18-11 victory at Wrigley Field in Chicago. Capping an eight-week tear, Cincinnati put together a ten-game win streak going into the All-Star break. On July 13, the Reds, with a record of 61-29, held a lead of 12½ games in the NL West. The second-place Dodgers were fading fast. They were hit by injuries early and got 100-game seasons out of just seven players.

By the end of August, Cincinnati was at 90-45 with an 18½ game lead over number two Los Angeles. During the month, Tony Perez hit .398 with three homers and 26 RBIs. He also tied and broke Frank Robinson's old club record of 1,009 runs batted in. On August 17, Pete Rose passed the 2,500 hit mark with a single off Pittsburgh's Bruce Kison during a 3-1 triumph in Cincinnati.

On September 7, the Reds clinched the division flag—the earliest title victory in National League history. In game 142, Gullett got the win in Cincinnati as the Big Red Machine won the NL West, beating the San Francisco Giants, 8-4.

Among other things, the Reds won big at home in 1975, picking up a NL record 64 victories at Riverfront Stadium.

They also won with timely hitting, rallying to take 24 games during the season in their last at bats.

After sweeping Pittsburgh in the playoffs to win the NL pennant, the Reds squared off to face the AL Boston Red Sox (95-65, .594) in a rain-soaked World Series. It was one of the most memorable Fall Classics of all time.

Game six, in particular, is often called the best in any modern World Series. Going into the contest, Cincinnati led three games to two despite a strong Boston lineup that included Carl Yastrzemski, Dwight Evans and rookie star Fred Lynn. Red Sox ace Luis Tiant had both of his team's victories.

Back in Fenway Park, the Bosox tied the game, 6-6, in game six on Bernie Carbo's three-run homer in the bottom of the eighth inning. In the bottom of the ninth, Boston loaded the bases with no outs. But George Foster threw out a runner at home for a double play and the Red Sox failed to score. In the top of the 11th, Evans made a great catch in right field off Morgan to start another double play. In the bottom of the 12th, Carlton Fisk led off against Pat Darcy, Cincinnati's record-tying eighth pitcher of the contest. Fisk hit Darcy's first pitch down the left-field line, stood using body English to urge it on, and leaped for joy when it struck the foul pole for a game-winning home run. Afterwards, Fisk said: "I don't think anybody in the world could ask for a better game than this one. Pete Rose came up to me in the 10th and said, 'This is some kind of game, isn't it?' Pete Rose said that to *me*."

In game seven, the Cincinnati Reds triumphed, 4-3, to win the world championship. But the Big Red Machine had to overcome a 3-0 deficit before Joe Morgan won the game with a two-out run scoring single in the ninth inning.

"It was our 115th victory," noted Sparky Anderson, the 1975 NL manager of the year, later on. "And we took the seventh game with the qualities that got us into the Series—speed, power, defense, relief pitching and the best spirit I ever saw."

9

Baltimore Orioles 1970

108-54

.667

THREE 20-GAME WINNERS LEAD BIRDS ♦ MIKE CUELLAR IS 24-8; DAVE MCNALLY, 24-9; JIM PALMER, 20-10 ♦ AL MVP IS BOOG POWELL (35, 114, .297) ♦ FRANK ROBINSON (25, 78, .306) STARS ♦ BROOKS ROBINSON FOILS REDS IN WORLD SERIES.

Getting ready for the first trip of the season, Brooks Robinson tagged his suitcase with a label that underlined the goal of his entire team. It read: "Baltimore Orioles, 1970 World Champions."

It was the kind of winning year that is born out of frustration.

Recalling the journey home from New York in 1969, general manager Harry Dalton of the Orioles explained: "The 1970 season started for most of us the night we came back to Baltimore after losing the World Series to the Mets, and there were 5,000 cheering people at Friendship Airport to greet us."

The homecoming was bittersweet. The '69 Orioles, thought to have the makings of one of the best major-league teams ever, were upset in a five-game World Series by the Miracle Mets. So, the O's, with their impressive blend of hitting, pitching, and defense, felt they had something to prove in 1970.

This time they went all the way.

Following nearly the same pattern, the Orioles of '70 cruised to victory in the American League East. Again the O's swept Minnesota in the playoffs. And this five-game World Series had a happy ending. With his glove and his bat, Brooks Robinson shocked the NL champion Cincinnati Reds and carried Baltimore to its missing world title.

The 1969-70 Orioles, under manager Earl Weaver, won a total of 217 regular-season games during two consecutive years. Thus, they broke the AL record of 211 set by the legendary 1927-28 New York Yankees.

To do so, the O's relied on murderous pitching. The lords of Baltimore in 1970 were left-handers Mike Cuellar (24-8, .3.47) and Dave McNally (24-9, 3.22), plus right-hander Jim Palmer (20-10, 2.71). It was the first team with three 20-game winners since the 1956 Cleveland Indians of Early Wynn, Herb Score and Bob Lemon. The '70 Orioles topped the American League with 60 complete games as their big three finished 54 of the 119 games they started. Neither Jim Hardin (6-5, 3.54) nor Tom Phoebus (5-5, 3.07) emerged as a consistent fourth starter. But the bullpen was solid, if a bit erratic. It won 30 games and saved 30 others. Lefty Pete Richert (7-2, 1.96), who had the best ERA on the team, and righty Eddie Watt (7-7, 3.27) combined for a total of 25 saves. Dick Hall (10-5, 3.10), another righty, also worked in relief. And Baltimore led the AL with an ERA of 3.15.

Not only did the Orioles hold their opponents to fewer runs (574) than did any other AL team, they also were number one in scoring runs themselves (792). A big reason was John "Boog" Powell, who was 6-foot-4½ and weighed 230 pounds. Powell (35, 114, .297) was the American League MVP in 1970. The 31-year-old first baseman had a slugging average of .549. It was his second banner year in a row. A left-handed swinger, Powell took his lumberjack cuts in the heart of the lineup. He teamed there with 35-year-old Frank Robinson (25, 78, .306), a right-handed hitter. In 1970, "F. Robby" had a slugging percentage of .520. After getting off to a good start, though, he ran into a few walls and was bothered by a shoulder injury. He was one of the two Robinsons—both of them future Hall of Famers—who for years were the heart and soul of the Baltimore Orioles. "B. Robby" was the magician who played third base. At age 33, Brooks Robinson (18, 94, .276) had a fine year. He saved his best for last in 1970.

"Mr. Third Base" was the star of the AL's best defensive infield. Powell, at first base, had size and grace. Dave Johnson, the top AL fielder at second base, finished the year with an errorless streak of 43 games. Next to him was shortstop Mark Belanger, who is considered one of the best fielders ever to play that position. That distinction is also accorded to center fielder Paul Blair, who was fast and sure-handed. He also had a good arm. By 1970, Ted Williams was calling Blair the best defensive player he had ever seen in center field. Three of the Orioles won Gold Gloves in 1970: Brooks Robinson (his 11th straight), Johnson and Blair.

"We just seem to do things automatically at times," said B. Robby about the Oriole defense. "I believe we do it that way because our guys are good enough that they don't need too many lessons to pick things up. Sure, we work in spring training on hitting the cutoff man and backing up the plays. If you make a mistake on things like those, a whole big inning will open up against you." That seldom happened, though. Admitted manager Earl Weaver: "We like to think that we do not have too many holes."

For years, the Orioles, who won their first world championship in 1966, had been plugging gaps with remarkable home-grown talent. Twenty-two of the 39 athletes who made the Baltimore roster in 1970 were originally signed and developed by the club. Among those who came up through the ranks were Powell, Brooks Robinson, Blair, Johnson, Belanger, McNally and Palmer. The man on top who had built the team was Harry Dalton.

For Weaver, 40, it was also a triumph. He had managed in

the Oriole farm system for 11 seasons before taking over as first-base coach in 1968. He became the manager later in the year. The fiery strategist led Baltimore to a pair of pennants and a world championship in his first two full seasons at the helm. From Hank Bauer, he had inherited a team that was 43-37. Weaver, who doted on statistics and percentages, pushed Baltimore to more than 100 games over .500 in less than three years. As a second baseman, he had gone to spring training with the St. Louis Cardinals in 1952. But Weaver never played a game in the major leagues. Now the bright, young manager had a World Series ring.

The 1970 season had unfolded against a turbulent background. The Apollo 13 astronauts, endangered by an oxygen tank explosion on the way to the moon, returned without making the third U.S. lunar landing. At Kent State University in Ohio, National Guardsmen opened fire during a Vietnam protest, killing four persons and wounding others. And one of the summer's top records was the Edwin Starr rock song "War." Baseball, of course, provided happier memories.

From the start, the Orioles were determined to succeed. They opened the season with an 8-2 victory in Cleveland as Dave McNally struck out 13. That was the first of five straight wins, including the home opener in Baltimore. In that game, the O's beat Detroit, 3-2, on Brooks Robinson's two-out single in the 10th inning. By April 26, the O's were in first place to stay. That day they scored five runs in the first inning in Kansas City and won, 10-9, with the help of left fielder Don Buford's three-run homer in the eighth. Buford (18, 94, .276; with 109 walks), was the best leadoff man in the AL in 1970. On April 29, Baltimore pounded out an 18-2 victory over the White Sox in Chicago as Blair hit three home runs and Palmer went the distance. The O's ended the month with a record of 13-6.

By May 30, Baltimore was 23-9 and led the second-place New York Yankees by six games. The next day, tragedy struck. In a West Coast game, a pitch by reliever Tom Tatum of California struck Blair in the face and nearly ended his career. It took three hours of surgery to repair a broken nose and bone damage to an eye socket. Blair spent three weeks on the disabled list. After that, he was always a bit gun-shy at the plate, although he finished the season with decent stats (18, 65, .267). From the day before Blair got hurt until July 19, Baltimore played just .500 ball over a 46-game stretch. McNally and Cuellar fell into slumps. Meanwhile, New York and Detroit stayed in contention.

Not that everything was bleak during those seven weeks. On June 20, Brooks Robinson's 2,000th hit, a three-run homer, gave the O's a 5-4 victory over Washington. Two days later, Blair returned to the lineup, going three-for-six with two doubles in a 9-8 Orioles victory in Boston. On June 26, the Orioles scored five runs in the 14th inning at Fenway Park and held on the beat the Red Sox, 13-8. It was a wild game that lasted five hours. Coming back from a 7-0 deficit, Baltimore tied a club record with 21 hits. Each team used seven pitchers. In the bottom of the 13th, Frank Robinson saved the game with a leaping catch in right field to rob Reggie Smith of a home run. The next night, F. Robby won the game with his bat. He belted a pair of grand slams in Washington as the O's triumphed, 12-2.

The pennant race heated up when the Yankees arrived in Baltimore on July 7. New York was in second place and trailing by just 5½ games. In the first game, the Orioles beat New York, 6-2, when Brooks Robinson hit a grand slam in the 10th inning. The next night, Baltimore was losing, 8-6, going into the botttom of the ninth. F. Robby hit a lead-off homer. Then singles by B. Robby and Davey Johnson, plus Andy Etchebarren's walk, loaded the bases. Yankee hurler Lindy McDaniel struck out two batters, but Don Buford's two-run single gave the Orioles a 9-8 win. The following day, New York coach Elston Howard said, "Last night's loss was the toughest I can remember as a Yankee." After winning a rain-shortened contest, the Yanks left town six games back. It was the most exciting series of the season in Baltimore. In 1970, New York, the runner up in the AL East, finished 15 games in back of the Orioles.

The O's took off and began to fly away from the

opposition in late July following their long slump. Detroit pulled to within three games of Baltimore and then fell to 6½ back on July 30. By August 15, the Orioles, with a record of 74-44, led New York by 8½ games and Detroit by 12. The big three of Cuellar, McNally and Palmer went 18-2 in August. McNally won his 20th on August 21 (vs. California, 5-0); and Cuellar did it on August 27 (vs. Oakland, 6-4). Palmer, who had a bit of trouble, didn't get his 20th win until September 20 (vs. Cleveland, 7-0). It came three days after Baltimore clinched the AL East title.

In September, the O's went 22-7. They won 19 of their last 22 games, including the final 11 in a row. Next, the Orioles swept Minnesota in three games to win the AL pennant. Then Baltimore pushed its streak to 17 straight victories by winning the first three games of the World Series.

The Orioles didn't get another shot at the Mets in the Fall Classic. Instead, they faced the Cincinnati Reds (102-60, .630), the NL pennant winner. The Big Red Machine of 1970 was led by Johnny Bench (45, 148, .293), Tony Perez (40, 129, .317), and Pete Rose (.316, with 205 hits and 120 runs).

Quickly, the World Series turned into "The Brooks Robinson Show."

In game one, Baltimore triumphed, 4-3, as B. Robby tormented the hometown fans in Cincinnati. He made three great plays at third base and won the game with a solo homer. That was only the beginning.

In the first inning of game two, Robinson made a diving stop at third base and turned it into a force play. Later, he drove in the tying run and the Orioles won again, 6-5.

In game three, Brooks did it again. This time it was before a friendly audience in Baltimore. The best of Robinson's plays during the game was a diving catch of Bench's line drive. B Robby also hit two doubles and scored on Dave McNally's grand slam, the first by a pitcher in World Series history. The O's won, 9-3. After a loss, Baltimore came back with another 9-3 victory to win the Fall Classic, four games to one.

Besides his spectacular fielding, Robinson batted .429 with two homers. He and Paul Blair each had nine hits to tie the record for a five-game Series. Boog Powell and Frank Robinson also had a pair of homers each.

"Certain people believe that we have had the finest team in baseball for the past two years," Weaver had pointed out during the World Series.

And Dalton repeated that it was the "Welcome, home!" crowd in Baltimore a year before that steered the Orioles toward the top in 1970.

Said Dalton: "There are those who would have you believe that a rah-rah spirit in professional sports doesn't mean anything. But it does."

10

New York Yankees 1936

102-51

.667

FIRST YANKEE WORLD CHAMPIONSHIP WITHOUT BABE RUTH ♦ LOU GEHRIG (49, 152, .354) IS AL MVP ♦ JOE DIMAGGIO (29, 125, .323) IS STAR ROOKIE ♦ BILL DICKEY HITS .362 ♦ YANKS BEAT GIANTS, 4-2, IN WORLD SERIES.

For the first time ever, the New York Yankees reached the top without the legendary Babe Ruth. It was easy, too—surprisingly so. The Bronx Bombers of 1936 became the most dominant team in the history of the American League, winning the pennant by a record margin of 19½ games. Never before had the chase for the AL flag turned into a one-team runaway for most of the season. Widely expected to finish third (or maybe fourth), manager Joe McCarthy's revamped Yanks went 102-51 (.667). They even outhit the great Yankees of 1927 in most categories. And they crushed the National League champion New York Giants in the World Series to begin an unprecedented four-year dynasty.

Early in the season, Eddie Brannick, secretary of the Giants (who were out of town), drove from the Polo Grounds to see a game at Yankee Stadium. It was a typical day for his powerful American League host. Asked what he thought of the Yanks, Brannick just said: "Window breakers."

Leading the Yankees in 1936 was Lou Gehrig, the familiar Iron Horse, who delivered one of his best efforts. He finally received the American League's MVP award, which was denied him as a Triple Crown winner (it went to Detroit's Mickey Cochrane) in 1934. That was Ruth's last year in New York; and the Babe, 40, retired in 1935 after a brief unseemly return to Boston to try to play in the National League. So, the 33-year-old Gehrig, no longer overshadowed by baseball's number one spectacle, had a shot at glory of his own.

As the Yankees triumphed in 1936, Gehrig hit .354, drove in 152 runs and belted a career-high 49 homers. He led the AL in home runs, slugging (.696), runs scored (167), and walks (130); he was number two in RBIs and total bases (403). His physical endurance, meanwhile, kept setting records day after day. Going into the season, the quiet Yankee first baseman already had played in more than 1,600 consecutive games. And he didn't miss a day's work in '36.

Yet, for all of that, the year belonged to a rookie—Joe DiMaggio. The 21-year-old newcomer stole the spotlight in New York by flashing what seemed like effortless skill. Young Joe broke in fast, hitting .323 with 29 home runs and 125 RBIs. He set an AL record by scoring 132 runs in his first season. And the kid from California ran, caught and threw with unique grace. It was the major-league debut of the greatest all-around star in baseball history. Thus, the Yankees did the virtually impossible: they replaced one all-time great outfielder with another. The 1-2 punch in the heart of the pinstriped lineup was no longer Ruth and Gehrig; it was now DiMaggio and Gehrig. In 1936, DiMaggio had 206 hits and Gehrig had 205. Together with their manager, they created the New York Yankee image of class, professionalism and superiority. Babe Ruth's boisterous, free-wheeling style was forever replaced by the McCarthy-Gehrig-DiMaggio blend of cool, efficient dominance. Once again, though, the Iron Horse failed to emerge by himself.

"Joe became a big star almost as soon as he joined the Yankees," explained pitcher Lefty Gomez, who roomed with DiMaggio. "The man I felt sorry for was Lou Gehrig. He had always played behind Ruth, and finally Ruth quit and he had it all to himself in 1935. Now in '36 Joe comes along. Lou had another big year, but Joe was the rookie sensation, so he got all the attention.

"The relationship between Joe and Lou was very good. They never had a cross word that I know of. They were both quiet fellows and they got along.

"But it just seemed a shame that Lou never got the attention he deserved. He didn't seem to care—but maybe he did. Anyway, I always felt a little sorry for him because of it."

The '36 Yankees were anything but a two-man club. Five of the Bronx Bombers drove in more than 100 runs, still a major-league record. Besides Gehrig and DiMaggio, the big hitters were: catcher Bill Dickey (22, 107, .362); right fielder George Selkirk (18, 107, .308), who once was booed for being the guy who replaced Ruth, and second baseman Tony Lazzeri (14, 109, .287). The Yanks also hit a record 182 home runs, with seven batters in double figures. Their 2,703 total bases (nearly 18 a game) was another record; and so was their 580 extra-base hits. New York led the American League in slugging percentage (.483, more than 20 points higher than anybody else), in runs (1,065) and in walks (700). The Yankee lineup contained six .300 hitters; in fact, the team batting average was an even .300. All in all, they did the hardest hitting during a year in which most American League bats boomed (the AL's batting average was .289; its ERA, 5.04).

On top of that, New York came up with the best staff of hurlers in the league in 1936. Thanks to pre-season trades and McCarthy's constant juggling, the Yankee pitching, which had figured to keep the team out of first place, suddenly became a strength. New York's pitchers more than got the job done. They led the league in ERA (4.17), in strikeouts (624), and—with the help of the AL's second-best defense—in opponents' runs (731). The New York ace was Red Ruffing (20-12, 3.85); it was the first of four 20-win seasons in a row for the right-hander. Monte Pearson (19-7, 3.71), newly acquired from Cleveland, led the league with a win percentage of .731. But it was an off-year for Lefty Gomez (13-7), one of five future Hall of Fame players on the club (along with Gehrig, DiMaggio, Dickey and Ruffing). Veteran Bump Hadley (14-4), newly acquired from Washington, took up some of the slack. And the Yanks got solid relief from Pat Malone (12-4, 9 saves) and Johnny Murphy (9-3, 5 saves).

Even without Babe Ruth, New York had finished just three games in back of Detroit in 1935—its third season in a row in the number two spot. McCarthy, who hadn't won since Ruth's last great year (1932), was being called "Second Place Joe." But there was plenty of reason for optimism during spring training in St. Petersburg, Florida. Filling the gap in the outfield, Joe DiMaggio arrived from the San Francisco Seals of the Pacific Coast League. In 1933, DiMaggio, at age 18, was the hottest minor-league prospect in America. He batted .340 (with a 61-game hitting streak) and drove in 169 runs. But the Seals tried to increase his value by keeping him for one more year. In the middle of 1934 DiMaggio injured his left knee while getting off a bus. Lost for much of the season, he became a doubtful property. The Yanks gambled. They acquired his contract for $25,000 and a bunch of minor leaguers, but agreed to let San Francisco keep its popular star for one final season. In 1935, DiMaggio batted .398 in the PCL with 270 hits in 172 games. Now he was a Yankee.

In spring training, the shy, aloof rookie (known in the minors as "Dead Pan Joe") got a New York-style press buildup. The fans began to anticipate big things. But the young outfielder injured his foot slightly during an exhibition game, and he suffered severe burns while being treated with a diathermy machine. The heat-lamp accident was to keep DiMaggio out of the Yankee lineup until May.

"He looked real good in spring training that first year—what was it, '36—and then he burned his foot in that machine," McCarthy recalled much later. "Well, we knew he could play, so we just waited for him to get well. . . .

"DiMaggio had never played center field. I watched him

go back on a ball and I knew he could play it. I started him in left field after his foot got better. And then I moved him over to right field for a while. I wanted to make sure he was comfortable before I put him in center field. Finally, I decided he was ready, so I moved him to center field (on August 8).

"He never would have become the great outfielder he was if I hadn't moved him. He needed room to roam in Yankee Stadium. That's the toughest center field in baseball and only the real great ones can play out there. That's a lot of ground for a man to cover."

With DiMaggio sitting on the bench, the Yankees opened the '36 season in Washington. The traditional baseball game in the nation's capital offered a bit of relief from Depression-era politics on the afternoon of April 14. Throwing out the first ball was President Franklin D. Roosevelt, who was to defend his New Deal later that year in the election campaign against Governor Alf Landon of Kansas. The Senators beat New York, 1-0, on a run-scoring double by Carl Reynolds in the bottom of the ninth. Bobo Newsom's four-hitter topped Lefty Gomez. Newsom, hit in the face by a throw on a play at first, stayed in the game despite a broken jaw. "When the President of the United States comes out to see old Bobo pitch," he vowed, "old Bobo ain't gonna let him down."

In April, the Bronx Bombers got off to a 10-5 start in their bid to depose the world champion Tigers. Quickly, Detroit was hurting. After playing just 12 games, Tiger slugger Hank Greenberg broke his arm when Washington's Jake Powell crashed into his glove hand on a play at first base. Greenberg was out for the season. It was that kind of a year for Detroit (which finished 83-71, .539). Schoolboy Rowe had a sore pitching arm and player-manager Mickey Cochrane, a chronic worrier, caught only 42 games. Mocking his distress, the Yanks chanted: "Mickey's going crazy! Mickey's going crazy!" Eventually, Cochrane had a nervous breakdown and left to recover in Wyoming.

The Yankees, meanwhile, were unveiling red-hot Joe DiMaggio. Wearing number 9, he made his big-league debut on May 3 in Yankee Stadium. New York beat St. Louis, 14-5, as

DiMaggio rapped out two singles and a triple, scored three times and drove in a run. In his first at bat, he singled to left off Browns hurler Jack Knott. Four days later, DiMaggio threw out Detroit's Pete Fox at home plate in the ninth inning at Yankee Stadium to save a 6-5 New York win. (The rookie Yank led AL outfielders in 1936 with 22 assists, a rare feat for somebody who played most of his games in left.) Three days later, DiMaggio belted his first career homer, a 400-foot shot in Yankee Stadium off George Turbeville of Philadelphia. He drove in three runs and made a great catch in left field as New York beat the A's, 7-2.

After that game, on Sunday, May 10, Babe Ruth walked into the Yankee clubhouse, went up to DiMaggio, shook hands and said: "Hello, Joe." Some of the veteran Yanks thought they were hearing things. Later, Lefty Gomez explained: "Joe, the Babe has just paid you a terrific compliment. He's famous for never paying attention to anybody's name. For him, veterans are always, 'Hi, Doc,' and the rookies are, 'Hi, Kid.' You're the first guy in all these years I've ever heard him call by name."

In only his first week of play, DiMaggio already had displayed each one of the all-around skills that would carry him to the Hall of Fame. As if to celebrate, he stroked four hits—three doubles and a single—as the Yanks triumphed, 6-1 in St. Louis on May 14.

But everything didn't come easy for young Joe. This was a long time before his days as a sophisticated idol who could deal smoothly with hero-worshipping fans of all ages. In the beginning, he was callow. "I can remember a reporter asking for a quote," DiMaggio once said, "and I didn't know what a quote was. I thought it was some kind of soft drink." Explained *New York Times* columnist Arthur Daley: "His shyness was mistaken for sullenness by some and for swell-headedness by others. The DiMaggio of 1936 was silent and uncomfortable. He was monosyllabic and uncommunicative with writers. He was ill at ease with all strangers." On the baseball field, though, he was eloquent. And he knew from the start that he would make it. "If you think I was cocky, you're right," DiMaggio eventually admitted. "It was more than self-confidence. But I kept it within myself—inside the shell so to speak." When general manager Ed Barrow warned about the pitfalls of sudden success, young Joe said: "Don't worry about me, Mr. Barrow. I never get excited."

Through it all, DiMaggio, who earned $8,000 in his first year, showed genuine respect for Lou Gehrig, the older Yankee star. DiMaggio was grateful when the Iron Horse stuck up for him early in the season. It happened in Detroit: batting in the number three spot, DiMaggio let a high pitch go by. "Strike one!" shouted umpire George Moriarity, a stiff old-timer. The rookie hitter said nothing. Next came an eye-level pitch. "Strike two!" called Moriarity. DiMaggio glanced back. "Turn around," ordered the ump. From the on-deck circle, Gehrig told Moriarity: "Leave the kid alone, George. If you call 'em right, he won't have to turn around."

Hinting at things to come, DiMaggio got started in May (when New York went 20-8) on a 17-game batting streak. His teammates were hitting, too—especially Gehrig and Bill Dickey. Even Tony Lazzeri, the 32-year-old veteran of the great '27 club, was hot. On May 23, the Yanks swept a double-header in Philadelphia, 12-6 and 15-1, as Lazzeri hit three home runs—one in the first game and two in the second. Next day he ran wild. New York bombed the A's, 25-2, scoring the most runs in the franchise's history. "Poosh 'em up" Tony, who hit three home runs, became the first major leaguer ever to belt two grand slams in one game. And his two-run triple fell just inches short of going out. In all, Lazzeri drove in an American League record 11 runs. He had six homers in three games in just two days; and five HRs and 15 RBIs in back-to-back games. During the 1936 season, every other Yankee regular hit higher than Lazzeri's .287. He batted eighth in the lineup.

On top of the AL by just a few games in mid-June, New York surprised everybody by trading Ben Chapman to Washington for Jake Powell. The exchange of outfielders was seen as a poor deal for the Yanks. But McCarthy disliked Chapman's unruly temperament. The manager made the swap even though the less-talented Powell, who had broken Greenberg's arm without apology, was also fiery. As it turned out,

Powell hit .306 for New York in 87 games. But the key to the controversial deal was that it made room for Joe DiMaggio's eventual shift to center field. So, the trade actually stabilized the Yankee outfield.

New York's pitchers already looked solid—on the mound and at bat. In Cleveland, the Yanks on June 17 swept a double-header, 15-4 and 12-2, collecting 19 hits in each game. Red Ruffing, who started the opener, belted two homers and made four hits. His ten total bases were a record for an AL pitcher. (A career .269 batter, Ruffing sometimes pinch hit). In the nightcap, pitcher Monte Pearson contributed four hits and four RBIs to the Yankee attack.

On June 22, New York, playing in Chicago, led the American League by five games over the White Sox. The Yanks won three of their four games in the Windy City. The highlight was New York's 18-11 victory on June 24—DiMaggio became the third player in AL history to hit two home runs in one inning. He also had two doubles in the game. And Powell, the newcomer, hit a grand slam. At the end of the month, the Bombers had a record of 47-22 and a lead of 9½ games. Gehrig was hitting .400. And it was all over in the American League.

The only thing the New York Yankees didn't dominate in 1936 was the All-Star Game. The National League won, 4-3, on July 7 at Braves Field in Boston. The NL got its first victory in the four-year old series despite the presence of Gehrig (who hit a solo homer) along with Dickey, Selkirk, Crosetti and DiMaggio. Looking like a rookie, young Joe had a sloppy day in the outfield, mishandling a couple of balls. At bat, he went 0 for 5 and hit an infield pop to end the game with the potential tying run on second base. "Don't let it get you down, Joe," said McCarthy, the AL manager. "I won't," DiMaggio promised. "But I won't ever forget it, either."

That summer of '36 left much for everybody to remember—both on and off the baseball field. Civil war erupted in Spain. Italy defied worldwide pleas to pull its invasion force out of Ethiopia. And U.S. sprinter Jesse Owens upstaged Hitler's Germany at the Olympics in Berlin.

In the Bronx, August was happy. The runaway Yanks went 21-8, their best month of the season. They swept troubled Detroit, 14-5 and 19-4, on August 28 in a twin bill at Yankee Stadium. In the nightcap, another of New York's pitchers had a good time at the plate. In a rare start, Johnny Murphy hit five singles (two of them in the Yanks' 11-run second inning), collected five RBIs and scored three runs. (In his career, the reliever hit just .154.) But there was no longer any hope for the Tigers, anyway.

On September 3, front-running New York treated the AL's other rookie sensation of 1936—Cleveland strikeout phenom Bob Feller—to a rude welcome in Yankee Stadium. They knocked out the 17-year-old high schooler in the first inning when they scored five times off the Indians on the way to a 6-4 win. The Yanks clinched the pennant in Cleveland on September 9, the earliest date an American League champion was ever crowned. Playing a double-header, New York won 11-3 and 12-9. It was sweet revenge for ex-Indian Monte Pearson, who won the opener. On the day, Lou Gehrig collected his second grand slam in less than a month. Fourteen of his homers during the season were hit against Cleveland, another major-league record.

Next came the first Subway Series since 1923. The Yanks squared off against the New York Giants (92-62, .597), who had just won the National League pennant by five games over both Chicago and St. Louis. Not for 13 years had the Fall Classic been confined to New York alone. No longer were the Yankees underdogs in the battle against their Manhattan rivals. In 1936, the Yanks had scored 323 more runs than the Giants while collecting 85 more homers, 70 more doubles and 35 more triples.

Playing his final season, 37-year-old Giants manager Bill Terry hit .310. But because his knee constantly filled up with fluid, he got into just 79 games. Mel Ott, the NL home run champ (with 33) did much of the heavy hitting. And "King Carl" Hubbell was the best pitcher in baseball. The veteran lefty went 26-6 for the Giants, winning his last 16 decisions. He was on the mound, therefore, when the Series began on September 30 in the rain-swept, muddy Polo Grounds.

In game one, the Yanks saw why Hubbell's screwballs

had baffled the National League. He pitched the Giants to a 6-1 victory (over Red Ruffing). It was the first time in ten years that the Yankees—coming off sweeps in 1927, 1928 and 1932—had lost a World Series game. But the Bombers regained their form in game two. They pounded the Giants, 18-4. Ten World Series records were broken or tied in the game. Every batter in the Yankee lineup, including Lefty Gomez, got at least one hit and one run. Lazzeri hit the second grand slam in World Series history; and Dickey belted a three-run homer. On the mound, Goofy Gomez was so relaxed that he took a break in the middle of the game to watch a transport plane fly overhead. Everybody in the Polo Grounds was kept waiting, including President Roosevelt. Later on, Joe DiMaggio made a spectacular catch in deep center field. He robbed Hank Leiber of a 475-foot hit to end the game. As his departing limousine passed the clubhouse steps, FDR gave the Yankee rookie a big wave.

Shifting to Yankee Stadium, the Bombers won two out of the next three games. That included a 5-2 victory in game four over Hubbell, who lost for the first time since mid summer; Gehrig's two-run homer into the bleachers in right field was enough to win the contest. The Yanks returned to the Polo Grounds to wrap up the Fall Classic in game six. With another 17-hit assault, they defeated the Giants, 13-5. Thus began a dynasty that would carry Joe McCarthy's New York Yankees to four consecutive world championships.

Years later, McCarthy, thinking of 1936, pointed out: "I remember after that Series, somebody came up to me and said my club was so good it didn't look like anybody was going to beat us for a long time. I'll tell you, that fellow knew what he was talking about."

11

New York Yankees 1937

102-52

.662

YANKEES REPEAT AS WORLD CHAMPS, BEATING GIANTS AGAIN IN ANOTHER SUBWAY SERIES ♦ JOE DIMAGGIO (46, 167, .346) IS AL HOMER KING ♦ LOU GEHRIG (37, 159, .351) AND BILL DICKEY (29, 133, .332) STAR ♦ LEFTY GOMEZ, RED RUFFING WIN 20.

Rookie Tommy Henrich joined the world champion New York Yankees at the beginning of the season in 1937. They had paid $25,000 to the minor-league sensation when he was ruled a free agent by Commissioner Kenesaw Mountain Landis. But the 24-year-old outfielder got a rude welcome to New York.

"I'll never forget the bellboy who showed me to my hotel room," Henrich recalled years later. "He really gave me a hard time. 'So you're Henrich,' he said. 'The papers say you're going to break into the lineup right away. Hey, wait till you see DiMaggio and Hoag and Selkirk. You ever seen those guys play?'"

In fact, the '37 Yankees were loaded with talent. Center fielder Joe DiMaggio, 22, following his own remarkable debut as a rookie, batted third. He was backed up by first baseman Lou Gehrig, 34, the legendary clean-up hitter who was having his last great season. Next came Bill Dickey, 29, the best catcher in baseball. On the mound, New York relied on a pair of aces: Lefty Gomez and Red Ruffing.

No wonder the Yanks, building a dynasty for manager Joe McCarthy, easily remained on top in 1937. After taking first place for keeps before Memorial Day, New York pulled away to win the American League pennant by 13 games over Detroit. In the World Series, the Yankees defeated the National League champion New York Giants for the second year in a row.

What about Tommy Henrich? The newcomer played in 67 games during the season and hit .320 with eight home runs and 42 RBIs. He shared time in the outfield with Myril Hoag; George "Twinkletoes" Selkirk, who suffered a broken collar bone; and Jake Powell, who was plagued by illness. Henrich went on to earn the nickname "Old Reliable" and become a fixture in the Bronx until 1950. To begin with, though, he was free to sign with the Yanks only because Landis ruled that Cleveland was unfairly hiding him in the minors. Though offered more money by other clubs, Henrich wanted to play in New York. "I'd been a Yankee fan since I was eight years old," he said later. "I was a Babe Ruth man."

Going into 1937, the Yanks were coming off their first triumphant season ever without the Babe. And McCarthy's club made it two straight, winning the ninth Yankee pennant and sixth world championship. Leading the way was DiMaggio (46, 167, .346), who topped the AL in homers and slugging (.673) in his second season. Gehrig (37, 159, .351), who led the league in walks (127), and Bill Dickey (29, 133, .322), who set an RBI record for catchers, both had solid years. The pitching was topped by Lefty Gomez (21-11, 2.33) and Red Ruffing (20-7, 2.99), the only 20-game winners in the league. Gomez led the AL in wins, ERA and strikeouts (194). And then there was Johnny Murphy, who was tagged "Fireman" as baseball's first relief star. He went 13-4 and saved ten games out of the bullpen.

The Yankees were first in the American League in 1937 in runs (979), homers (174), RBIs (922), slugging (.456) and walks (709). Their pitchers led the AL in ERA (3.65) for the fourth year in a row. They also posted the most shutouts (15) and complete games (82). On defense, New York gave up fewer runs (671) than any of its rivals. In the outfield, DiMaggio was unrivaled. The Yankee infield—Red Rolfe at third, Frankie Crosetti at shortstop, Tony Lazzeri at second and Lou Gehrig at first—also featured smooth golves.

In spring training, Gehrig, the Iron Horse, said he was hoping to extend his playing streak to 2,500 consecutive games before retiring in a few years. His only remaining teammate from the great 1927 New York Yankees was Lazzeri. By now, Yankee Stadium looked much different, too. As the 1937 season began, the Stadium took on its modern appearance for the first time. The triple-decked grandstand was extended past the foul pole and into right field, matching similar renovations that had been made in 1928 in left.

Off the field, major developments during the 1937 season included the crash of the German dirigible Hindenburg in New Jersey; the disappearance of aviator Amelia Earhart in the Pacific; and the approval by the Supreme Court of key New Deal laws despite President Roosevelt's failure to expand the panel.

On Opening Day, Washington triumphed, 3-2, in Yankee Stadium. But Joe DiMaggio missed the opener for the second year in a row. He sat out the first six games after his tonsils were removed. On May 1, DiMaggio returned to the lineup with three hits off Rube Walberg of Boston. New York won, 3-2, as DiMaggio had a hand in all of the Yankee scoring. By May 23, the Yanks moved into first place to stay with a 7-3 victory over Cleveland at Yankee Stadium.

Detroit suffered a tragic blow at the Stadium just two days later. Catcher Mickey Cochrane, who also managed the Tigers, was accidentally struck in the head by a fastball thrown by Bump Hadley. The near-fatal beaning ended Cochrane's playing career. It also destroyed Detroit's chances of overtaking the Yankees, even though Black Mike returned to the dugout late in the season.

TOP: *Former Cleveland Indians (from left) Elmer Smith, Tris Speaker and Bill Wambsganss donned old uniforms during a get-together in 1936. They were stars of the 1920 world championship team.* LEFT: *Babe Ruth belts his record 60th home run on Sept. 30, 1927, in Yankee Stadium. His two-run homer in the eighth inning off Washington's Tom Zachary broke a tie and gave New York a 4-2 victory.*

Three top hitters for the 1929 Philadelphia Athletics were (from left) Jimmie Foxx, 21 years old, Mickey Cochrane, 26, and Al Simmons, 27. They are shown at Shibe Park on Sept. 3, 1929.

RIGHT: *National League batting champ Chick Hafey waits for the World Series to begin on Oct. 1, 1931. During the regular season, he hit .3489 for the St. Louis Cardinals, who became world champions.* BELOW: *Connie Mack (left), owner-manager of the Philadelphia Athletics, poses with his star pitcher, Lefty Grove, on Sept. 25, 1931. That year Grove was 31-4.*

TOP: *Photo reproduced from movie film taken by Matt M. Kandle of Chicago apparently shows Babe Ruth calling his World Series shot on Oct. 1, 1932, at Wrigley Field. In a journal, Kandle cited his presence at the game, and referred to his movie film of "Babe Ruth slamming out one of his famous home runs."*
RIGHT: *Babe Ruth is congratulated by New York teammate Lou Gehrig after crossing the plate following his "called shot" home run in game three off Chicago's Charlie Root.*

LEFT: *Veteran first baseman Lou Gehrig (left) and rookie centerfield Joe DiMaggio pose on Aug. 31, 1936, in front of the New York dugout at Yankee Stadium.*
BELOW: *Stars of the 1938 New York Yankees include (from left): shortstop Frankie Crosetti, third baseman Red Rolfe, right fielder Tommy Henrich, center fielder Joe DiMaggio, first baseman Lou Gehrig, catcher Bill Dickey, left fielder George Selkirk, outfielder Myril Hoag and second baseman Joe Gordon.*

REDS

FAR LEFT TOP: *Manager Bill McKechnie (center) of the Cincinnati Reds and his two ace pitchers, Paul Derringer (left) and Bucky Walters, celebrate winning the National League pennant at home on Sept. 28, 1939. They led Cincinnati to the world championship in 1940.* FAR LEFT BOTTOM: *Former New York star Babe Ruth (left), who had retired, and Lou Gehrig, recently sidelined by a fatal illness, await the start of game two of the World Series at Yankee Stadium on Oct. 5, 1939.* LEFT: *Center fielder Joe DiMaggio of New York poses in the visitor's locker room at League Park in Cleveland after hitting in his record 56th consecutive game on July 16, 1941.* BELOW: *DiMaggio homers in Philadelphia on June 27, 1941, during the 39th game of his batting streak.*

TOP: *Rival managers Billy Southworth of the Cardinals and Joe McCarthy of the New York Yankees get together before the first game of the World Series in St. Louis on Sept. 30, 1942.* ABOVE: *Rookie left fielder Stan Musial hit .315 with 10 homers and 72 RBIs for the world champion St. Louis Cardinals in 1942.*

Manager Casey Stengel of the New York Yankees offers advice to rookie Mickey Mantle before an exhibition game at Ebbetts Field in Brooklyn on April 14, 1951. In his debut in New York that day, Mantle homered.

ABOVE: *Shortstop Phil Rizzuto of the New York Yankees leaps over Al Dark of the New York Giants at Yankee Stadium in game six of the 1951 World Series.* TOP RIGHT: *Dodger fans and players celebrate in Yankee Stadium after Brooklyn's 2-0 victory in game seven of the 1955 World Series.* BOTTOM RIGHT: *Whitey Ford of New York pitches in Yankee Stadium during the opening game of the 1961 World Series.*

77

LEFT: *Roger Maris of the New York Yankees hits his record 61st home run on Oct. 1, 1961. The fourth-inning homer off Boston's Tracy Stallard—with a count of two balls and no strikes—was the only run in a 1-0 New York victory at Yankee Stadium.* ABOVE: *Maris strikes out against Stallard in the sixth inning of the same game on a three and two pitch with one out. However, superimposed arrow shows the trajectory of homer No. 61. The ball landed about 10 rows deep in the right field stands. It was retrieved by 19-year-old Sal Durante. The official attendance that Sunday afternoon was 23,154.*

FAR LEFT TOP: *Third baseman Brooks Robinson of the Baltimore Orioles makes one of the diving plays that earned him the MVP award in the 1970 World Series. He catches a line drive by Johnny Bench of Cincinnati in the ninth inning of game five in Baltimore.* FAR LEFT BOTTOM: *Third baseman Pete Rose of the Cincinnati Reds fields a ball in the first inning of the second game of the 1975 National League playoffs.* LEFT: *Pitcher Willie Hernandez celebrates with Dave Bergman (back) and Lance Parrish (front) after the Detroit Tigers won the 1984 World Series.* TOP: *Detroit's Sparky Anderson in 1984 became the first manager ever to win 100 games in one season in both the American and National Leagues, and the first ever two win world championships in both major leagues.*

Led by catcher Gary Carter (arms raised), members of the 1986 New York Mets celebrate their 8-5 win against the Boston Red Sox at Shea Stadium in the seventh game of the World Series. It was their 116th victory of the season

CREDITS: *All photographs courtesy of AP/Wide World Photos (unless otherwise identified).*

By the All-Star break, New York had built its record to 44-22. The 8-3 AL triumph in Washington was a Yankee show. Gomez, the starter, earned his third All-Star victory while DiMaggio, Gehrig, Dickey and Rolfe played the entire game. Gehrig homered off Dizzy Dean and drove in four runs in the game.

In July, DiMaggio's hitting was spectacular. He belted the first two grand slam homers of his career during the month. And his 15 home runs were the most ever hit during July. DiMag led the Yanks to a 20-8 record during the month. On July 9, he hit for the cycle, collecting a single, double, triple and two homers as New York pounded the Senators, 16-2. On July 18, DiMaggio accounted for all the Yankee scoring in Cleveland with a double, triple and homer. His grand slam with two outs in the ninth inning clinched a 5-1 victory. On August 1, DiMaggio hit No. 31, his third homer in two days, to go one game ahead of Babe Ruth's record pace of 1927. Gehrig, the Babe's old teammate, hit for the cycle that day as New York beat the Browns, 14-5. Two days later the Iron Horse played in his 1,900th consecutive game. It happened on Lou Gehrig Appreciation Day at Yankee Stadium. In the first game of a doubleheader, Gehrig and DiMaggio each hit three-run homers as the Yanks beat Chicago, 7-2. In the nightcap, Dickey's grand slam keyed a 5-3 Yankee win. The next day, Dickey hit another grand slam as New York beat the White Sox, 13-8.

After going 21-8 in August, the Yanks closed out the regular season with a 20-14 record in September. They won a memorable twin bill on September 8 in Yankee Stadium against Boston. Hoag's run-scoring single in the bottom of the ninth won the opener, 3-2. In the second game, New York trailed 6-1 with two outs in the ninth. But Gehrig capped a big rally with a three-run homer to give the Yanks a 9-6 win. They clinched the American League pennant on September 23.

In the World Series, the Yankee firepower prevailed against the Giants (95-57, .625), the NL pennant winner. The Yankees defeated the Giants, 8-1, 8-1 and 5-1 in the first three games. After losing 7-3 to Carl Hubbell in game four, the Yanks ended the Series with a 4-2 victory. Lefty Gomez earned two Series wins against a pair of 20-game winners. He beat Hubbell in the opener and Cliff "Mountain Music" Melton in the finale. Meanwhile, Joe DiMaggio hit his first World Series homer, and Lou Gehrig his last. And 33-year-old Tony Lazzeri, just days away from being released, hit .400 in the Series to lead both teams.

Yankee manager Joe McCarthy knew the future was bright. There was more young talent about to join DiMaggio and Tommy Henrich. The 1937 Newark Bears, the Yanks' top farm team, were pehaps the greatest minor-leauge club in baseball history. They won the International League title by 25 games behind several players who were soon to be promoted. Among them were Joe Gordon, Charlie Keller, Babe Dahlgren, Atley Donald and Spud Chandler. A lot of people believed Newark could finish in the first division in the American League.

For assembling such talent, Ed Barrow, the long-time general manager of the Yankees, was named the 1937 Executive of the Year by The Sporting News.

And the New York Yankees, putting together their first dynasty, were half way to an unprecedented four straight world championships.

12

Philadelphia Athletics

1930

102-52

.662

CONNIE MACK'S LAST WORLD CHAMPIONS ♦ LEFTY GROVE (28-5) AND GEORGE EARNSHAW (22-13) TOP PITCHERS ♦ AL SIMMONS (36, 165, .381) IS BAT KING ♦ JIMMIE FOXX (37, 156, .335) STARS ♦ A'S REPEAT IN WORLD SERIES (VS. CARDS).

"To be considered great," said Connie Mack, "a team must repeat."

Coming off his first world championship in 16 years, Mack expected the Philadelphia Athletics to do it again in 1930. The 67-year-old manager was finally on the verge of a second A's dynasty in the American League.

"I knew I had another good club and would have been disappointed if we hadn't won again," said Mack, whose Hall of Fame career as an owner and manager in Philadelphia lasted from 1901 until 1950.

Despite stiffer AL competition, the '30 Athletics wound up on top once more. They finished eight games ahead of much-improved Washington. The previous runner-up, New York, fell to third place, 16 lengths behind.

In the 1930 World Series, Philadelphia beat St. Louis, four games to two.

It was a year in which hitting prevailed in baseball. Worried about the Depression, the owners in both leagues juiced up the ball in order to sell tickets. Thus, for example, the earned run average in the AL climbed to 4.65.

Not that it bothered Lefty Grove, the hard-throwing A's ace. He led the league with an ERA of 2.54 (no other AL pitcher finished below 3.00). Grove, who went 28-5, also was tops in wins, strikeouts (209) and games pitched (50). Next in appearances on the mound (49) was Philadelphia's big righthander, George Earnshaw. He went 22-13 and struck out 193 batters. Talking about his club's success, Mack once said: "I just remember two names, Lefty Grove and George Earnshaw, and pitch them every four days." Backing up those two in 1930 were Rube Walberg (13-12), Bill Shores (12-4), Eddie Rommel (9-4) and Roy Mahaffey (9-5). Even 46-year-old Jack Quinn (9-7) contributed.

The '30 Athletics also featured the American League batting champ, Al Simmons. The left fielder hit .381 with 36 homers and 165 RBIs, and he led the league in runs (152). The other two big hitters in the A's lineup were first baseman Jimmie Foxx (37, 156, .335) and catcher Mickey Cochrane (10, 85, .357). Mack relied further on right fielder Bing Miller (9, 100, .303), third baseman Jimmy Dykes (6, 73, .301) and center fielder Mule Haas (2, 68, .299).

Summing up the 1930 A's, sportswriter Ford Frick, who years later served as commissioner of baseball, declared: "They can hit, they can field, they can run bases with at least average ability—and in the pitching box they are supreme. Nowhere in either league is there a pitching staff that can match Connie Mack's collection."

Even so, the Athletics got off to a slow start in April. They rebounded in May, but moved in and out of first place a couple of times before capturing the lead for good in mid-July. In particular, Philadelphia had trouble against manager Walter Johnson's Senators, who were sparked all season long by shortstop Joe Cronin. Walberg shut out Washington, 9-0, on April 19 in Philadelphia in the first game of the year between the two clubs. But the Senators beat the A's in their next seven meetings. "What's the matter with you fellows whenever you play Washington?" scolded Mack. "You look like a bunch of old women."

Going into their two contests on Memorial Day, the first-place Senators led the A's by 4½ games. Two Nat hurlers, Ad Liska and Bump Hadley, were sent to Philadelphia 48 hours ahead of time to rest before their morning and afternoon starts on May 30. But the A's won both games, anyway.

In the first game, Washington led 6-3 with two outs in the bottom of the ninth inning. Facing Liska, Simmons belted a three-run homer into the left field seats in Shibe Park to tie the contest. In the 13th, Simmons doubled, went to third on Foxx's infield hit and limped home when Boob McNair singled to win the game, 7-6. Big Al had popped a blood vessel going into third base.

In game two, Simmons, briefly confined to the bench, was asked to pinch hit with the bases loaded in the fourth inning. At the time, Washington led, 7-4. "See whether you can walk around the bases," Mack suggested. Simmons did. He belted a grand slam to give the A's the lead and they eventually won the wild game, 15-11. Simmons called it the most memorable day of his career.

Thereafter, Philadelphia, in the midst of winning seven consecutive times against the Senators, gained the edge. The A's went 21-9 in May. On June 4, they completed a 10-game win streak, their longest of the season. Within a month, Washington responded with a 10-game winning streak of its own. But Philadelphia pushed the Senators out of first once and for all on July 13.

For the A's, July was the best month of the season. They went 23-9 with the help of an eight-game winning streak. Grove lost, 7-4, in Washington on July 30 as President Hoover and his wife watched. And the Senators defeated Earnshaw, 4-3, the following day. But it was Philadelphia's year.

By the end of August, the Athletics had a record of 88-44. And Connie Mack set an American League record when he clinched his eighth pennant on September 18. That happened when the A's beat the White Sox, 14-10, in Chicago. The Chisox pounded Earnshaw for five runs in the first inning of the game. But the Macks scored five runs in the fourth and seventh innings, collected a total of 20 hits and held on to win. The hit parade included a home run and three singles by Simmons, who ripped AL hurlers throughout the season.

"I was a fighting, snarling player on the field," he later said. "I am proud, not ashamed of that reputation. I played to win. So did Dykes, Cochrane, Grove, Earnshaw, Mule [Haas], Foxx, and the rest of that crowd. We were champions, and we battled. . . . Connie held a bridle on us if anybody got too tough. But he wanted us to fight. There was a spirit in those later-day Mack champions that I've never seen on any other club of which I was a member."

That fighting spirit helped Philadelphia in 1930 to come back and win in the late innings of many games. The A's went 13-4 in contests decided in the seventh inning; 7-7 in those decided in the eighth, and 13-5 in those decided in the ninth. And they were 6-1 in extra-inning battles.

In the six-game World Series, Philadelphia demonstrated its tenacity against the National League champion St. Louis Cardinals (92-62, .597). The Redbirds, whose eight regular players had batted over .300, were led by Frankie Frisch and Chick Hafey. But Grove and Earnshaw, respectively, won the first two games (5-2 and 6-1) and the last two (2-0 and 7-1).

Game five in St. Louis was the key victory. The Cardinal starter was Burleigh Grimes, who still threw legal spit balls. As Jimmie Foxx recalled: "Mr. Mack took me to one side of the dugout before the game started. 'Jimmie,' he said, 'you watch out for that pitcher out there. He figures he has your number and I think he'll try to get you if he gets in a pinch. And watch for that curveball. Don't let him fool you with that spitter motion. Just because he goes through like he's going to throw it is no sign he will.'"

Grimes and Earnshaw battled 0-0 through seven innings; and Grove relieved in the eighth. In the ninth, Grimes faced Foxx with Cochrane on first base. Just as Mack predicted, the

Cards hurler faked a spitter and threw a curve. Double XX belted the pitch into the left-field bleachers for the only runs of the game. "He hit it so hard I couldn't feel sorry for myself," said Grimes.

Back in Philadelphia, Earnshaw, pitching on only one day of rest, tossed a five-hitter to give the Mackmen their second world championship in a row.

Before the Fall Classic, Ford Frick, the journalist, had written that the A's were "perhaps the most colorless outfit ever to engage in a World Series battle. Their leader, the ancient and venerable Connie Mack, lovable in character and interesting in conversation, is none the less a man who shuns the spotlight and avoids the spectacular."

With dignity, the Tall Tactician won it all in 1930—for the last time.

13

New York Yankees 1941

101-53

.656

JOE DIMAGGIO (30, 125, .357), THE AL MVP, HITS IN RECORD 56 STRAIGHT GAMES ♦ CHARLIE KELLER HITS 33 HRS; TOMMY HENRICH 31 ♦ LEFTY GOMEZ (15-5), RED RUFFING (15-6) STAR ♦ YANKS WIN FIRST WORLD SERIES VS. BROOKLYN.

Who started baseball's famous streak /
That's got us all aglow /
He's just a man and not a freak /
Jolting Joe DiMaggio.

1941 belonged to 26-year-old Joe DiMaggio. He hit safely in 56 consecutive games, setting perhaps the most glamorous record of them all. That summer the hottest question in America was: "Did Joe get a hit today?" And his batting was heralded throughout the country in a popular Big Band tune.

It was Joe DiMaggio's peerless hitting that led the New York Yankees to their fifth world championship in six years. The '41 Yanks seized first place during his mid-season streak and went on to clinch the American League pennant on September 4, the earliest finish in big-league history.

For the first time, the World Series matched the Yankees against the National League champion Brooklyn Dodgers. The result: manager Joe McCarthy's Bronx Bombers triumphed, four games to one.

All in all, The Streak by DiMaggio was the top event of the season. It earned the Yankee Clipper his second AL MVP award even though Boston's Ted Williams hit .406, a level unapproached ever since. In 1941, DiMaggio hit .357 with 30 homers and a league-leading 125 runs batted in.

Jolting Joe hit safely in 56 games in a row from May 15 until July 16. He also began a 16-game batting streak on July 18 and thus hit safely in 72 of 73 games. And he reached base for 84 consecutive games.

What does Ted Williams think of DiMaggio's accomplishments? Williams, known as the all-time number one expert on hitting, has said: "I believe there isn't a record in the books that will be harder to break than Joe's 56 games. It may be the greatest batting achievement of all."

DiMaggio's hitting in 1941 overshadowed the performance of his entire team. For instance, the Yankees put together a streak of their own in June: they homered in 25 consecutive games. In fact, the Yanks topped the American League with 151 home runs. New York's starting outfielders—possibly the best trio on offense and defense in baseball history—combined to hit 94 homers. Left fielder Charlie "King Kong" Keller (33, 122, .298) and right fielder Tommy "Old Reliable" Henrich (31, 85, .277) had big seasons. It was the first time three big-league teammates each hit at least 30 homers. And they each scored more than 100 runs during the season.

Besides DiMaggio, rookie shortstop Phil Rizzuto (3, 46, .307) was the only other Yankee regular player to hit .300. But second baseman Joe Gordon (24, 87, .276) and catcher Bill Dickey (7, 71, .284) were key contributors. And the combination of Rizzuto and Gordon helped New York to lead the league with 196 double plays. Dickey led AL catchers in fielding. For the 13th consecutive season, he caught at least 100 games.

Their defense and pitching enabled the Yanks to hold opponents to the fewest runs (631) scored against any team in the league. New York's mound staff had an ERA of 3.53, just .001 behind Chicago, the top club. For the Yankees, 31-year-old Lefty Gomez (15-5, 3.75) and 37-year-old Red Ruffing (15-6, 3.53) combined solidly for the last time. Gomez had the top AL winning percentage (.750) and Ruffing tied for the second best (.714). Marius Russo (14-10, 3.09) led Yankee starters in ERA; and Spud Chandler (10-4, .3.18) won effectively. Out of the bullpen, "Fireman" Johnny Murphy (8-3, 1.99) had 15 saves.

Despite such talent, New York in 1941 was coming off a third-place finish that snapped McCarthy's dynasty of four consecutive world championships. Early on, the situation was bleak. The Yankees, with a record of 14-14, were in fourth place, 5½ games behind Cleveland, when DiMaggio began his batting streak. It started in Yankee Stadium on May 15 when DiMag singled in the first inning off Chicago's Edgar Smith. But the White Sox triumphed, 13-1, handing New York its eighth loss in ten games. "Yank Attack Weakest in Years," shouted the headline in the New York *Journal-American*.

DiMaggio's hitting during the next nine weeks propelled the Yanks to the top. In those 56 games, he batted .408 with 91 hits in 223 at-bats. He belted 15 homers, drove in 55 runs, scored 56 times and collected 160 total bases. DiMaggio hit 56 singles, 16 doubles and four triples. He drew 41 walks and was hit twice by a pitch. He struck out seven times. He never bunted.

Among the highlights of baseball's most celebrated streak:

June 16 (in New York)—Going one for four, DiMaggio ties the Yankee mark of hitting safely in 29 consecutive games. The previous record holders, Roger Peckinpaugh and Earle Combs, look on. The Yanks win their eighth straight game, beating Cleveland, 6-4.

June 17 (New York)—Jolting Joe, getting one of the few

lucky breaks during his batting streak, lifts the club record to 30 straight games. His bad-hop bouncer off Chicago shortstop Luke Appling's shoulder is ruled a hit by the official scorer. But the Yanks lose, 8-7, and fall to third place.

June 28 (Philadelphia)—DiMaggio hits in his 40th straight game despite Yankee killer Johnny Babich's vow to stop him. Forced to chase bad pitches, the Clipper socks one back through the legs of the A's hurler. "That was one of the most satisfying hits I ever got," DiMaggio once admitted, "because Babich had great control and he wasn't even going to give me a chance to hit." New York wins, 7-4, and moves into first place.

July 2 (New York)—Setting a new big-league record, DiMag hits safely in his 45th straight game to beat Wee Willie Keeler's old batting mark. The Jolter's three-run homer off Boston's Dick Newsome sparks an 8-4 Yankee triumph. About that day, DiMaggio recalled: "My teammates never mentioned the streak. They'd never say, 'Come on, Joe, get that base hit,' or anything like that. You knew all the time they were pulling for me, though. Finally, in the game I did break the record, the whole bunch ran out to congratulate me. That was a real thrill—the fact that the players themselves were excited about it."

July 6 (New York)—DiMaggio hits safely in games 47 and 48 as the Yanks sweep Philadelphia, 8-4 and 3-1, in a doubleheader. The wins mean that New York reaches the All-Star break with a record of 48-26 and a 3½ game lead over second-place Cleveland. But that day at Yankee Stadium was also somber. A monument was dedicated in center field to Lou Gehrig, who died June 2 after a two-year battle with amyotrophic lateral sclerosis.

July 16 (Cleveland)—The Streak reaches 56 games when DiMag singles off Indian hurler Al Milnar as the Bombers win, 10-3.

July 17 (Cleveland)—Before 67,468 fans at Municipal Stadium, Joe DiMaggio goes hitless in a game for the first time since mid-spring. Indian third baseman Ken Keltner robs him of two sure doubles against starter Al Smith. In his last at bat, the Yankee Clipper, facing reliever Jim Bagby, hits into a double play. That takes the edge off of a 4-3 Yankee win. "I wanted to keep on going," said DiMaggio. "I wanted it to go on forever."

During the Jolter's 56-game streak, New York pulled away from its foes with a record of 55-16, for a winning percentage of .775. The Yanks finished July, their best month of the season, with a 25-4 mark. In August, they went 21-14. On September 4, New York clinched the pennant with a 6-3 victory against the Red Sox in Fenway Park. The Yankees ended the season 17 games ahead of Boston.

In the first two games of the World Series, the Yanks and manager Leo Durocher's Dodgers exchanged 3-2 victories. Then the Yankees earned the world title by winning three straight games—2-1, 7-4 and 3-1. Game 4 was the killer. The Dodgers led 4-3 at Ebbets Field with two outs in the top of the ninth and two strikes on Tommy Henrich. On the next pitch from Hugh Casey, Henrich swung and missed. But the curve ball got by catcher Mickey Owen and Henrich reached first base. Then successive hits by DiMaggio, Keller, Dickey and Gordon won the game. Looking back, DiMaggio noted: "Well, they say everything happens in Brooklyn."

Not exactly. It was an unforgettable year because of goings-on in the American League. And the young Yankee Clipper was triumphant.

"He'll live in baseball's Hall of Fame /
He got there blow by blow /
Our kids will tell their kids his name /
Joe, Joe DiMaggio . . ."

14

St. Louis Cardinals 1931

101-53

.656

NL MVP FRANKIE FRISCH (4, 82, .311) LEADS CARDS ♦ CHICK HAFEY (16, 95, .3489) IS BATTING CHAMP ♦ WILD BILL HALLAHAN IS 19-9; PAUL DERRINGER, 18-8 ♦ PEPPER MARTIN BEATS A'S IN WORLD SERIES.

Frankie Frisch, the "Fordham Flash." Chick Hafey. Wild Bill Hallahan. Pepper Martin, the "Wild Hoss of the Osage." Sunny Jim Bottomley. Burleigh Grimes. 'Oom Paul Derringer. And manager Gabby Street, the Old Sarge.

There was no shortage of distinctive characters on the St. Louis Cardinals in 1931. Yet Street's odd collection of heroes—a bunch of whom stuck around and played for Frisch's rowdy Gas House Gang in 1934—fit together smoothly.

The '31 Cardinals, relying on speed, defense and teamwork, easily repeated as National League champs. Without power hitters, the Cards became the first NL team of the home-run era to win at least 100 games. They finished 13 games ahead of New York and 17 ahead of Chicago.

In the World Series, the Redbirds took revenge on Connie

Mack's dynasty and defeated perhaps the best Philadelphia Athletics team ever.

Following the 1931 season, the *Spalding Official Base Ball Guide* praised St. Louis, reporting: "There was no preeminent player on the team. It was splendidly matched—infield, outfield, pitchers and catchers. . . . Toward the latter part of the year, and in the World Series, it was called an old-fashioned ball team of nine players and not a team of one player and trimmings, and no greater compliment could have been paid to it."

Even so, some Cardinals flew higher than others.

Thirty-two-year-old second baseman Frankie Frisch (4, 82, .311) won the first National League MVP Award for his heads-up play in 1931. And center fielder Pepper Martin (7, 75, .300), completing his first full season at age 27, ran crazy in the World Series. He stole America's heart in the midst of the Depression.

St. Louis left fielder Chick Hafey (16, 95, .3489) was the top hitter in the National League. And he was the first batting champion to wear glasses. To win the batting title, Hafey, 28, edged New York Giants star Bill Terry (.3486) and Cardinal first baseman Sunny Jim Bottomley (9, 75, .3482). It was the closest three-man race for the hitting crown in NL history.

"For Hafey, wearing glasses to lead in a department where keen vision is most essential is nothing short of remarkable," claimed the *Reach Official Base Ball Guide*. It added: "Perhaps Hafey's achievement will remove the prejudice against players wearing glasses in the future."

But the '31 Cards were known more for their daring on the basepaths than for their batting eyes. Frisch led the NL with 28 stolen bases. Tied at number three with 16 steals each were Martin and third baseman Sparky Adams (1, 40, .293) of St. Louis. Next came Cardinal right fielder George Watkins (13, 51, .288) with 15 steals. In all, the Redbirds collected 114 stolen bases, one of the few offensive categories in which they were able to lead the league.

On defense, St. Louis was tops in fielding (.974). And Cardinal pitchers led the NL in strikeouts (626) and saves (20);

and they tied for number one in shutouts (17). The Cardinal pitching staff had the second-best ERA (3.45) in the league in 1931, a year in which the rabbit ball was outlawed and batting figures dropped closer to normal.

The best St. Louis pitcher was Wild Bill Hallahan (19-9, 3.29), who topped the National League in wins and strikeouts (159). The 29-year-old ace was the only left-hander on the Card staff. Paul Derringer (18-8, 3.35), a 24-year-old rookie, had the league's best winning percentage (.692). Next came two mound veterans: Burleigh Grimes (17-9, 3.65) and Jesse Haines (12-3, 3.02). Both 37 years old, Grimes and Haines were each future Hall of Famers—along with Frisch, Hafey and Bottomley.

"I've seen a lot of great ballclubs in my day," Gabby Street once said, "but for pitching, spirit and all-around balance, I would back my 1931 Cardinal team against any of them."

Street, an ex-catcher whose major-league career dated back to 1904, deserved plenty of credit for his team's success. It was reported by the *Spalding Guide*, for example, that the '31 Cardinals were duly impressed by their manager's "quiet insistence" day after day that they could go all the way.

On the field, leadership of another sort prevailed. Frisch's dynamic ability and brash spirit inspired his teammates. He was recognized as the greatest switch-hitter the game had ever known. And the 12-year National League veteran also was considered one of the best "money" players.

St. Louis had won the world championship in 1926, for manager Rogers Hornsby. It also had won NL pennants in 1928, for Bill McKechnie (and Billy Southworth); and 1930, for Street. In each of those years, the Cards won the flag by only two games.

1931 was a different story. They broke fast, climbed on top right away, spent 154 days in first place and won the season's series with every rival. Other than the Cards, the Giants spent two days alone in first place early in the season and the Boston Braves held first for just one day.

The Redbirds went 8-3 in April. On April 28, they began

an eight-game winning streak, their longest of the season. It got underway in Sportsman's Park in St. Louis when Grimes earned an 8-2 win against the visiting Pirates. In May, the Cardinals had a record of 21-8.

On Memorial Day, St. Louis seized first place for good. They did so by winning two May 30th games at home against the Cincinnati Reds. The Cards triumphed, 12-4, with Haines on the mound in game one. Then they won, 5-4, behind Hallahan, Allyn Stout and Jim Lindsey. In fact, Lindsey (6-4, 2.76; with 7 saves) went on to provide great relief pitching all season long.

On July 15, general manager Branch Rickey made room for one of his best prospects. In an exchange of outfielders, he sent Taylor Douthit to the Reds for Wally Roettger. That cleared the way for little-used Pepper Martin to become the regular center fielder. Martin had been a utility player and a pinch hitter. Finally, though, he confronted Rickey. "I'm tired of riding that bench," vowed Martin. "I want to get into the game—or I want you to trade me to some club that will play me." Fortunately, Rickey kept Martin.

In the middle of a one-sided pennant race, St. Louis drew a record number of fans to a game at Sportsman's Park: On Sunday, July 12, they saw a doubleheader with the Chicago Cubs. Attendance was put at 45,715, about 13,000 more than the park seated. The overflow crowd swarmed onto the field, stood along the foul lines and ringed the outfield walls. That forced the outfielders on both teams to move in and play shallow. It was ruled that pop flies into the crowd would be ground-rule doubles. There were nine doubles in the first game, which Chicago won, 7-5. The Cards won, 17-13, in game two. That contest produced 33 hits, including 23 doubles—a major-league record.

St. Louis went 21-13 in July; then 21-8 in August. The Cardinals clinched the pennant on September 16, when Hallahan defeated the Phillies, 6-3, in St. Louis.

Connie Mack's Athletics (107-45, .704) were favored in the 1931 World Series. But the Cardinals won, four games to three, as the Wild Hoss of the Osage galloped to fame.

Pepper Martin hit .500 on 12 hits in 24 at bats. He belted one homer, drove in five runs and scored five times. Martin also stole five bases against Mickey Cochrane, the great A's catcher.

The Cards won despite the efforts of Philadelphia hurlers Lefty Grove, who had gone 31-4 to win the American League MVP title, and George Earnshaw, who was 21-7. In game seven, the Cards won, 4-2, as Martin snared Max Bishop's low liner to center in the ninth inning with two outs and two runners on base.

That ended Connie Mack's second dynasty.

After the World Series, Martin began a vaudeville tour to capitalize on his glory. But he called it off before long. Said Pepper: "I ain't an actor. I'm cheating the public and the guy who's paying me the $1,500 a week. Besides, the hunting season's on in Oklahoma."

15

New York Yankees 1928

101-53

.656

BABE RUTH (54, 142, .323) LEADS AL IN HRS ♦ LOU GEHRIG (27, 142, .374) TIES HIM FOR RBI CROWN ♦ INJURY-PLAGUED YANKS LEAD IN RUNS, HRS AND BATTING ♦ GEORGE PIPGRAS WINS 24; WAITE HOYT, 23 ♦ N.Y. SWEEPS CARDS IN SERIES.

Baseball's "greatest team ever" returned essentially the same lineup to Murderer's Row in 1928. But the New York Yankees, paced by Babe Ruth's 54 home runs, had to rally in the stretch to finish on top again. The Yanks were forced to overcome a string of injuries in order to repeat as world champions.

The '28 Yankees, who broke fast and led the American League on the Fourth of July by a record 12 games, ultimately limped to victory. To win the AL pennant, New York fended off Connie Mack's Philadelphia Athletics, a budding dynasty, by just 2½ games. However, the Yanks won 16 of their 22 contests with the A's during the season. And there was no other challenger—the St. Louis Browns finished third, 19 games behind the Yankees.

Ignoring aches and pains, the Bronx Bombers swept the National League champion St. Louis Cardinals in the 1928 World Series. The Babe and Lou Gehrig dominated in that Series as no two hitters have in any other. Thus, New York became the first club to sweep back to back Fall Classics.

For Babe Ruth, it was a good year. The Sultan of Swat reigned from start to finish in 1928. Though bothered by minor injuries, Ruth easily won his eighth HR title. The AL runner-up, Gehrig, had 27 homers, half as many as the Babe. It was Ruth's hitting in the first months of the season that sparked the Yanks to a remarkable 53-17 record by Independence Day. He belted No. 42 on August 1 to move 27 games ahead of his record 1927 pace. Finally, the Babe wound up just six homers below his previous mark. He also finished first in the AL in slugging (.709), runs (163) and walks (136). And Ruth, who hit .323, and Gehrig, who hit .374, tied for the league lead in RBIs with 142 each.

Like the Bambino, the other two starters in New York's outfield, Bob Meusel (11, 113, .297) and Earle Combs (7, 56, .310), were solid contributors. Yet all three were off a bit from the previous year. So were the infield regulars, including Gehrig at first base. Second baseman Tony Lazzeri (10, 82, .332), shortstop Mark Koenig (4, 63, .319) and third baseman Joe Dugan (6, 34, .276) fought various ailments in 1928. Newcomers Leo Durocher (0, 31, .270) and Gene Robertson (1, 36, .291) filled in often at second, short or third.

The Bronx attack still led the American League in runs (894), homers (133), walks (894), RBIs (817), slugging (.450) and batting (.296). But the defense wasn't as good as it was in 1927. This time New York finished sixth in fielding (.968). And the pitchers dropped to second in ERA (3.74).

Three right-handed Yankee starters did fine work in 1928. George Pipgras (24-13, 3.38) led the AL in starts (38) and innings pitched (301); and he tied Lefty Grove of the A's for the most wins. Waite Hoyt (23-7, 3.36) was number two in the league in wins and winning percentage (.767). And 22-year-old Hank Johnson (14-9, 4.30) beat the Athletics five times. But the Yanks nearly lost the pennant when left-hander Herb Pennock (17-6, 2.56) was sidelined by an arm injury with several weeks to go. Pennock, 34, had a strong first half on the way to his last great season. In 1928, reliever Wilcy Moore (4-4, 4.20; with two saves) fizzled. Worst of all was the plight of Urban Shocker. He had gone 18-6 in 1927 while secretly fighting a heart ailment. In 1928, Shocker pitched only two innings early in the season. He died on September 9 at the age of 37.

Little seemed difficult in the Bronx in April. Now the former boys of '27 wanted to be paid like the greatest players ever. And so they were, for the most part. Babe Ruth, king of the Roaring '20s, got a raise to $80,000 a year. And Yankee manager Miller Huggins, who had become wealthy through investments, offered a Wall Street tip to his affluent players. "If you're in the market, get out," Huggins warned. "It can't last." Most of them did.

On the field, the Yanks also thrived. They opened the '28 season in Philadelphia by knocking out Lefty Grove in the third inning and winning 8-3 behind Pennock's seven-hitter. The opener in Yankee Stadium unveiled the extension of the triple-decked stands beyond the foul line in left field. But Philadelphia spoiled the day with a 2-1 victory.

New York pulled away from the A's by going 10-3 in April, 24-5 in May and 16-8 in June. One of the highlights was a 15-7 victory on June 12 in Chicago. In the game, Gehrig hit two homers and two triples, drove in six runs, scored five times and collected 14 bases. Ruth also homered and scored four runs. Little more than two weeks later the Yanks led the A's by 13½ games.

But injuries caught up to the New Yorkers in the second half. They slumped to 20-15 in July and 14-11 in August. During 1928, Dugan was increasingly hobbled by a trick knee and missed 60 games; Lazzeri's right shoulder limited his batting and throwing; Koenig was also often hurting; Meusel sat out for a while with a bum ankle; Combs had various woes, including a broken finger; and Ruth was slowed by a bad ankle and a severe charley horse.

One of the low points was July 29. In Cleveland, the

Yankees lost 24-6, their worst beating ever. The Indians collected 27 hits off New York pitching. Even worse, Philadelphia was catching up fast. The A's went 25-8 in July.

When Pennock injured his arm in late August, New York purchased Washington's Tom Zachary, who had given up Ruth's 60th homer in 1927. Zachary went 3-3 in the final weeks as the Yanks battled the rising Athletics.

On September 1, the Yankees triumphed, 8-3, in Washington. Before the game, Ruth stirred up a bit of a controversy by declining to pose for a campaign photograph with Republican presidential candidate Herbert Hoover. "Nothing doing," said the Babe. "I'm for Al Smith."

The Athletics caught up to New York on September 7 by sweeping a doubleheader against Boston while the Yanks dropped two in the Stadium vs. Washington. Next day, the Mackmen beat the Red Sox twice more while the Yanks defeated the Senators. That left the A's in first place by half a game.

On September 9, more than 85,000 fans turned out for a do-or-die twin bill at Yankee Stadium between New York and Philadelphia. Pipgras blanked the Macks, 3-0, in the first game. And the Yanks won, 7-3, behind Hoyt in the second. A homer by Meusel supplied the key runs. After a day off, the Yankees beat Philadelphia, 5-3, on September 9 as Hank Johnson outpitched Lefty Grove. With the score tied 3-3 in the bottom of the eighth, Ruth blasted a two-run homer to give New York the three-game sweep. The A's left town 2½ games behind, which is where they eventually wound up. The Yanks clinched the AL flag on September 28.

In the World Series, New York defeated the Cardinals, 4-1, 9-3, 7-3 and 7-3. It was the Cards who had beaten the Yanks in the 1926 Series. Because of their injuries, the Yankees were slight underdogs in the '28 Fall Classic. But Doc Woods, their trainer, patched up all the regulars except Combs.

The Yanks only needed two batters, anyway.

In the Series, Ruth hit .625, the highest batting average in World Series history, and Gehrig hit .545. In all, the Babe belted three homers, drove in four runs and scored nine times.

Gehrig hit four home runs, collected nine RBIs and scored five runs.

The peak moments came during game four in St. Louis. Ruth homered three times. His second blast tied the score in the seventh inning, and Gehrig followed with a homer that put the Yanks on top. The game ended with the Babe making a one-hand running stab on a foul ball near the left-field stands.

For the second year in a row, the Yankees were world champions, which created a stir in rival cities. Thus, a new cry was heard for the first time in baseball: "Break up the Yankees!"

16

New York Yankees 1953

99-52

.656

CASEY STENGEL'S DYNASTY WINS RECORD FIFTH STRAIGHT WORLD SERIES ♦ YANKS BEAT DODGERS ♦ WHITEY FORD (18-6) IS TOP N.Y. WINNER ♦ EDDIE LOPAT'S 2.42 ERA LEADS AL ♦ YOGI BERRA (27 HRS), MICKEY MANTLE (21 HRS) STAR.

On the 50th anniversary of the World Series, the New York Yankees formed an unprecedented dynasty. They won their fifth consecutive world championship in 1953. How did the Yankees do what had never been done before in the history of baseball? Manager Casey Stengel's explanation was uncharacteristically simple. Said the Old Perfessor: "I got the players who can execute."

The '53 New York Yankees, combining remarkable depth and talent, won 18 games in a row early on and virtually cruised to the American League pennant. Along the way, Stengel platooned his young and old "regulars" brilliantly and effectively juggled an aging pitching staff.

The season was marked by the rise of two 24-year-old Yankees heroes. Center fielder Mickey Mantle (21, 92, .295) clouted several mammoth homers and pitcher Whitey Ford (18-6, 3.00) became a big winner. Typically, they were backed by a pair of veteran performers. Catcher Yogi Berra (27, 108, .296) was a star at age 28 and Eddie Lopat (16-4, 2.42) won the AL ERA crown at age 35.

In the six-game World Series, the Yanks once more halted the powerful Brooklyn Dodgers, who were thought to have perhaps their best team ever. The Dodgers had captured three National League pennants in five years and lost the other two on the final day of the season. Yet the Subway Series, which made New York City the capital of baseball in October, still belonged to the Yanks.

Looking back on the 1949-53 Yankee dynasty, "Steady Eddie" Lopat pointed out: "In those five years, 96 players went through that club. People say how can you win a pennant five years in a row with 96 players going through a club? Well, the nucleus of the club was there the whole time and they just filled in around it where they needed.

"Actually, of the five World Series we won, there were only 12 of us who were on that club through it all: Berra, Joe Collins, [Phil] Rizzuto, Gene Woodling, Hank Bauer, [Vic] Raschi, [Allie] Reynolds, and myself, and Charlie Silvera [plus Ralph Houk and Jerry Coleman]. . . . Johnny Mize we got in the middle of '49, so he was there the whole time. . . ."

In 1953, Stengel was anxious to surpass both his old New York Giants mentor John McGraw and former Yankee manager Joe McCarthy. McGraw had won four straight pennants (1921-24) and McCarthy had won four straight World Series (1936-39). Now Stengel, 62, who had all of his regulars and his best pitchers back from the previous year, reasoned: "If the players are good enough to win four years they should be good enough to win five."

They were. Behind Mantle and Berra, the rest of the starting players in '53—except for Rizzuto, the shortstop—had HR totals in double figures. That included first baseman Collins (17, 44, .269), second baseman Billy Martin (15, 75, .257), third baseman Gil McDougald (10, 83, .285), left fielder Woodling (10, 58, .306) and right fielder Bauer (10, 57, .304).

And even Rizzuto (2, 54, .274) was a solid contributor.

The Bronx Bombers scored the most runs (801) in the American League in 1953. They also held their opponents to the fewest runs (547). New York's hitters led the league in batting (.273) and slugging (.417) while its pitchers led in ERA (3.20) and saves (39). On defense, the Yankees missed tying for the AL lead in fielding average by only .001.

Ford, just back from two years in the Army, was the young star of a pitching staff with an average age of 32. Besides Lopat, the veteran starters were Johnny Sain (14-7, 3.00) and Raschi (13-6, 3.33). Reynolds (13-7, 3.41), who also started 15 games, led the Yankees in saves (13).

Four games into the season, Mantle, the most powerful switch-hitter ever, made history during a 7-3 New York triumph at Griffith Stadium in Washington. Off Chuck Stobbs, the Mick hit his most famous right-handed blast—perhaps the longest homer in baseball history. The ball sailed high over the wall in left center at the 391-foot mark, hit the top of a 60-foot high beer sign at the back of the bleachers, flew out of the stadium and rolled into the backyard of a house two blocks away. The total distance from home plate was walked off and put at 565 feet. Thus, the age of the "tape measure" home run was born. In 1953, Mantle hit epic homers in New York, Washington, Detroit, Philadelphia and St. Louis. And he became the talk of baseball as the successor to Yankee great Joe DiMaggio, once the young star of McCarthy's dynasty.

"I'd say that Mantle today is the greatest player in either league," St. Louis Browns manager Marty Marion noted, pointing to his hitting, fielding, running and throwing. No weaknesses? "Let's see—uh, yes," said Marion. "There's one thing he can't do very well. He can't throw left-handed."

The Mick, batting right-handed, hit his big homer in St. Louis on April 28, helping New York to a 6-0 lead during a wild game at Sportsman's Park. The three-run homer soared over the left-field wall and out of the ballpark. Distance: 500 feet. With the game tied 6-6 in the top of 10th, McDougald scored the eventual winning run by slamming into catcher

Clint Courtney and knocking the ball out of his glove. Vowing to get somebody, "Old Scrap Iron" Courtney spiked Rizzuto while trying for a double in the bottom of the tenth. That ignited one of the roughest two-team brawls ever. But the Yanks won the game, 7-6.

New York went 11-3 in April, taking over the lead in the American League for good in 1953. The Yanks won 16 of 24 games in May, including the last four in a row. The Bombers also triumphed in their first 14 games in June as Stengel shrewdly hounded them to a near-record AL winning streak. They missed by one game—but 15 of their 18 consecutive wins were on the road. In St. Louis, Satchel Paige, working in relief, beat Ford, 3-1, to snap the streak. It was Ford's first loss in '53. He won his first seven decisions of the season (and so did Lopat). In the game that broke the Yank victory string, Johnny Mize got his 2,000th hit, driving in his team's only run. Big Jawn led the AL in pinch hits that season (19 for 61, .311).

The Yankees, who had streaked to a 10½ game lead over Cleveland, were being called the best baseball team since World War II. But they turned around in late June and began a nine-game losing streak. Stengel, who left them alone until they won again, drove his players to a 20-12 record in July.

At that point, the Yankees were 66-33. But Chicago trailed by just five games when the White Sox arrived at Yankee Stadium on August 7. New York won the opener, 6-1. Next day the Yanks swept Chicago in a doubleheader, winning 1-0 (on Ford's five-hitter) and 3-0 (on Bob Kuzava's one-hitter).

That ended the AL race. The Yankees clinched their 20th pennant on September 14 at Yankee Stadium. They defeated Cleveland, 8-5, after Berra hit a two-run homer and Martin drove in four runs. The Indians finished second, 8½ games behind New York. Chicago was third, 11½ games back.

Against the National League champion Dodgers (105-49, .682), Billy Martin set a World Series record. His 12 hits were the most ever in a six-game Series. Martin batted .500 with two homers and eight RBIs. Mantle, who struck out eight times, also hit two homers. Brooklyn's hitters did well, too.

But the Dodgers made seven errors, paving the way to defeat.

The Yankees had won their 16th world championship—their record fifth in a row. Said Stengel: "Everybody contributed."

17

Cincinnati Reds 1940

100-53

.654

STRONG PITCHING AND DEFENSE SPARK THE REDS ♦ BUCKY WALTERS LEADS NL IN WINS (22), ERA (2.48) ♦ PAUL DERRINGER WINS 20 ♦ NL MVP IS FRANK MCCORMICK (19, 127, 309) ♦ CINCINNATI BEATS TIGERS IN WORLD SERIES.

Behind solid pitching and record fielding, the Cincinnati Reds triumphed in 1940. It was the first legitimate world championship for baseball's oldest pro team. Cincinnati's original World Series crown in 1919 had been tainted by the notorious Chicago Black Sox, who were secretly paid by gamblers to lose.

The 1940 Reds, earning the satisfaction denied to the franchise a generation before, defeated the Detroit Tigers in an honest World Series. More immediately, the seven-game victory by manager Bill McKechnie's Cincinnati team made up for being swept in 1939 by the New York Yankees.

On the way to their second National League pennant in a row, the Reds of '40 had to overcome a personal tragedy. Reserve catcher Willard Hershberger, 29, become depressed and killed himself on August 2. He cut his throat in a Boston hotel room during a road trip with his first-place team.

Six weeks later, starting catcher Ernie Lombardi (14, 74, .319) sprained his ankle and was sidelined. Thus, 40-year-old Reds coach Jimmie Wilson, who stepped in and caught the rest of the way, was in a position to become the surprise hero of the World Series. Wilson batted .353 in the Series.

Cincinnati in 1940 was short on hitting—and long on pitching and fielding. First baseman Frank McCormick (19, 127, .309), who extended his playing streak to 462 consecutive games, earned the NL MVP award. But he was the team's only strong hitter besides Lombardi, who had won the award in 1938. The NL MVP in '39, Bucky Walters, pitched for Cincinnati.

In 1940, Walters (22-10, 2.48) and Paul Derringer (20-12, 3.06) were the team's best pitchers. Next came Junior Thompson (16-9, 3.32), Jim Turner (14-7, 2.89) and reliever Joe Beggs (12-3, 1.99; with seven saves). But Johnny Vander Meer (3-1, 3.75), who had pitched back-to-back no-hitters in 1938, was bothered by injuries. Briefly farmed out, he started only seven games in 1940.

Walters led the NL for the second consecutive season in wins, ERA, innings (305) and complete games (29). Derringer was number two in wins and complete games (26); he was tied for second in innings (297).

"We were a one-run club," said Vander Meer. "As Joe Beggs would say if we got one run in the first inning, 'Brother, there's your lead and go hold 'em.' We lacked one more good hitter to win games by two or three runs . . . they could pitch around Ernie Lombardi [and McCormick]."

So Cincinnati in 1940 scratched out runs here and there. For the third season in a row, the Reds led the NL in sacrifice hits (125). Left fielder Mike McCormick (1, 30, .300) paced the club with 20 sacrifices. Third baseman Bill Werber (12, 48, .277) topped the club with by scoring 105 runs, third best in the league. Second baseman Lonny Frey (8, 54, .266) scored 102 runs. He also led the NL in stolen bases with 22; and Werber was fourth with 16.

On defense, the Reds had the best fielders in baseball. The team set a major-league record in 1940 by committing only 117 errors. Cincinnati topped the National League with a fielding average of .981. McCormick (.995) led NL first baseman in fielding; Werber (.962) led third basemen; center fielder Harry Craft (.997) led outfielders; and Lombardi (.988) led catchers.

During the 1940 season, Cincinnati allowed the fewest runs (528) of any NL team. It held the opposition scoreless 10 times, to one run 22 times and to two runs 31 times. In those games, the Reds won 59, lost three and tied one.

Cincinnati also had the longest winning streak of the year in the National League—they won 11 games in a row. But that happened in mid September, when the pennant race was over. The Reds had finished 12 games ahead of runner-up Brooklyn and 16 games ahead of third place St. Louis.

Much of the credit belonged to McKechnie. Before he took over, the Reds finished last in 1937—40 games out of first place. McKechnie became manager in 1938 and the Reds climbed to fourth before winning two straight pennants.

"Bill was an outstanding defensive manager," said Vander Meer about the ex-National League catcher. "He wasn't much of an offensive manager because he never had a club where he could be one."

Cincinnati opened the 1940 season at home. The Reds began with a pair of 2-1 victories at Crosley Field against Chicago. There was more of that to come. They set an NL record in 1940, winning 41 games by just one run.

For the first half of the season, Cincinnati and the Dodgers moved in and out of first place. No other teams reached the top in 1940 once the early tie between undefeated NL teams was broken.

Brooklyn broke on top, winning its first nine games. The ninth Dodger victory was Tex Carleton's 3-0 no-hitter in Cincinnati on April 30.

But the Reds, who won 15 of their first 19 games, were also hot.

They first gained a lead over the Dodgers in the pennant

race with a 12-5 victory in St. Louis on May 11. Three days later, the Dodgers regained first place. They did it by beating Cincinnati, 6-5, in a 13-inning game in Brooklyn.

Thereafter, the lead kept shifting back and forth between the two teams until the Reds moved on top for the seventh time on July 7. The Reds were in the lead to stay. They held first place for the final 85 days of the season.

In early August, the suicide of Hershberger disrupted the team. The number two catcher had hit .309 in 48 games in 1940. He became despondent over his play in three tough losses on the road. Hershberger told McKechnie he was thinking about killing himself. But the manager talked him back to normal. Or so McKechnie thought. Next day, Hershberger called in sick; later, his body was found.

After coming off the road, the Reds were still troubled by the incident. But their play had improved by the time they headed East in early September on their final trip. And then Lombardi sprained his ankle, in Brooklyn on September 15, and was sidelined for the rest of the year. Coach Jimmie Wilson took over the catching and the team kept on winning.

Three days later, the Reds clinched the pennant in Philadelphia. They won, 4-3, in 13 innings. Vander Meer, still worried about his sore arm, pitched 12 strong innings, scored the winning run and got relief help from Beggs. "That was one of the highlights of my career," Vander Meer recalled.

In the World Series, Cincinnati beat the American League champion Detroit Tigers (90-64, .584), four games to three. Walters won game two and game six; Derringer won game four and game seven. The steady work of Wilson behind the plate was crucial, particularly in Walters' 4-0 shutout in game six at Crosley Field. That set up Derringer's 2-1 final-game victory in Cincinnati.

There was only one stolen base in the entire 1940 Series. But it wasn't at the expense of old Jimmie Wilson. He stole the base himself.

And the Reds voted Willard Hershberger's widowed mother a full World Series share of nearly $6,000.

18

New York Yankees 1938

99-53

.651

MANAGER JOE MCCARTHY'S FAVORITE TEAM ♦ HIS YANKEE DYNASTY SWEEPS CUBS FOR UNPRECEDENTED THIRD STRAIGHT WORLD TITLE ♦ LED BY JOE DIMAGGIO (32, 140, .324), FIVE YANKS HIT MORE THAN 20 HOMERS ♦ RED RUFFING WINS 21 GAMES, LEFTY GOMEZ WINS 18.

Joe McCarthy called this team the best he ever managed. His New York Yankees had so much talent in 1938 that the American League was dubbed "Snow White and the Seven Dwarfs." Vowed a rival manager: "If the Yankees don't win the pennant by August 1, there should be a grand jury investigation."

The '38 Yanks, combining rare strength and balance, became the first major-league team to win a third consecutive world championship. New York ran away from the competition in August, clinched its tenth flag in September and won its seventh World Series in October. The Yankees swept the National League champion Chicago Cubs in the Fall Classic.

Led by center fielder Joe DiMaggio (32, 140, .324), five

Yanks hit more than 20 home runs during the regular season. They included 35-year-old first baseman Lou Gehrig (29, 114, .295), who played his last full season. The power was also supplied by catcher Bill Dickey (27, 115, .313), second baseman Joe Gordon (25, 97, .255) and right fielder Tommy Henrich (22, 91, .270).

New York's other regulars made solid contributions. Third baseman Red Rolfe (10, 80, .311) led the team with 132 runs. Shortstop Frankie Crosetti (9, 55, .263) led the league with 27 stolen bases. And left fielder George "Twinkletoes" Selkirk (10, 62, .254) used his 335 at bats productively.

The new Yankee starting players in 1938 were Henrich, who had broken in the previous season, and Gordon, promoted from the great 1937 Newark Bears of the International League. "Flash" Gordon's AL debut created excitement. "He made tremendous plays," recalled Crosetti. "He was just a jumping jack. He was an acrobat in college and a tumbler, and he was really quite a fielder."

In 1938, New York scored the most runs (966) in the American League and held their opponents to the fewest (710). The Yanks led the AL in homers (174), RBIs (917), walks (749), stolen bases (91) and slugging (.446). For the fifth straight time, their pitchers led in ERA (3.91). Yankee hurlers were also tops in complete games (91) and shutouts (10).

King of the hill in '38 was AL victory champ Red Ruffing (21-7, 3.31), who put together his third 20-win season in a row. Lefty Gomez (18-12, 3.35) set a record by allowing only three homers in 239 innings. Monte Pearson (16-7, 3.97) counted the first no-hitter in Yankee Stadium history among his wins. And Spud Chandler (14-5, 4.03) won effectively. Out of the bullpen, Johnny Murphy (8-2, 4.24) had more saves (11) than any other pitcher in the league.

Despite their talent, the Yanks got off to a slow start, partly because of DiMaggio's holdout. He was demanding a raise to $40,000 after being paid $8,000 in his first year and $15,000 in his second. Not until late April did DiMaggio accept the original Yankee offer of $25,000 and report to the club. That made the 23-year-old star the third highest-paid player in baseball. For a while, the great DiMaggio heard boos in Yankee Stadium. He responded silently, without complaining. Soon his hitting, running and fielding won back the fans.

The Yanks went 7-6 in April, 13-8 in May and 17-11 in June—for a combined record of only 37-25. The first-half highlight was a big doubleheader on Memorial Day. New York swept Boston, 10-0 and 5-4, on May 30 before 81,841 fans, the largest official crowd in Yankee Stadium history.

On July 1, the Yanks, in the midst of a nine-game winning streak at home, beat Washington, 8-0, as Bill Dickey hit a grand slam and a three-run homer. On July 12, New York defeated St. Louis, 7-3 and 10-5, at Yankee Stadium. That moved them ahead of Cleveland and into first place to stay. Eventually, they wound up 9½ games in front of Boston, and 13 games in front of Cleveland.

After improving to 20-5 in July, the Yankees pulled away by winning an AL record 28 games in August (while losing only eight). Key victories:

On August 7, the Yanks won 7-0 in Cleveland. Ruffing lost a no-hitter with one out in the bottom of the ninth inning when Roy Weatherly doubled.

On August 12, New York beat the Philadelphia A's, 16-3, in the nightcap of a twinbill at Yankee Stadium. Selkirk hit a grand-slam, a three-run homer and a run-scoring single. He had a solo homer in the opener, but the Yanks lost, 5-4.

On August 20, Gehrig, still the Iron Horse, hit the 23rd and final grand slam of his career—for a major-league record. His blast off Buck Ross led the Yankees to an 11-3 win in Philadelphia.

On August 27, Pearson pitched a no-hitter to beat the Indians, 13-0, in the second game of a doubleheader at Yankee Stadium. He faced the minimum of 27 batters, striking out seven and walking two (who were erased in double plays). In the first game, New York won, 8-7, as DiMaggio contributed three triples.

A month later, Lou Gehrig hit the 493rd and final homer of his career. In the September 27 game, the Yanks, who had clinched the pennant more than a week before, defeated Washington, 5-2. Gehrig homered against Dutch Leonard in Yankee Stadium. It happened exactly 15 years to the day after he hit his first home run in the major leagues. Of course, it was believed in 1938 that Gehrig still had a few seasons remaining—even though he was obviously slowing. He finished the year by both driving in and scoring more than 100 runs for the 13th consecutive time in his brilliant career.

In the World Series, the Yanks swept Chicago, 3-1, 6-3, 5-2 and 8-3.

Dickey hit .438. Gordon, whose emergence had sent ex-New York second baseman Tony Lazzeri packing to the Cubs, hit .400. And Gordon and Crosetti each drove in six runs, more than half the Yankee total of 22.

But Gehrig, unaware that he was fatally ill, struggled. He had just four singles in his final World Series.

Only game two in Chicago was dramatic. The Cubs starter was ex-St. Louis Cardinal ace Dizzy Dean, who was trying to make a comeback without his fastball. For seven innings, sore-armed Dean held off the Bronx Bombers with curves and off-speed pitches. But Crosetti's two-run homer dashed his hopes.

"Congratulations, Joe," said Dean to McCarthy after game four. "You got a great ball club."

"Thanks, Diz," replied the Yankee manager. "I was sorry we had to beat you the other day. You pitched a great game."

"That's all right," Dean said. "I got beat by a great team."

And the New York Yankees celebrated their historic dynasty.

19

New York Yankees 1923

98-54

.645

CLUB'S FIRST WORLD CHAMPIONSHIP ♦ YANKEE STADIUM, "THE HOUSE THAT RUTH BUILT," OPENS ♦ THE BABE (41, 131, .393) STARS ♦ SAD SAM JONES IS 21-8 ♦ YANKS WIN ON PITCHING, DEFENSE ♦ BEAT GIANTS IN WORLD SERIES.

Yankee Stadium, "The House That Ruth Built," opened on April 18, 1923. The $2.5 million steel-and-concrete stadium in the Bronx was a modern marvel—the first three-tiered ballpark ever constructed. It housed what was to become the most celebrated franchise in the history of sports.

The New York Yankees won their first world championship in 1923 and their third consecutive American League pennant. In little more than half a century, Yankee Stadium would be the home of 22 world titles and 33 AL flags.

The '23 Yanks, managed by Miller Huggins, earned the World Series crown by defeating the New York Giants, their former Polo Grounds landlord. The Giants, under John McGraw, had beaten the Yankees in the World Series in 1921 and 1922. But National Leaguers were being outdrawn in their own park during the regular season by the increasingly popular Yankees.

Why? Babe Ruth had ushered in the home-run era by hitting 54 home runs in the Polo Grounds in 1920. That season the Yankees became the first baseball team ever to draw one million fans. Ordered to move, the Yanks decided to build their own park a quarter-mile away on the other side of the Harlem River.

The debut of Yankee Stadium attracted an Opening Day crowd of 62,281, about 20,000 more than the previous major-league record. At mid-afternoon, John Philip Sousa led the Seventh Regiment Band in the national anthem. Governor Al Smith of New York threw out the first ball. And pitcher Bob Shawkey of the Yankees went to work against the Boston Red Sox.

The Babe, of course, rose to the occasion. "I'd give a year of my life if I can hit a home run in the first game in the new park," Ruth had vowed. He delivered, too. Breaking a scoreless tie in the bottom of the fourth inning, Ruth belted a three-run homer off a slow curve by Boston's Howard Ehmke. His 199th career home run, a line-drive to right field, was enough to win the game. Shawkey tossed a three-hitter for a 4-1 New York victory.

From there, the Yankees went on to the finest season in their 20-year history. The Yanks went 8-4 in April; and 21-6 in May. They led the American League by eight games on June 1. For the next four weeks, New York played .500 baseball. But the club went 23-8 in July to boost its record to 65-30. At the end of the season, the Yanks led second-place Detroit by 16 games and third-place Cleveland by 16½.

Leading the way was Babe Ruth (41, 131, .393). Not only did he collect 205 hits for the highest batting average of his career, but the Babe also reached base 379 times with the help of 170 walks—both major-league records. At least half of his walks were either intentional or thereabouts; once he was even walked on purpose with the bases loaded. Ruth's on-base percentage was .542. He topped the AL in homers, RBIs, runs (151), total bases (399) and slugging (.764).

The Yanks of '23 led the league in home runs (105) and slugging (.422). But that was because of Ruth. No other Yankee hit more than ten homers. And both Cleveland and Detroit scored more runs than New York did that season.

Where the Yankees really succeeded was on defense. New York held opponents to fewer runs (622) than did any other club. Yankee pitchers led the AL in ERA (3.66), complete games (102) and strikeouts (506). Also, New York had the best fielding percentage (.977) and made the fewest errors (144).

"People forget that the Yankees in the '20s were more than a great offensive club," Sad Sam Jones, one of their ace pitchers, once said. "They were the best defensive team in both leagues, as well. That outfield, terrific pitching, a great infield—it was a well-balanced club in every way."

In 1923, Jones (21-8, 3.63) won the most games on an experienced pitching staff that was dubbed "The Six-Star Final." He was joined by Herb Pennock (19-6, 3.34), Bullet Joe Bush (19-15, 3.42), Waite Hoyt (17-9, 3.01), Shawkey (16-11, 3.51) and Carl Mays (5-2, 6.22).

"What's the matter with you, Hoyt?" asked Yankee owner Jacob Ruppert at one point in 1923. "You win all your games by scores of 1 to 0, and 2 to 1, and 3 to 2. Pennock, Shawkey, Bush, those fellows—they win their games by 9 and 10 to 1. Why don't you win some of your games like that?"

New York's attack was led by a .300-hitting outfield. Ruth was joined by center fielder Whitey Witt (6, 56, .314) and left fielder Bob Meusel (9, 91, .313). Second baseman Aaron Ward (10, 82, .284) was the only Yankee besides the Babe to reach double figures in homers. The other regular players were: first baseman Wally Pipp (6, 108, .304), shortstop Everett Scott (6, 60, .246), third baseman Joe Dugan (7, 67, .283) and catcher Wally Schang (2, 29, .276).

Four Yanks—Witt, Ward, Scott and Dugan—were the best AL fielders at their positions in 1923. And Scott, the captain of the team, pushed his playing streak beyond 1,000 games early that season. It was thought at the time to be an unbreakable record. Yet later in the year, "Columbia Lou" Gehrig, 20, who was destined to surpass Scott, got his first few at bats with the Yankees—and hit his first major-league home run.

Among the other highlights of 1923:

April 24: In New York, President Warren G. Harding spends the afternoon at brand-new Yankee Stadium. He watches New York beat Washington, 4-0.

May 22: In Chicago, the Yanks get a telegram from Ruppert. It reads: "I now am the sole owner of the Yankees. Miller Huggins is my manager." Ruppert had paid $1.5 million to buy out partner Til Huston, ending a feud that, for a time, had undermined the authority of Huggins.

September 4: In Philadelphia, Sad Sam Jones fires a no-hitter to beat the Athletics, 2-0. "I'm going to break it up if I can," yelled Chick Galloway, the last man up. But Jones fielded his bunt and threw him out.

September 20: In St. Louis, New York wins, 4-3, clinching the AL pennant in the 141st game of the season.

Nearly half of the 24 Yankees eligible for the World Series of '23 had been acquired through the years from the Red Sox. Ruth was the best known. Among the others: Dugan, Scott, Schang—and the Yankee pitchers who started five of the six Series games: Hoyt, Pennock, Jones and Bush.

In the Series, the Yankees beat the Giants, four games to two. Casey Stengel, who later managed the Yanks to seven world titles, won a pair of games for the "Jints." His inside-the-park homer in the ninth inning at Yankee Stadium was the winning run in the opener; and his solo blast was the only run in game three.

But the Yankees won the Series. The Babe hit .368 with three home runs ("The Ruth is mighty and shall prevail," reported Heywood Broun). Ward batted .417. Meusel drove in eight runs. And Pennock won two games.

Thrilled to see his New York Yankees celebrate their first world championship, Ruppert crowed: "I have the greatest park, the greatest players and the greatest team."

20

Detroit Tigers 1984

104-58

642

TIGERS GET OFF TO RECORD 35-5 START ♦ SPARKY ANDERSON IS FIRST MANAGER TO WIN 100 GAMES IN BOTH AL AND NL; FIRST TO WIN WORLD SERIES IN BOTH ♦ WILLIE HERNANDEZ (32 SAVES) GETS AL MVP, CY YOUNG AWARDS.

Not since the legendary New York Yankees of 1927 had a major-league team owned first place from Opening Day until the final out of the regular season.

Leaping into the 1984 campaign, the Detroit Tigers won their first nine games-including a no-hit victory by Jack Morris over the Chicago White Sox on national TV. The Tigers won the home openers in Minnesota, Chicago, Detroit and Boston. They went 18-2 in April, tying a major-league record. Then Detroit set the record by going 26-4 over the first 30 games.

By late May, the club had tied another major-league record: 17 consecutive road victories. And the Tigers had won 35 of their first 40 games, the hottest streak right off the bat in the history of baseball. Second-place Toronto won at a sizzling rate of .659 meanwhile. But the Blue Jays found themselves trailing by eight games. The AL East race was just about over before summer even began.

No wonder Sparky Anderson, on his way to becoming the first manager ever to win 100 games in each major league, began to size up his Detroit Tigers against his Cincinnati Reds dynasty of the 1970s.

"This team has better pitching, defense and depth," he said about his red hot Tigers.

By October, Anderson, 50 years old, gray-haired and wordy, was able to rejoice. His players blew away Kansas City in three AL playoff games and beat San Diego in a five-game World Series mismatch—which also made him the first manager to win world championships in both leagues.

"The 1984 Tigers were truly a team in the real sense of the word," claimed Anderson, who won the AL Manager of the Year award. "We didn't have one player to hit 35 homers. Yet we led the league in home runs. We didn't have one pitcher to win 20 games or pitch 250 innings. Yet we led the league in ERA-and that's with playing half our games in Tiger Stadium where the fences scratch the backs of the outfielders."

None of which bothered ace reliever Willie Hernandez, the newly acquired left-hander who set a Tigers pitching record with 80 trips to the mound. Over his seven previous seasons in the National League (at Chicago and Philadelphia), Hernandez was only a .500 hurler with a total of 27 saves. But the AL batters, who knew nothing about him, didn't like his looks. They saw tough screwballs, sinking fastballs, sharp curves—and pinpoint control. For Detroit, Hernandez saved 32 games in 33 chances and posted a 9-3 record with a dazzling 1.92 ERA. He became the 1984 AL Most Valuable Player and the Cy Young Award winner.

Certainly, the Tigers got solid pitching-and 54 wins-from their best three starters: Morris (19-11, 3.60 ERA), Dan Petry (18-8, 3.24) and Milt Wilcox (17-8, 4.00). But the Latin bullpen duo worked magic: Puerto Rico-born Hernandez teamed with Mexico-born Aurelio Lopez (10-1, 2.94 ERA and 14 saves), a righty known as Senior Smoke. Even before Detroit finished the season 15 games ahead of Toronto, Anderson had prepared an epitaph for the Blue Jays. "I can tell you the difference between Detroit and Toronto in two words," he said. "Hernandez and Lopez. If Toronto had them instead of us, we'd be trailing by as many games, if not more, than the Blue Jays."

Well, perhaps. But the Tigers did have the best strength up the middle in baseball in 1984. Catcher Lance Parrish, second baseman Lou Whitaker and center fielder Chet Lemon all started for the American League in the All-Star game; shortstop Alan Trammell also made the team and later was named the MVP in the World Series.

The fielding and hitting of Parrish (33 HRs, 98 RBIs, .237 avg.), Whitaker (13, 56, .289), Lemon (20, 76, .287) and Trammell (14, 69, .314) helped to keep Detroit in front of its rivals. And right fielder Kirk Gibson, coached by Tiger Hall of Famer Al Kaline, drove himself to become a star. Gibson (27, 91, .282) emerged as the first Tiger ever to hit more than 20 homers and steal more than 20 bases in one season.

"Depending on the time of year, we had a different most valuable player just about every week," said Lemon. "Everyone can feel the satisfaction of being a contributor, and that's one of the best feelings of all. Nobody was left out."

What everyone also felt was the pressure on Detroit to keep on winning after its quick start. Explained Trammell: "We would have been labeled as chokers." From May 17 until the end of the season, they never played at Tiger Stadium before less than 25,000 fans; in all, home attendance reach 2.7 million. While Detroit spectators performed. "The Wave" and media coverage boomed, the players tried to go about their business.

"If anything, that fast start put pressure on us that no other team ever experienced before," said Anderson. "Every place we went, everytime we played, everybody expected us to win and everyone tried to knock the bully down. Every time we played a game, it was like a playoff atmosphere. Writers followed us around the country. We bumped into TV cameras every time we turned around. That was pressure.

And my guys handled it better than anyone could possibly imagine."

For a total of 177 days in mid 1984—while President Reagan campaigned for re-election, Mary Lou Retton captured Olympic glory, John De Lorean survived a cocaine trial and Vanessa Williams gave up her Miss America crown—the Tigers were in first place alone. That set an AL record. Detroit had shared first place with the Cleveland Indians for only five days.

The best Toronto ever did was close the gap to three games on June 6, the 40th anniversary of D-Day.

On the following day, more than 40,000 fans turned out in Detroit for a Thursday afternoon game against the Blue Jays, who had just taken two out of three from the Tigers. Detroit beat Toronto, 5-3, as Morris went the distance, allowing seven hits, and newcomer Ruppert Jones hit a game-winning three-run homer. Then Detroit won three of four games in a weekend series at Baltimore.

Which brought the Tigers to Toronto for what the local newspapers called "The June World Series." After winning two of the three contests, the Blue Jays were still six games behind Detroit. For Toronto, it had gotten late early.

Of course, the Tigers did have an inevitable mid-season slump. They were 16-12 in July and 16-15 in August. Hot-tempered Morris struggled, refusing all interviews. Knee and shoulder injuries forced Trammell to DH some and to ride the bench for a while. Yet Detroit still fell just one short of winning 70 of its first 100 games.

In early September, the Blue Jays were eight games back when they began a three-game visit to Detroit for one last try. The Tigers swept the series. And that was that.

Detroit clinched the AL East flag on September 18.

"I have to be honest," noted Anderson. "I've waited for this day since they fired me in Cincinnati. I think they made a big mistake when they did it."

Detroit beat Kansas City in the AL playoffs (winning, 8-1, 5-3 and 1-0), then the Tigers defeated San Diego in a dull World Series (winning, 3-2, losing, 5-3, and winning, 5-2, 4-2 and 8-4). Finally, they had it all. It was the first time Detroit had clinched a World Series in Tiger Stadium since 1935.

"I'm not saying that this was a great team," Anderson concluded. "But it was a great season."

21

Brooklyn Dodgers 1955

98-55

.641

BROOKLYN WINS ITS FIRST WORLD SERIES CROWN (VS. YANKS IN SEVEN GAMES) ♦ OFF A RECORD 10-0 START, DODGERS ROLL TO PENNANT ♦ NL MVP: ROY CAMPANELLA (32, 107, .318) ♦ DUKE SNIDER (42, 136, .309) STARS; DON NEWCOMBE: 20-5, 3.19.

"This is next year!" No longer did the Brooklyn Dodgers have to wait. In 1955, Brooklyn won its first (and only) world championship. The Dodgers finally beat the New York Yankees. It was something the Bums had failed to do in their five most recent World Series—in 1941, 1947, 1949, 1952 and 1953.

To his Dodger teammates, Jackie Robinson had urged: "We gotta win this one. If we lose again, they'll be calling us choke-up guys the rest of our lives. Do we want that?" No. They didn't. And all of Brooklyn celebrated the World Series of '55. Years later, Johnny Podres, whose 2-0 shutout won game seven, recalled: "There was a whole city that now could raise its head, look across the river to the Bronx and Manhattan, and say, 'We're number one.' "

They really were. The '55 Dodgers dominated the National League like no other team ever had. Brooklyn was in first place on 166 of 168 days in the regular season. Only because the opener at Ebbets Field came two days into the NL campaign were the Dodgers denied a chance to lead all the way.

Setting a modern record, Brooklyn won its first ten games of the year—and 22 of its first 24. On July 4, the Dodgers (55-22) led by 12½ games. They clinched the pennant on September 8, the earliest victory in NL history. The Bums went on to finish 13½ games in front of Milwaukee, the pre-season favorite; and 18½ ahead of the defending champion New York Giants.

Going into '55, second-year manager Walter Alston had yet to gain full control of his veteran team. The Dodgers were tempestuous and frustrated. But Alston took charge early in the season, both in the clubhouse and on the field. That squelched lingering rumors that Brooklyn's aging stars ran the club.

Winning smoothed the way. To combat Dodger aches and pains, Alston deftly platooned in three places: second base, third base and left field. Meanwhile, he juggled an ailing staff on which ten pitchers won at least five games.

Catcher Roy Campanella (32, 107, .318) won his third NL MVP award. Center fielder Duke Snider (42, 136, .309), the only left-handed slugger in the lineup, was the RBI champ. The Duke of Flatbush also scored 126 runs, the most in the league. Right fielder Carl Furillo (26, 95, .314) and first baseman Gil Hodges (27, 102, .289) each had big seasons. Meanwhile, Robinson (8, 36, .256), the third baseman, was fading at age 36. But team captain Pee Wee Reese (10, 61, .282) had one of his best years at shortstop. His 37th birthday on July 23 drew more than 30,000 fans to a candlelight celebration at Ebbets Field.

In 1955, the only Dodger ace was Don Newcombe (20-5, 3.19). He won his first ten decisions and then soared to 18-1 on July 31 before tailing off. Used mostly in relief, Clem Labine (13-5, 3.25; with 11 saves) was Brooklyn's next biggest winner. He started eight of the 60 games in which he pitched;

and he led the NL in appearances. The only other Dodger winners in double figures were Carl Erskine (11-8, 3.78) and Billy Loes (10-4, 3.59). Reliever Ed Roebuck (5-6, 4.71; with 12 saves) worked in 47 games as a rookie.

"What I remember most about the Dodger club," Roebuck once said, "was how businesslike and serious it was, and how much character the club had. There was no fooling around.... With Robinson, Hodges, Reese, and those guys, you weren't expected to be a clown. You were expected to be a ballplayer."

Together, Brooklyn's heroes of '55 scored the most runs (857) by any NL team and allowed the fewest (650). They led the league in batting (.271), slugging (.448), home runs (201) and stolen bases (79). At the same time, Dodger hurlers were number one in ERA (3.68), strikeouts (773) and saves (37).

This is how Brooklyn's Bums surged and coasted to the NL flag: they went 14-2 in April, 18-9 in May; 20-8 in June; 19-13 in July; 13-14 in August; and 14-9 in September. The Dodgers clinched the pennant in Milwaukee with a 10-2 triumph—rookie Roger Craig started and Karl Spooner came on to get the win.

In the World Series, Brooklyn did it the hard way. The Dodgers became the first team ever to reach the top in seven games after losing the first two. The surprise Series MVP was young Podres, who had a pair of complete-game wins.

Game 7 was played in Yankee Stadium. In the sixth inning, Podres faced Yogi Berra with no outs and the tying runs on first and second base. Berra, the AL MVP in '55, sliced an opposite-field fly down the line in left. But Dodger outfielder Sandy Amoros made a running left-handed catch and fired a perfect throw to Reese, who relayed to first for a double play. The grab by Amoros ("I run and run and run," said the happy Cuban) was historic. As it turned out, that play won it all for Brooklyn. At long last.

Next day, the New York *Daily News* headline shouted: "WHO'S A BUM?"

22

New York Yankees 1951

99-56

.636

CASEY STENGEL, YANKS WIN THIRD STRAIGHT WORLD SERIES CROWN (VS. "MIRACLE" GIANTS) ♦ JOE DIMAGGIO, 36, RETIRES; MICKEY MANTLE, 19, ARRIVES ♦ YOGI BERRA (27, 88, .294) IS AL MVP ♦ ALLIE REYNOLDS (17-8, 3.05) FIRES TWO NO-HITTERS.

For the New York Yankees, one era ended as another began. 1951 was Joe DiMaggio's last big-league season and Mickey Mantle's first. That year Casey Stengel managed his Bronx dynasty to its third straight world championship.

During '51, the Yankee Clipper and his rookie successor displayed only flashes of the talent that made them Hall of Famers. But DiMaggio (12, 71, .263; in 116 games) was 36 years old. It was his 13th season as the regular center fielder in Yankee Stadium. And Mantle (13, 65, .267; in 96 games) was only 19. His raw home-run power and speed—"My God, the boy runs faster than Cobb!" said Stengel—had created a sensation in spring training. So, the Mick was tested in right field before and after one last trip to the minors.

The '51 Yankees relied most heavily on catcher Yogi Berra (27, 88, .294), the American League MVP, and a veteran pitching staff. Also, Stengel wisely manipulated a deep bench on the way to the 18th Yankee pennant.

Collecting their 14th World Series crown, the Yanks beat the New York Giants, four games to two. It followed the "Miracle of Coogan's Bluff"—the Giants had come from 13½ lengths back to force Brooklyn into a playoff game at the Polo Grounds. Bobby Thomson's homer won the NL flag.

In the AL, the Yankees finished five games ahead of second-place Cleveland and 11 ahead of third-place Boston. On September 28, they clinched the pennant by defeating Boston, 8-0 and 11-3, in a doubleheader at Yankee Stadium.

The opener featured the second no-hit victory of 1951 by "Super Chief" Allie Reynolds, a half-blood Cherokee from Oklahoma. Reynolds had tossed a 1-0 no-hitter in Cleveland on July 12. Against the Red Sox, he ended the game by getting Ted Williams to hit two pop fouls in a row. Of Berra's miscue on the first foul, Reynolds later recalled, "I said, 'Well, let's try it again.' So we did, and he popped it up again. This time Yogi caught it. And I told him, 'That was your last chance. I was going to take the rest of 'em' "

In the nightcap, Vic Raschi's victory gave the Yanks the AL flag. DiMaggio padded New York's big lead in the second game with a three-run home run off Chuck Stobbs. It was Joltin' Joe's 361st and last regular-season homer.

At age 36, Reynolds (17-8, 3.05) was the oldest Yankee starting pitcher in 1951. He threw seven shutouts. And "the Indian" relieved and earned seven saves. Eddie Lopat (21-9, 2.91; with five shutouts) and Raschi (21-10, 3.28) lead the club in wins. Lopat was 33 years old; Raschi was 32. The only other Yankee to pitch more than 100 innings was rookie Tom Morgan (9-3, 3.67).

Both Stengel and Berra fully exercised their own Hall of Fame skill in 1951. They did a masterful job of controlling 19 different Yankee pitchers. The Yanks led the AL with 24 shutouts—four during the pennant race in September.

New York, knocked out of first place a couple of times

earlier in the season, didn't take the lead for good until September 16. It edged .003 points ahead of Cleveland with a 5-1 victory (by Reynolds) over the Indians before 68,000 fans at Yankee Stadium. In the fifth inning, Mantle doubled, Berra drew an intentional walk and DiMaggio tripled for the key runs. The next day, New York won, 2-1, as Lopat got his 20th victory. DiMaggio scored the winning run on Phil Rizzuto's perfect suicide squeeze bunt in the ninth inning.

After DiMaggio, shortstop Rizzuto (2, 43, .274), at the age of 33, was the oldest Yankee regular. But 38-year-old Johnny Mize (10, 49, .259) saw a lot of action at first base behind Joe Collins (9, 48, .286). Outfielders Gene Woodling (15, 71, .281) and Hank Bauer (10, 54, .296) were key players. So was utility infielder Gil McDougald (14, 63, .306), the AL Rookie of the Year.

The Yanks played their best late in the '51 campaign. They were 21-12 in August and 18-9 in September—thanks to Stengel's effective platooning. He juggled in '51 at every spot but catcher and, for the most part, shortstop.

"If you've got a number of good men setting around on the bench you'll do yourself a favor playing them," the Old Perfessor once said. "I decided I'd never count on one player taking care of one position for an entire season."

In the World Series, DiMaggio, who was embarrassed by the publication of a critical scouting report in *Life* magazine, batted only .261—with one last homer. Mantle's career nearly ended also. He stepped on a drain cover and tore up a knee while chasing a fly ball hit by Giants rookie Willie Mays.

But the Yanks prevailed again. Lopat won twice. And Hank Bauer's three-run triple in Yankee Stadium was the winning blow in Game 6. His sliding catch in right field ended the Series with the tying run on second in the 4-3 contest.

Afterwards, Joe DiMaggio sat in front of his locker with a beer in his hand as the Yankees enjoyed their third straight world title.

Said the once great DiMaggio: "I've played in my final game."

23

New York Yankees 1950

98-56

.636

YANKS WIN SECOND OF FIVE CONSECUTIVE WORLD CHAMPIONSHIPS ♦ JOE DIMAGGIO (32, 122 .301) HAS LAST BIG YEAR ♦ AL MVP IS PHIL RIZZUTO (7, 66, .324) ♦ YOGI BERRA (28, 124, .322) STARS ♦ VIC RASCHI IS 21-8 ♦ N.Y. TOPS PHILLIES IN SERIES.

Joe DiMaggio, the Yankee Clipper, was 35 years old. Scooter Phil Rizzuto was 32. Big Jawn Mize? He was 37. Vic Raschi, the Springfield Rifle, was 31. Ed Lopat was 32 years old. Chief Allie Reynolds was 35.

Behind the Old Guard of 1950, the New York Yankees earned the second of Casey Stengel's record five straight world titles. Sixty-year-old Stengel proved that his successful Yankee debut the season before was no fluke. Now the ex-National League "clown" was building a Hall of Fame record.

The Yanks in 1950, moving in and out of first place several times, had to battle hard to win their 17th American League pennant. But they remained in contention all season long in the four-team race. At the finish, New York led Detroit by three games, Boston by four and Cleveland by six.

In the World Series, the experienced Yanks taught Philadelphia's "Whiz Kids" a lesson. New York beat the youthful NL champions, four games to none. It was the sixth sweep and 13th triumph by the Yankees in 17 World Series.

In his last big year, Joe DiMaggio (32, 122, .301) had an uneasy time. He led the American League in 1950 with a slugging average of .585. But he was old; he couldn't throw; and his sore right heel, which had benched him for much of 1949, was still a problem. In fact, DiMaggio had been reluctant to return at all. In 1950, the center fielder stroked his 2,000th hit and played in 139 games. Yet DiMaggio admitted: "I haven't got that feeling that I used to have—that I can walk up there and hit any pitcher who ever lived."

Another veteran Yankee, Phil Rizzuto (7, 66, .324), was the AL MVP in '50. Once again, the 5-foot-6, 150-pound shortstop led the league in fielding (.982) at his position. And he collected 200 hits, 125 runs, 91 walks and 12 stolen bases. Rizzuto was also perhaps the greatest bunter of all time. "Pound for pound he's the best baseball player alive today," claimed Ty Cobb. "I like to watch him field as well as bat. He picks off grounders like picking cherries, and he has the opposition jittery every time he comes to bat. They don't know what to expect. If it were not for Honus Wagner, who was a superman in every respect, I would make Phil Rizzuto my all-time, all-star shortstop."

Aging Johnny Mize, the part-time Yankee first baseman, recaptured some old-time glory, too. In only 274 at bats, he belted 25 homers and drove in 72 runs. The Big Cat even socked three HRs in one game in 1950. Wrote sports reporter Dan Parker: "Your arm is gone; your legs likewise, / But not your eyes, Mize, not your eyes."

How about the younger Yanks? At age 25, catcher Yogi Berra (28, 124, .322) was rock solid. Two 27-year-old outfielders—Hank Bauer (13, 70, .320) and Gene Woodling (6, 60, .283)—were steady performers. And a 21-year-old rookie pitcher named Eddie Ford (9-1, 2.81; in 112 innings) wowed everybody after being called up from the minors at midseason.

For the most part, however, the pitching was in older hands. Raschi (21-8, 3.99), Lopat (18-8, 3.47) and Reynolds (16-12, 3.73) were the big three. Tommy Byrne (15-9, 4.74), fast and wild, also contributed. Working in relief for the Yanks were Joe Page (13 saves) and Tom Ferrick (9 saves).

On Opening Day, New York beat Boston, 15-10, at Fenway Park. The Yanks fell behind early, but fought back to win—just what they did during the season itself. Down 9-0, New York rallied. In a nine-run eighth inning, Yankee rookie Billy Martin got a pair of hits in his first two big-league at bats.

The Yanks, after a slow start, led the AL for the first time during a nine-game winning streak in May, a month in which they went 20-6. Then New York played just under .500 in June. DiMaggio, who was slumping, agreed reluctantly to try first base in early July. But he rushed back to center field after a shaky one-game trial. That month the Yanks went 19-8.

In August, the Bronx Bombers were 20-11. Then they went 18-9 in September to win the pennant. Ater "resting" for a week, DiMaggio returned to the lineup on August 18 and hit .376 the rest of the way. In September, he belted nine homers and drove in 30 runs. DiMaggio's hot hitting—including three homers in an 8-1 victory on September 10 in Washington—led New York back into first place to stay. They clinched the AL flag on September 29.

The World Series was a mismatch. New York beat the Phillies, 1-0, 2-1, 3-2 and 5-2. DiMaggio won game two in Philadelphia with a homer off Robin Roberts in the 10th inning. The Yanks allowed only three earned runs in four games.

"We just didn't hit," said Phillies manager Eddie Sawyer. "Of course, we were facing four guys named Raschi, Reynolds, Lopat and Ford."

Another guy, Charles D. Stengel, was on his way to a historic dynasty.

24

Cleveland Indians 1920

98-56

.636

MGR-CF TRIS SPEAKER (8, 107, .388) LEADS INDIANS TO FIRST WORLD TITLE ♦ HISTORIC AL PENNANT RACE OPENS HR ERA ♦ SS RAY CHAPMAN IS BEANED, DIES ♦ JIM BAGBY IS 31-12; STAN COVELESKI IS 24-14, 3-0 IN WORLD SERIES VS. BROOKLYN.

It was a tumultuous season. Baseball's home run era began in 1920 in the midst of a historic pennant race in the American League. Despite the livelier ball, the Cleveland Indians won their first AL flag and world championship the old-fashioned way. They relied on strong pitching and timely base hits.

Led by the steadiness of player-manager Tris Speaker, the Indians survived and triumphed under dramatic circumstances. Tragedy, scandal and the rising power of Babe Ruth shook the great American pastime in 1920:

• Shortstop Ray Chapman of Cleveland was fatally beaned. He became the only player ever to die after being injured during a major-league game.

• The Chicago White Sox, one of three AL contenders,

were decimated just days before the season ended. Eight "Black Sox" were suspended when it was revealed that Chicago's loss of the 1919 World Series was fixed by gamblers.

• The Babe's arrival in New York transformed the other AL contender and the rest of baseball. For the Yankees, Ruth hit an unprecedented 54 home runs, pleasing fans at a time when his sport most needed a heroic lift.

The Indians, who shook off a slump in mid-August following the death of Chapman, battled down to the wire to win the pennant. Cleveland finished two games ahead of dissension-torn Chicago and three games ahead of New York.

Through most of the exciting race, Cleveland remained on top. The Indians first gained the lead more than briefly on May 9. Thereafter, they surrendered first place only for two days in May (to Boston), four days in July (to New York), ten days in August (to Chicago) and two days in September (to New York).

Did the "Black Sox" suspensions on September 28 deny the pennant to Chicago, which lost two of its last three games (vs. St. Louis)?

"I don't know whether we could have won or not," said ex-Cleveland catcher Steve O'Neill years later. "But we did stay in front of Chicago (nearly) all year, even when it was at full strength."

Three future Hall of Famers—Speaker, Stan Coveleski and Joe Sewell—played key roles in Cleveland. Known as the Gray Eagle, Speaker (8, 107, .388), the 32-year-old center fielder, was the only player-manager in baseball in 1920. His sensational pitching staff featured not only Coveleski (24-14, 2.48), but also Jim Bagby (31-12, 2.89) and Ray Caldwell (20-10, 3.86). And Sewell (0, 12, .329; in 22 games) was the rookie shortstop who replaced Chapman. Another late arrival from the minors was Duster Mails (7-0, 1.85), a left-hander.

Speaker was virtually the first major-league manager to platoon widely. Against right-handed pitching, he used Charlie Jamieson (1, 40, .319) in left field, Elmer Smith (12, 103, .316) in right and Doc Johnston (2, 71, .292) at first base. Against lefties, Speaker used Smokey Joe Wood (1, 30, .270) and Joe Evans (0, 23, .349) in the outfield, and George Burns (0, 13, .268) at first.

Along with Chapman (3, 49, .303), Cleveland's infielders also included third baseman Larry Gardner (3, 118, .310); and Bill Wambsganss (1, 55, .244), the second baseman known in the box scores as "Wamby." O'Neill (3, 55, .321) led the catching delegation.

The entire Tribe of 1920 hit only 35 home runs, not even two-thirds of Ruth's total. But Cleveland led the AL in runs (857), hitting the ball hard enough to take advantage of various developments. Trick pitches were banned, the spitball was being phased out and better yarn made the ball more lively.

The Chapman incident on August 17 also led to the use of cleaner baseballs. He was crowding the plate in the Polo Grounds and apparently failed to pick up a tight pitch by Yankee hurler Carl Mays, a submarine-style thrower. Mays was exonerated. Agreed Speaker: "There was time for Chappie to duck when the ball was coming at him, but he never moved." Chapman died the next day.

Speaker got much of the credit for rallying Cleveland to victory despite the tragedy. On October 2, the Indians clinched the AL pennant when they triumphed, 10-1, in Detroit as Bagby won his 31st game of the year.

In the World Series, Cleveland beat Brooklyn, five games to two. It was the last best-of-nine Series, and one of the most historic. Covaleski won three games. But Bagby's 8-1 victory in Game 5 in Cleveland was the most memorable contest. Elmer Smith hit the first grand slam in World Series history in the first inning. In the fifth, Wamby, at second base, pulled off an unassisted triple play. He caught Clarence Mitchell's line drive, stepped on second before Pete Kilduff could get back and tagged Otto Miller steaming in from first base.

It was considered an honest World Series, even though Cleveland was a hotbed of betting in those days. And it produced the kind of excitement needed to get the game of baseball back on the right track.

25

Detroit Tigers 1968

103-59

.636

DENNY MCLAIN (31-6, 1.96) TOPS "YEAR OF THE PITCHER" ♦ MICKEY LOLICH (17-9) BEATS CARDINALS IN GAMES 2, 5 AND 7 OF WORLD SERIES WILLIE HORTON (36, 85, .285) AND BILL FREEHAN (25, 84, .263) STAR ♦ AL KALINE HITS .287.

In the "Year of the Pitcher," Denny McLain was king of the hill. The brash, outspoken 24-year-old went 31-6 with a sizzling 1.96 earned run average. He led the Detroit Tigers to their first world championship since 1945.

The Tigers, who also earned their first pennant in 23 years, dominated the American League in 1968. They outdistanced the second-place team, Baltimore, by 12 games—the biggest AL winning margin in more than two decades. The New York Yankees of the 1950s and 1960s never finished so far ahead.

"Fantastic!" affirmed McLain on September 14 after beating the Oakland A's, 5-4, in Detroit for his 30th victory. He was the first such winner since Dizzy Dean of the St. Louis Cardinals went 30-7 in 1934. McLain tied Jim Bagby (31-12 with Cleveland in 1920) and Lefty Grove (31-4 with the Philadelphia A's in 1931) for the most wins in any season during the home-run era.

Pitchers controlled the major leagues in 1968. Batting averages plunged in both the American (.230) and National Leagues (.243). So did ERAs in both the AL (2.98) and NL (2.99). In '68, there was a total of 335 shutouts.

McLain reeled off five straight victories to begin the season. His fifth was a 12-1 triumph in Washington on May 10, when manager Mayo Smith's Tigers moved into first place to stay. McLain never let them stumble too far. Thirteen times the 6-foot-1 right-hander won games that followed losses by Detroit.

Known as a rebellious free-spirit, McLain, on the mound, was a classic pitcher. His high kick was matched by a flawless follow-through and superb control. He threw hard and tricky—fastballs, curves and sliders.

In 1968, McLain was the unanimous choice as the AL MVP and Cy Young Award winner. He completed 28 of his 41 starts. He struck out 280 batters in 336 innings and walked 63. Also, he pitched six shutouts. In one of his losses, the Tigers were shut out; in two, they scored one run; in two, they scored twice.

Next on the staff came Mickey Lolich (17-9, 3.19), a 27-year-old lefty who fanned 197 hitters. Right-handers Earl Wilson (13-12, 2.85) and Joe Sparma (10-10, 3.71) were the only other Detroit hurlers to win in double figures. Fred Lasher (5-1, 3.31; with five saves) was the most effective reliever.

The Tiger players who followed McLain in the AL MVP voting were (in order): catcher Bill Freehan (25, 84, .263); left fielder Willie Horton (36, 85, .285); second baseman Dick McAuliffe (16, 56, .249); right fielder Jim Northrup (21, 90, .264); first baseman Norm Cash (25, 63, .263); and center fielder Mickey Stanley (11, 60, .259).

Outfielder Al Kaline (10, 53, .287; in 102 games) was hurt in 1968, but he came back in the closing months to demonstrate his Hall of Fame talents.

The Tigers of '68 scored the most runs (671) in the

American League and gave up the fewest (492). They led the AL in home runs (185) and slugging (.385). They were tops in fielding (.983) and made the fewest errors (105).

"This bunch of kids has grown up into men," said Detroit owner John Fetzer of his hitters and pitchers, who averaged 28 years old in both categories. They wiped away the frustration of having finished one game behind the Boston Red Sox in "The Great Race" of 1967.

In 1968, it wasn't only pitching that made the Tigers fierce. About four in every ten runs they scored were due to homers. Detroit tallied the winning run in the seventh inning or later in a total of 40 games.

On August 27, Baltimore creeped to within four games of first place. But they lost two in a row before traveling to Detroit. The Tigers ended the AL race by winning two of the three games with the Orioles. In the third contest, McLain's 7-3 victory on September 1 pushed McLain's record to 27-5.

Detroit clinched the pennant on September 17 in dramatic fashion before 46,512 fans in nearly full Tiger Stadium. Don Wertz's bases-loaded single with two outs in the bottom of the ninth scored Kaline and beat New York, 2-1.

"These guys are the greatest," said Manager Mayo Smith.

The World Series of 1968 was billed as a showdown between McLain and St. Louis Cardinals ace Bob Gibson (22-9, 1.12; with 268 strikouts). Instead, Lolich became the star. He went the distance each time and won Games 2, 5 and 7. Gibson struck out a record 17 hitters as he earned a 4-0 victory (over McLain) in the opener. Next Detroit fell behind, three games to one. But the pitching of Lolich and McLain (who won Game 6) saved the day.

Never again would major-league teams reach the World Series without first surviving the playoffs. Both leagues expanded in 1969 from 10 to 12 teams, creating four division races and two championship series.

Thus, the Detroit Tigers of '68—the team of McLain, Lolich, Kaline and Horton—were the last of their kind. They were the last world champions to win the pennant during the regular season.

Pennant Winners

1. Cleveland Indians (1954) 111-43 .721

The winningest team in American League history lost the World Series in four straight games. Until October, the Cleveland Indians were the heroes of 1954. But the New York Giants (97-57, .630) stopped them cold.

No team since the beginning of the home-run era in 1920 has won as many games as the '54 Indians. Even so, Cleveland is seldom compared to the New York Yankees of 1927. The Tribe, which had been picked to finish third, suddenly exploded to win the AL pennant. Yet it has never reached the World Series since.

For nearly all of 1954, though, Cleveland was sensational.

"It had power, defense and great pitching," said ex-center fielder Larry Doby (32, 126, .272), one of Manager Al Lopez' stars. "We were a little short on team speed, but made up for that in timely hitting."

Doby, who led the AL in homers and RBIs, was supported by second baseman Bobby Avila (15, 67, .341), who led the league in hitting, and third baseman Al Rosen (24, 102, .300). First baseman Vic Wertz added 14 home runs.

The pitching was remarkable. It was led by Bob Lemon (23-7, 2.72), Early Wynn (23-11, 2.72), Mike Garcia (19-8, 2.64), Art Houtteman (15-7, 3.35) and Bob Feller (13-3, 3.09). In the bullpen were Hal Newhouser (7-2, 2.49; with 7 saves), Don Mossi (6-1, 1.94, 7 saves) and Ray Narleski (3-3, 2.22; 13 saves).

In the World Series, Willie Mays' famous catch in the Polo Grounds and key pinch hits by Dusty Rhodes won it all for Leo Durocher's Giants.

2. Philadelphia Athletics (1931) 107-45 .704

Connie Mack's dynasty was halted in 1931. These Athletics—led by AL MVP Lefty Grove (31-4, 2.05)—were being called Mack's best club ever. In the World Series, however, the St. Louis Cardinals triumphed, four games to three.

The '31 A's were virtually unchanged from Mack's two previous world champions. But the heavily favored Mackmen failed to get excited about facing the Cardinals (101-53, .656), a team they had easily beaten the year before.

It's been said that the '31 Athletics, a bust at the box office in the midst of the Depression, were gloomy about their salary outlook. And they knew tiny Sportsman's Park in St. Louis limited the size of World Series checks.

The Series belonged to Pepper Martin of the Cards. He batted .500 (12 for 24), with one homer, five RBIs, five runs and five steals. "What is he hitting?" asked Mack. "Everything we throw," replied pitcher George Earnshaw.

Along with Grove, "Moose" Earnshaw (21-7, 3.67) and Rube Walberg (20-12, 3.74) gave the Tall Tactician three 20-win aces in 1931. And Mickey Cochrane (17, 89, .349) had one of his finest seasons behind the plate.

Left fielder Al Simmons (22, 128, .390) and first baseman Jimmie Foxx (30, 120, .291) wielded big bats for the '31 A's. Center fielder Mule Haas (8, 56, .323) and right fielder Bing Miller (8, 77, .281) provided timely hitting.

But Philadelphia fell short in Connie Mack's final World Series.

3. Brooklyn Dodgers (1953) 105-49 .682

Were these the best "Boys of Summer"? Many thought so—until they were beaten in the World Series by the New York Yankees. Casey Stengel's Yanks (99-52, .656) won a historic fifth consecutive (1949-53) world championship.

To the Dodgers, it was a bitter defeat. Now Brooklyn had failed to surpass the Yankees in each of its five most recent World Series: in 1941, 1947, 1949, 1952 and 1953. "The Dodgers are the Dodgers," crowed Yankee Billy Martin. "If they had eight Babe Ruth's they couldn't beat us."

It was Martin who did much of the damage as the Yankees triumphed, four games to two. He collected a record 12 hits. Actually, Brooklyn (.300) outhit the Yanks (.279). But manager Chuck Dressen's Dodgers made seven errors.

In '53, Brooklyn was led by five .300 hitters: right fielder Carl Furillo (21, 92, .344), the NL batting champ; center fielder Duke Snider (42, 126, .336); left fielder Jackie Robinson (12, 95, .329); catcher Roy Campanella (41, 142, .312), the NL MVP; and first baseman Gil Hodges (31, 122, .302).

On the mound, Carl Erskine (20-6, 3.53) was the big winner. Next came two more right-handers: Russ Meyer (15-5, 4.57) and Billy Loes (14-8, 4.53). Erskine set a World Series record in game three by striking out 14 batters (one more than Philadelphia's Howard Ehmke fanned in 1929). But it just wasn't enough.

4. Boston Red Sox (1946) 104-50 .675

The Boston Red Sox reached the World Series in 1946 for the first time since selling Babe Ruth to the New York Yankees in 1920. Led by AL MVP Ted Williams (38, 123, .342), Boston finally won the pennant after finishing second to the Yanks in 1938, 1939, 1941 and 1942. But the World Series was disappointing.

The Bosox couldn't stop Enos "Country" Slaughter of the St. Louis Cardinals. He scored the winning run during game seven in St. Louis. With the score tied 3-3 in the bottom of the eighth inning, Slaughter, who had singled, raced all the way home on Harry Walker's two-out drive to left center field. Shortstop Johnny Pesky became the goat when he hesitated on the relay home.

In 1946, Pesky (2, 55, .335) was the only Boston regular to bat .300 besides Williams, who had returned to left field following World War II duty. But center fielder Dom DiMaggio (25, 95, .290), first baseman Rudy York (17, 119, .276) and second baseman Bobby Doerr (18, 116, .271) also hit well.

Manager Joe Cronin's pitching staff featured Boo Ferriss (25-6, 3.25), Tex Hughson (20-11, 2.75) and Mickey Harris (17-9, 3.63).

In the World Series, Williams was a bust. He hit .200 (five for 25) with no homers and just one RBI. But he was bothered by an elbow injury. His timing was off. And the Red Sox just couldn't make it all the way.

5. Baltimore Orioles (1969) 109-53 .673

It was one of the biggest upsets in the history of the World Series. The Baltimore Orioles, one of the strongest and best-balanced teams ever, were upset by the "Miracle" Mets (100-62, .617), the heroes of New York.

For manager Earl Weaver, Baltimore was beginning a string of American League titles. His pitching and defense led the AL in 1969. The top O's hurlers: left-handers Mike Cuellar (23-11, 2.38) and Dave McNally (20-7, 3.21), along with right-hander Jim Palmer (16-4, 3.24).

At bat, Baltimore relied most on the hitting of first baseman Boog Powell (37, 121, .304), right fielder Frank Robinson (32, 100, .308), center fielder Paul Blair (26, 76, .285) and left fielder Don Buford (11, 64, .291).

To open the World Series, the Orioles beat the Mets, 4-1, in Baltimore (Cuellar over Tom Seaver). But the New Yorkers won the next four in a row. Baltimore just couldn't overcome hot pitching by Jerry Koosman, great catches by Tommie Agee and Ron Swoboda—and that "Amazin'" Mets magic.

1

New York Yankees (1927)

Miller Huggins, Mgr.

BATTING	G by POS	B	AGE	G	AB	R	H	2B	3B	HR	RBI	BB	SO	SB	BA	SA
LOU GEHRIG	1B155	L	24	155	584	149	218	52	18	47	175	109	84	10	.373	.765
TONY LAZZERI	2B113, SS38, 3B9	R	23	153	570	92	176	29	8	18	102	69	82	22	.309	.482
MARK KOENIG	SS122	B	24	123	526	99	150	20	11	3	62	25	21	3	.285	.382
JOE DUGAN	3B111	R	30	112	387	44	104	24	3	2	43	27	37	1	.269	.362
BABE RUTH	OF151	L	32	151	540	158	192	29	8	60	164	138	89	7	.356	.772
EARL COMBS	OF152	L	28	152	648	137	231	36	23	6	64	62	31	15	.356	.511
BOB MEUSAL	OF131	R	30	135	516	75	174	47	9	8	103	45	58	24	.337	.510
PAT COLLINS	C89	R	30	92	251	38	69	9	3	7	36	54	24	0	.275	.418
RAY MOREHART	2B53	L	27	73	195	45	50	7	2	1	20	29	18	4	.256	.328
JOHNNY GRABOWSKI	C68	R	27	70	195	29	54	2	4	0	25	20	15	0	.277	.328
CEDRIC DURST	OF36, 1B2	L	30	65	129	18	32	4	3	0	25	6	7	0	.248	.326
MIKE GAZELLA	3B44, SS6	R	30	54	115	17	32	8	4	0	9	23	16	4	.278	.417
BEN PASCHAL	OF27	R	31	50	82	16	26	9	2	2	16	4	10	0	.317	.549
JULIE WERA	3B19	R	25	38	42	7	10	3	0	1	8	1	5	0	.239	.381
BENNY BENGOUGH	C30	R	28	31	85	6	21	3	3	0	10	4	4	0	.247	.353

PITCHING	T	AGE	W	L	PCT	SV	G	GS	CG	IP	H	BB	SO	ShO	ERA
WAITE HOYT	R	26	22	7	.759	1	36	32	23	256	242	54	86	3	2.64
WILCY MOORE	R	30	19	7	.731	13	50	12	6	213	185	59	75	1	2.28
HERB PENNOCK	L	33	19	8	.704	2	34	26	18	210	225	48	51	1	3.00
URBAN SHOCKER	R	36	18	6	.750	0	31	27	13	200	207	41	35	2	2.84
DUTCH RUETHER	L	33	13	6	.684	0	27	26	12	184	202	52	45	3	3.38
GEORGE PIPGRAS	R	27	10	3	.769	0	29	21	9	166	148	77	81	1	4.12
MYLES THOMAS	R	29	7	4	.636	0	21	9	1	89	111	43	25	0	4.85
BOB SHAWKEY	R	36	2	3	.400	4	19	2	0	44	44	16	23	0	2.86
JOE GIARD	L	28	0	0	.000	0	16	0	0	27	38	19	10	0	8.00
WALTER BEALL	R	27	0	0	.000	0	1	0	0	1	1	0	0	0	9.00

American League (1927)

							Batting						Pitching						Fielding		
	W	L	PCT	GB	R	OR	2B	3B	HR	BA	SA	SB	CG	BB	SO	ShO	SV	ERA	E	DP	FA
NY	110	44	.714		975	599	291	103	158	.307	.489	90	82	409	431	11	20	3.20	195	123	.969
PHI	91	63	.591	19	841	726	281	70	56	.303	.414	98	66	442	553	8	24	3.95	190	124	.970
WAS	85	69	.552	25	782	730	268	87	29	.287	.386	133	62	491	497	10	23	3.95	195	125	.969
DET	82	71	.536	27.5	845	805	282	100	51	.289	.409	141	75	577	421	5	17	4.12	206	173	.968
CHI	70	83	.458	39.5	662	708	285	61	36	.278	.378	90	85	440	365	10	8	3.91	178	131	.971
CLE	66	87	.431	43.5	668	766	321	52	26	.283	.379	63	72	508	366	5	8	4.27	201	146	.968
STL	59	94	.386	50.5	724	904	262	59	55	.276	.380	91	80	604	385	4	8	4.95	248	166	.960
BOS	51	103	.331	59	597	856	271	78	28	.259	.357	82	63	558	381	6	7	4.68	228	162	.964
					6094	6094	2261	610	439	.285	.399	788	585	4029	3339	59	115	4.12	1641	1150	.967

2

New York Yankees (1939)

JOE MCCARTHY, MGR.

BATTING	G by POS	B	AGE	G	AB	R	H	2B	3B	HR	RBI	BB	SO	SB	BA	SA
BABE DAHLGREN	1B144	R	27	144	531	71	125	18	6	15	89	57	54	2	.235	.377
JOE GORDON	2B151	R	24	151	567	92	161	32	5	28	111	75	57	11	.284	.506
FRANKIE CROSETTI	SS152	R	28	152	656	109	153	25	5	10	56	65	81	11	.233	.332
RED ROLFE	3B152	L	30	152	648	139	213	46	10	14	80	81	41	7	.329	.495
CHARLIE KELLER	OF105	L	22	111	398	87	133	21	6	11	83	81	49	6	.334	.500
JOE DIMAGGIO	OF117	R	24	120	462	108	176	32	6	30	126	52	20	3	.381	.671
GEORGE SELKIRK	OF124	L	31	128	418	103	128	17	4	21	101	103	49	12	.306	.517
BILL DICKEY	C126	L	32	128	480	98	145	23	3	24	105	77	37	5	.302	.513
TOMMY HENRICH	OF88, 1B1	L	26	99	347	64	96	18	4	9	57	51	23	7	.277	.429
RED RUFFING	P28	R	35	44	114	12	35	1	0	1	20	7	18	1	.307	.342
BUDDY ROSAR	C35	R	24	43	105	18	29	5	1	0	12	13	10	4	.276	.343
JAKE POWELL	OF23	R	30	31	86	12	21	4	1	1	9	3	8	1	.244	.349
JOE GALLAGHER	OF12	R	25	14	41	8	10	0	1	2	9	3	8	1	.244	.439
LOU GEHRIG	(IL) 1B8	L	36	8	28	2	4	0	0	0	1	5	1	0	.143	.143
BILL KNICKERBOCKER	2B2, SS2	R	27	6	13	2	2	1	0	0	1	0	0	0	.154	.231
ART JORGENS	C2	R	34	3	0	1	0	0	0	0	0	0	0	0	.000	.000

PITCHING	T	AGE	W	L	PCT	SV	G	GS	CG	IP	H	BB	SO	ShO	ERA
RED RUFFING	R	35	21	7	.750	0	28	28	22	233	211	75	95	5	2.94
ATLEY DONALD	R	28	13	3	.813	1	24	20	11	153	144	60	55	1	3.71
LEFTY GOMEZ	L	30	12	8	.600	0	26	26	14	198	173	84	102	2	3.41
BUMP HADLEY	R	34	12	6	.667	2	26	18	7	154	132	85	65	1	2.98
MONTE PEARSON	R	29	12	5	.706	0	22	20	8	146	151	70	76	0	4.50
STEVE SUNDRA	R	29	11	1	.917	0	24	11	8	121	110	56	27	1	2.75
ORAL HILDEBRAND	R	32	10	4	.714	2	21	15	7	127	102	41	50	1	3.05
MARIUS RUSSO	L	24	8	3	.727	2	21	11	9	116	86	41	55	2	2.41
SPUD CHANDLER (BL)	R	31	3	0	1.000	0	11	0	0	19	26	9	4	0	2.84
JOHHNY MURPHY	R	30	3	6	.333	19	38	0	0	61	57	28	30	0	4.43
WES FERRELL	R	31	1	2	.333	0	3	3	1	19	14	17	6	0	4.74
MARV BREUER	R	25	0	0	.000	0	1	0	0	1	2	1	0	0	9.00

American League (1939)

							Batting						Pitching						Fielding		
	W	L	PCT	GB	R	OR	2B	3B	HR	BA	SA	SB	CG	BB	SO	ShO	SV	ERA	E	DP	FA
NY	106	45	.702		967	556	259	55	166	.287	.451	72	87	567	565	12	26	3.31	126	159	.978
BOS	89	62	.589	17	890	795	287	57	124	.291	.436	42	52	543	539	4	20	4.56	180	147	.970
CLE	87	67	.565	20.5	797	700	291	79	85	.280	.413	72	69	602	614	9	13	4.08	180	148	.970
CHI	85	69	.552	22.5	755	737	220	56	64	.275	.374	113	62	454	535	5	21	4.31	167	140	.972
DET	81	73	.526	26.5	849	762	277	67	124	.279	.426	88	64	574	633	6	16	4.29	198	147	.967
WAS	65	87	.428	41.5	702	797	249	79	44	.278	.379	94	72	602	521	4	10	4.60	205	167	.966
PHI	55	97	.362	51.5	711	1022	282	55	98	.271	.400	60	50	579	397	5	12	5.79	210	131	.964
STL	43	111	.279	64.5	733	1035	242	50	91	.268	.381	48	56	739	516	3	3	6.01	199	144	.968
					6404	6404	2107	498	796	.279	.407	589	512	4660	4320	48	121	4.62	1465	1183	.969

3

New York Yankees (1932)

JOE McCARTHY, MGR.

BATTING	G by POS	B	AGE	G	AB	R	H	2B	3B	HR	RBI	BB	SO	SB	BA	SA
LOU GEHRIG	1B156	L	29	156	596	138	208	42	9	34	151	108	38	4	.349	.621
TONY LAZZERI	2B134, 3B5	R	28	142	510	79	153	28	16	15	113	82	64	11	.300	.506
FRANKIE CROSETTI	SS84, 3B33, 2B1	R	21	116	398	47	96	20	9	5	57	51	51	3	.241	.374
JOE SEWELL	3B123	L	33	125	503	95	137	21	3	11	68	56	3	0	.272	.392
BABE RUTH	OF128, 1B1	L	37	133	457	120	156	13	5	41	137	130	62	2	.341	.661
EARLE COMBS	OF139	L	33	144	591	143	190	32	10	9	65	81	16	3	.321	.455
BEN CHAPMAN	OF150	R	23	151	581	101	174	41	15	10	107	71	55	38	.299	.473
BILL DICKEY (SL)	C108	L	25	108	423	66	131	20	4	15	84	34	13	2	.310	.482
SAMMY BYRD	OF91	R	25	105	209	49	62	12	1	8	30	30	20	1	.297	.478
LYN LARY	SS80, 1B5, 2B2, 3B2, OF1	R	26	91	280	56	65	14	4	3	39	52	28	9	.232	.343
ART JORGENS	C56	R	27	56	151	13	33	7	1	2	19	14	11	0	.219	.318
RED RUFFING	P35	R	28	55	124	20	38	6	1	3	19	6	10	0	.306	.444
MYRIL HOAG	OF35, 1B1	R	24	46	54	18	20	5	0	1	7	7	13	1	.370	.519
DOC FARRELL	2B16, SS5, 1B2, 3B1	R	30	26	63	4	11	1	1	0	4	2	8	0	.175	.222
JACK SALTZGAVER	2B16	L	27	20	47	10	6	2	1	0	5	10	10	1	.128	.213
EDDIE PHILLIPS	C9	R	31	9	31	4	9	1	0	2	4	2	3	1	.290	.516
JOE GLENN	C5	R	23	6	16	0	2	0	0	0	0	1	0	5	.125	.125
DUSTY COOKE (BL)		L	25	3	0	1	0	0	0	0	0	1	0	0	.000	.000
ROY SCHALK	2B3	R	23	3	12	3	3	1	0	0	0	2	2	0	.250	.333

PITCHING	T	AGE	W	L	PCT	SV	G	GS	CG	IP	H	BB	SO	ShO	ERA
LEFTY GOMEZ	L	23	24	7	.774	1	37	31	21	265	266	105	176	1	4.21
RED RUFFING	R	28	18	7	.720	2	35	29	22	259	219	115	190	3	3.09
JOHNNY ALLEN	R	27	17	4	.810	4	33	21	13	192	162	76	109	3	3.70
GEORGE PIPGRAS	R	32	16	9	.640	0	32	27	14	219	235	87	111	2	4.19
HERB PENNOCK	L	38	9	5	.643	0	22	21	9	147	191	38	54	1	4.59
DANNY MACFAYDEN	R	27	7	5	.583	1	17	15	8	121	137	37	33	0	3.94
JUMBO BROWN	R	25	5	2	.714	1	19	3	3	56	58	30	31	1	4.50
ED WELLS	L	32	3	3	.500	2	22	0	0	32	38	12	13	0	4.22
WILCY MOORE	R	35	2	0	1.000	4	10	1	0	25	27	6	8	0	2.52
IVY ANDREWS	R	25	2	1	.667	0	4	1	1	25	20	9	7	0	1.80
HANK JOHNSON (VR)	R	26	2	2	.500	0	5	4	2	31	34	15	27	0	4.93
CHARLIE DEVENS	R	22	1	0	1.000	0	1	1	1	9	6	7	4	0	2.00
GORDON RHODES	R	24	1	2	.333	0	10	2	1	24	25	21	5	0	7.88
JOHNNY MURPHY	R	23	0	0	.000	0	2	0	0	3	7	3	2	0	18.00

American League (1932)

							Batting						Pitching						Fielding		
	W	L	PCT	GB	R	OR	2B	3B	HR	BA	SA	SB	CG	BB	SO	ShO	SV	ERA	E	DP	FA
NY	107	47	.695		1002	724	279	82	160	.286	.454	77	95	561	770	11	15	3.98	188	124	.969
PHI	94	60	.610	13	981	752	303	51	173	.290	.457	38	95	511	595	10	10	4.45	124	142	.979
WAS	93	61	.604	14	840	716	303	100	61	.284	.408	70	66	526	437	10	22	4.16	125	157	.979
CLE	87	65	.572	19	845	747	310	74	78	.285	.413	52	94	446	439	6	8	4.12	191	129	.969
DET	76	75	.503	29.5	799	787	291	80	80	.273	.401	103	67	592	521	9	17	4.30	187	154	.969
STL	63	91	.409	44	736	898	274	69	67	.276	.388	69	63	574	496	8	11	5.01	188	156	.969
CHI	49	102	.325	56.5	667	897	274	56	36	.267	.360	89	50	580	379	2	12	4.82	264	170	.958
BOS	43	111	.279	64	566	915	253	57	53	.251	.351	46	42	612	365	2	7	5.02	233	165	.963
					6436	6436	2287	569	708	.277	.404	544	572	4402	4002	58	102	4.48	1500	1197	.969

4

Philadelphia A's (1929)

Connie Mack, Mgr.

BATTING	G by POS	B	AGE	G	AB	R	H	2B	3B	HR	RBI	BB	SO	SB	BA	SA
FOXX	1B142, 3B7	R	21	149	517	123	183	23	9	33	117	103	70	9	.354	.625
MAX BISHOP	2B129	L	29	129	475	102	110	19	6	3	36	128	44	1	.232	.316
JOE BOLEY	SS88, 3B1	R	32	91	303	36	76	17	6	2	47	24	16	1	.251	.366
SAMMY HALE	3B99, 2B1	R	32	101	379	51	105	14	3	1	40	12	18	6	.277	.338
BING MILLER	OF145	R	34	147	556	84	186	32	16	8	93	40	25	24	.335	.493
MULE HAAS	OF139	L	25	139	578	115	181	41	9	16	82	34	38	0	.313	.498
AL SIMMONS	OF142	R	27	143	581	114	212	41	9	34	157	31	38	4	.365	.642
MICKEY COCHRANE	C135	L	26	135	514	113	170	37	8	7	95	69	8	7	.331	.475
JIMMY DYKES	SS60, 3B45, 2B12	R	32	119	401	76	131	34	6	13	79	51	25	8	.327	.539
WALT FRENCH	OF10	L	29	45	45	7	12	1	0	1	9	2	3	0	.267	.356
CY PERKINS	C38	R	33	38	76	4	16	4	0	0	9	5	4	0	.211	.263
HOMER SUMMA	OF24	L	30	37	81	12	22	4	0	0	10	2	1	1	.272	.321
OSSIE ORWOLL	P12, OF9	L	28	30	51	6	13	2	1	0	6	2	11	0	.255	.333
GEORGE BURNS	1B19	R	36	29	49	5	13	5	0	1	11	2	3	1	.265	.429
JIM CRONIN	2B10, SS9, 3B4	B	23	25	56	7	13	2	1	0	4	5	7	0	.232	.304
BEVO LEBOURVEAU	OF3	L	34	12	16	1	5	0	1	0	2	5	1	0	.313	.438
EDDIE COLLINS		L	42	9	7	0	0	0	0	0	0	2	0	0	.000	.000
BUD MORSE	2B8	L	24	8	27	1	2	0	0	0	0	0	2	0	.074	.074
JOE HASSLER	SS2	R	24	4	4	1	0	0	0	0	0	0	2	0	.000	.000
ERIC McNAIR	SS4	R	20	4	8	2	4	1	0	0	3	0	0	1	.500	.625
CLOY MATTOX	C3	L	26	3	6	0	1	0	0	0	0	1	1	0	.167	.167
DOC CRAMER	OF1	L	23	2	6	0	0	0	0	0	0	0	2	0	.000	.000
RUDY MILLER	3B2	R	28	2	4	1	1	0	0	0	1	3	0	0	.250	.250

PITCHING	T	AGE	W	L	PCT	SV	G	GS	CG	IP	H	BB	SO	ShO	ERA
GEORGE EARNSHAW	R	29	24	8	.750	1	44	33	13	255	233	125	149	2	3.28
LEFTY GROVE	L	29	20	6	.769	4	42	37	21	275	278	81	170	2	2.82
RUBE WALBERG	L	32	18	11	.621	4	40	33	20	268	256	99	94	3	3.59
EDDIE ROMMEL	R	31	12	2	.857	4	32	6	4	114	135	34	25	0	2.84
JACK QUINN	R	45	11	9	.550	2	35	18	7	161	182	39	41	0	3.97
BILL SHORES	R	25	11	6	.647	7	39	13	5	153	150	59	49	1	3.59
HOWARD EHMKE	R	35	7	2	.778	0	11	8	2	55	48	15	20	0	3.27
CARROLL YERKES	L	26	1	0	1.000	1	19	2	0	37	47	13	11	0	4.62
BILL BRECKINRIDGE	R	23	0	0	.000	0	3	1	0	10	10	16	2	0	8.10
OSSIE ORWOLL	L	28	0	2	.000	1	12	0	0	30	32	6	12	0	4.80

American League (1929)

							Batting						Pitching						Fielding		
	W	L	PCT	GB	R	OR	2B	3B	HR	BA	SA	SB	CG	BB	SO	ShO	SV	ERA	E	DP	FA
PHI	104	46	.693		901	615	288	76	122	.296	.451	61	72	487	573	8	24	3.44	146	117	.975
NY	88	66	.571	18	899	775	262	74	142	.295	.450	51	64	485	484	12	18	4.17	178	152	.971
CLE	81	71	.533	24	717	736	294	79	62	.294	.417	75	80	488	389	8	10	4.05	198	162	.968
STL	79	73	.520	26	733	713	276	63	46	.276	.380	72	83	462	415	15	10	4.08	156	148	.975
WAS	71	81	.467	34	730	776	244	66	48	.276	.375	86	61	496	494	3	17	4.34	195	156	.968
DET	70	84	.455	36	926	928	339	97	110	.299	.453	95	82	646	467	5	9	4.96	242	149	.961
CHI	59	93	.388	46	627	792	240	74	37	.268	.363	106	78	505	328	5	7	4.41	188	153	.970
BOS	58	96	.377	48	605	803	285	69	28	.267	.365	85	84	496	416	9	5	4.43	218	159	.965
					6138	6138	2228	598	595	.284	.407	631	604	4065	3566	65	100	4.24	1521	1196	.969

5

St. Louis Cardinals (1942)

Billy Southworth, Mgr.

BATTING	G by POS	B	AGE	G	AB	R	H	2B	3B	HR	RBI	BB	SO	SB	BA	SA
JOHNNY HOPP	1B88	L	25	95	314	41	81	16	7	3	37	36	40	14	.258	.382
CREEPY CRESPI	2B83, SS5	R	24	93	292	33	71	4	2	0	35	27	29	4	.243	.271
MARTY MARION	SS147	R	24	147	485	66	134	38	5	0	54	48	50	8	.276	.375
WHITEY KUROWSKI	3B104, SS1, OF1	R	24	115	366	51	93	17	3	9	42	33	60	7	.254	.391
ENOS SLAUGHTER	OF151	L	26	152	591	100	188	31	17	13	98	88	30	9	.318	.494
TERRY MOORE	OF126, 3B1	R	30	130	489	80	141	26	3	6	49	56	26	10	.288	.391
STAN MUSIAL	OF135	L	21	140	467	87	147	32	10	10	72	62	25	6	.315	.490
WALKER COOPER	C115	R	27	125	438	58	123	32	7	7	65	29	29	4	.281	.434
JIMMY BROWN	2B82, 3B66, SS12	B	32	145	606	75	155	28	4	1	71	52	11	4	.256	.320
RAY SANDERS	1B77	L	25	95	282	37	71	17	2	5	39	42	31	2	.252	.379
HARRY WALKER	OF56, 2B2	L	25	74	191	38	60	12	2	0	16	11	14	2	.314	.398
COAKER TRIPLETT	OF46	R	30	64	154	18	42	7	4	1	23	17	15	1	.273	.390
KEN O'DEA	C49	L	29	58	192	22	45	7	1	5	32	17	23	0	.234	.359
BUDDY BLATTNER	SS13, 2B3	R	22	19	23	3	1	0	0	0	1	3	6	0	.043	.043
ERV DUSAK	OF8, 3B1	R	21	12	27	4	5	3	0	0	3	3	7	0	.185	.296
SAM NARRON	C2	R	28	10	10	0	4	0	0	0	1	0	0	0	.400	.400
ESTEL CRABTREE		L	38	10	9	1	3	2	0	0	2	1	3	0	.333	.556
GUS MANCUSO	C3	R	36	5	13	0	1	0	0	0	1	0	0	0	.077	.077
JEFF CROSS	SS1	R	23	1	4	0	1	0	0	0	1	0	0	0	.250	.250

PITCHING	T	AGE	W	L	PCT	SV	G	GS	CG	IP	H	BB	SO	ShO	ERA
MORT COOPER	R	29	22	7	.759	0	37	35	22	279	207	68	152	10	1.77
JOHNNY BEAZLEY	R	24	21	6	.778	3	43	23	13	215	181	73	91	3	2.14
HOWIE KRIST	R	26	13	3	.813	1	34	8	3	118	103	43	47	0	2.52
MAX LANIER	L	26	13	8	.619	2	34	20	8	161	137	60	93	2	2.96
HARRY GUMBERT	R	32	9	5	.643	5	38	19	5	163	156	59	52	0	3.26
HOWIE POLLET	L	21	7	5	.583	0	27	13	5	109	102	39	42	2	2.89
ERNIE WHITE (SA)	L	25	7	5	.583	2	26	19	7	128	113	41	67	1	2.53
MURRY DICKSON	R	25	6	3	.667	2	36	7	2	121	91	61	66	0	2.90
LON WARNEKE	R	33	6	4	.600	0	12	12	5	82	76	15	31	0	3.29
BILL BECKMANN	R	34	1	0	1.000	0	2	0	0	7	4	1	3	0	0.00
BILL LOHRMAN	R	29	1	1	.500	0	5	0	0	13	11	2	6	0	1.39
WHITEY MOORE	R	30	0	1	.000	0	9	0	0	12	10	11	1	0	4.50
CLYDE SHOUN	L	30	0	0	.000	0	2	0	0	2	1	0	0	0	0.00

National League (1942)

							Batting						Pitching						Fielding		
	W	L	PCT	GB	R	OR	2B	3B	HR	BA	SA	SB	CG	BB	SO	ShO	SV	ERA	E	DP	FA
STL	106	48	.688		755	482	282	69	60	.268	.379	71	70	473	651	18	15	2.55	169	137	.972
BKN	104	50	.675	2	742	510	263	34	62	.265	.362	79	67	493	612	16	24	2.84	138	150	.977
NY	85	67	.559	20	675	600	162	35	109	.254	.361	39	70	493	497	12	13	3.31	138	128	.977
CIN	76	76	.500	29	527	545	198	39	66	.231	.321	42	80	526	616	12	8	2.82	177	158	.971
PIT	66	81	.449	36.5	585	631	173	49	54	.245	.330	41	64	435	426	13	11	3.58	184	129	.969
CHI	68	86	.442	38	591	665	224	41	75	.254	.353	61	71	525	507	10	14	3.60	170	169	.973
BOS	59	89	.399	44	515	645	210	19	68	.240	.329	49	68	518	414	9	8	3.76	142	138	.976
PHI	42	109	.278	62.5	394	706	168	37	44	.232	.306	37	51	605	472	2	6	4.12	194	147	.968
					4784	4784	1680	323	538	.249	.343	419	541	4068	4195	92	99	3.31	1312	1156	.973

6

New York Yankees (1961)

RALPH HOUK, MGR.

BATTING	G by POS	B	AGE	G	AB	R	H	2B	3B	HR	RBI	BB	SO	SB	BA	SA
BILL SKOWRON	1B149	R	30	150	561	76	150	23	4	28	89	35	108	0	.267	.472
BOBBY RICHARDSON	2B161	R	25	162	662	80	173	17	5	3	49	30	23	9	.261	.316
TONY KUBEK	SS145	L	24	153	617	84	170	38	6	8	46	27	60	1	.276	.395
CLETE BOYER	3B141, SS12, OF1	R	24	148	504	61	113	19	5	11	55	63	83	1	.224	.347
ROGER MARIS	OF160	L	26	161	590	132	159	16	4	61	142	94	67	0	.269	.620
MICKEY MANTLE	OF150	B	29	153	514	132	163	16	6	54	128	126	112	12	.317	.687
YOGI BERRA	OF87, C15	L	36	119	395	62	107	11	0	22	61	35	28	2	.271	.466
ELSTON HOWARD	C111, 1B9	R	32	129	446	64	155	17	5	21	77	28	65	0	.348	.549
HECTOR LOPEZ	OF72	R	28	93	243	27	54	7	2	3	22	24	38	1	.222	.305
JOHNNY BLANCHARD	C48, OF15	L	28	93	243	38	74	10	1	21	54	27	28	1	.305	.613
BOB CERV	OF30, 1B3	R	35	57	118	17	32	5	1	6	20	12	17	1	.271	.483
BILLY GARDNER	3B33, 2B6	R	33	41	99	11	21	5	0	1	2	6	18	0	.212	.293
JOE DEMAESTRI	SS18, 2B5, 3B4	R	32	30	41	1	6	0	0	0	2	0	13	0	.146	.146
JACK REED	OF27	R	28	28	13	4	2	0	0	0	1	1	1	0	.154	.154
EARL TORGESON	1B8	L	37	22	18	3	2	0	0	0	0	8	3	0	.111	.111
JESSE GONDER		L	25	15	12	2	4	1	0	0	3	3	1	0	.333	.417
DERON JOHNSON	3B8	R	22	13	19	1	2	0	0	0	2	2	5	0	.105	.105
BOB HALE	1B5	L	27	11	13	2	2	0	0	1	1	0	0	0	.154	.385

PITCHING	T	AGE	W	L	PCT	SV	G	GS	CG	IP	H	BB	SO	ShO	ERA
WHITEY FORD	L	32	25	4	.862	0	39	39	11	283	242	92	209	3	3.21
RALPH TERRY	R	25	16	3	.842	0	31	27	9	188	162	42	86	2	3.16
LUIS ARROYO	L	34	15	5	.750	29	65	0	0	119	83	49	87	0	2.19
BILL STAFFORD	R	21	14	9	.609	2	36	25	8	195	168	59	101	3	2.68
JIM COATES	R	28	11	5	.688	5	43	11	4	141	128	53	80	1	3.45
ROLLIE SHELDON	R	24	11	5	.688	0	35	21	6	163	149	55	84	2	3.59
BUD DALEY	L	28	8	9	.471	0	23	17	7	130	127	51	83	0	3.95
BOB TURLEY (SA)	R	30	3	5	.375	0	15	12	1	72	74	51	48	0	5.75
HAL RENIFF	R	22	2	0	1.000	2	25	0	0	45	31	31	21	0	2.60
ART DITMAR	R	32	2	3	.400	0	12	8	1	54	59	14	24	0	4.67
TEX CLEVENGER	R	28	1	1	.500	0	21	0	0	32	35	21	14	0	4.78
DANNY MCDEVITT	L	28	1	2	.333	1	8	2	0	13	18	8	8	0	7.62
AL DOWNING	L	20	0	1	.000	0	5	1	0	9	7	12	12	0	8.00
RYNE DUREN	R	32	0	1	.000	0	4	0	0	5	2	4	7	0	5.40
JOHNNY JAMES	R	27	0	0	.000	0	1	0	0	1	1	0	2	0	0.00
DUKE MAAS	R	32	0	0	.000	0	1	0	0	0	2	0	0	0	0.00

American League (1961)

							Batting						Pitching						Fielding		
	W	L	PCT	GB	R	OR	2B	3B	HR	BA	SA	SB	CG	BB	SO	ShO	SV	ERA	E	DP	FA
NY	109	53	.673		827	612	194	40	240	.263	.442	28	47	542	866	14	39	3.46	124	180	.980
DET	101	61	.623	8	841	671	215	53	180	.266	.421	98	62	469	836	12	30	3.55	146	147	.976
BAL	95	67	.586	14	691	588	227	36	149	.254	.390	39	54	617	926	21	33	3.22	128	173	.980
CHI	86	76	.531	23	765	726	216	46	138	.265	.395	100	39	498	814	3	33	4.06	128	138	.980
CLE	78	83	.484	30.5	737	752	257	39	150	.266	.406	34	35	599	801	12	23	4.15	139	142	.977
BOS	76	86	.469	33	729	792	251	37	112	.254	.374	56	35	679	831	6	30	4.29	144	170	.977
MIN	70	90	.438	38	707	778	215	40	167	.250	.397	47	49	570	914	14	23	4.28	174	150	.972
LA	70	91	.435	38.5	744	784	218	22	189	.245	.398	37	25	713	973	5	34	4.31	192	154	.969
KC	61	100	.379	47.5	683	863	216	47	90	.247	.354	58	32	629	703	5	23	4.74	175	160	.972
WAS	61	100	.379	47.5	618	776	217	44	119	.244	.367	81	39	586	666	8	21	4.23	156	171	.975
					7342	7342	2226	404	1534	.256	.395	578	417	5902	8330	100	289	4.02	1506	1585	.969

7

New York Mets (1986)

Dave Johnson, Mgr.

BATTING	G by POS	B	AGE	G	AB	R	H	2B	3B	HR	RBI	BB	SO	SB	BA	SA
KEITH HERNANDEZ	1B149	L	32	149	551	94	171	34	1	13	83	94	69	2	310	.446
WALLY BACKMAN	2B113	B	26	124	387	67	124	18	2	1	27	36	32	13	.320	.385
RAFAEL SANTANA	SS137 2B1	R	28	139	394	38	86	11	0	1	28	36	43	0	.218	.254
RAY KNIGHT	3B132 1B1	R	33	137	486	51	145	24	2	11	76	40	63	2	.298	.424
DARRYL STRAWBERRY	OF131	L	24	136	475	76	123	27	5	27	93	72	141	28	.259	.507
LEN DYKSTRA	OF139	L	23	147	431	77	127	27	7	8	45	58	55	31	.295	.445
MOOKIE WILSON (SJ-IJ)	OF114	B	30	123	381	61	110	17	5	9	45	32	72	25	.289	.430
GARY CARTER	C122 1B9 OF4 381	R	32	132	490	81	125	14	2	24	105	62	63	1	.255	.439
KEVIN MITCHELL	OF68 SS24 387 1B2	R	24	106	328	51	91	22	2	12	43	33	61	3	.277	.466
TIM TEUFEL	2B84 1B3 3B1	R	27	93	279	35	69	20	1	4	31	32	42	1	.247	.369
HOWARD JOHNSON	3B45 SS34 OF1	B	25	88	220	30	54	14	0	10	39	31	64	8	.245	.445
DANNY HEEP	OF56	L	28	86	195	24	55	8	2	5	33	30	31	1	.282	.421
GEORGE FOSTER	OF62	R	37	72	233	28	53	6	1	13	38	21	53	1	.227	.429
ED HEARN	C45	R	25	49	136	16	36	5	0	4	10	12	19	0	.265	.390
LEE MAZZILLI	OF10 1B8	B	31	39	58	10	16	3	0	2	7	12	11	1	.276	.431
KEVIN ELSTER	SS19	R	21	19	30	3	5	1	0	0	0	3	8	0	.167	.200
STAN JEFFERSON	OF7	B	23	14	24	6	5	1	0	1	3	2	8	0	.206	.375
DAVE MAGADAN	1B9	L	23	10	18	3	8	0	0	0	3	3	1	0	.444	.444
JOHN GIBBONS	C8	R	24	8	19	4	9	4	0	1	1	3	5	0	.474	.842
BARRY LYONS	C3	R	26	6	9	1	0	0	0	0	2	1	2	0	.000	.000
TIM CORCORAN	1B1	L	33	6	7	1	0	0	0	0	0	2	0	0	.000	.000

PITCHING	T	AGE	W	L	PCT	SV	G	GS	CG	IP	H	BB	SO	ShO	ERA
BOB OJEDA	L	28	18	5	.783	0	32	30	7	217	185	52	148	2	2.57
DWIGHT GOODEN	R	21	17	6	.739	0	33	33	12	250	197	80	200	2	2.84
SID FERNANDEZ	L	23	16	6	.727	1	32	31	2	204	161	91	200	1	3.52
RON DARLING	R	25	15	6	.714	0	34	34	4	237	203	81	184	2	2.81
ROGER MCDOWELL	R	25	14	9	.609	22	75	0	0	128	107	42	65	0	3.02
RICK AGUILERA	R	24	10	7	.588	0	28	20	2	142	145	36	104	0	3.88
JESSE OROSCO	L	29	8	6	.571	21	58	0	0	81	64	35	62	0	2.33
DOUG SISK	R	28	4	2	.667	1	41	0	0	71	77	31	31	0	3.06
RICK ANDERSON	R	29	2	1	.667	1	15	5	0	50	45	11	21	0	2.72
BRUCE BERENYI	R	31	2	2	.500	0	14	7	0	40	47	22	30	0	6.35
RANDY NIEMANN	L	30	2	3	.400	0	31	1	0	36	44	12	18	0	3.79
RANDY MYERS	L	23	0	0	--	0	10	0	0	11	11	9	13	0	4.22
ED LYNCH (KJ)	R	30	0	0	--	0	1	0	0	2	2	0	1	0	0.00
TERRY LEACH	R	32	0	0	--	0	6	0	0	7	6	3	4	0	2.70
JOHN MITCHELL	R	20	0	1	.000	0	4	1	0	10	10	4	2	0	3.60

National League (1986)

	W	L	PCT	GB	R	OR	Batting 2B	3B	HR	BA	SA	SB	Pitching CG	BB	SO	ShO	SV	ERA	Fielding E	DP	FA
EAST																					
NY	108	54	.667		783	578	261	31	148	.263	.401	118	27	509	1083	11	46	3.11	138	145	.978
PHI	86	75	.534	21.5	739	713	266	39	154	.253	.400	153	22	553	874	11	39	3.85	137	157	.978
STL	79	82	.491	28.5	601	611	216	48	58	.236	.327	262	17	485	761	4	46	3.37	123	178	.981
MON	78	83	.484	29.5	637	688	255	50	110	.254	.379	193	15	566	1051	9	50	3.78	133	132	.979
CHI	70	90	.438	37	680	781	257	27	155	.256	.397	132	11	557	962	6	42	4.49	124	147	.980
PIT	64	98	.395	44	663	700	273	33	111	.250	.374	152	17	570	924	9	30	3.90	143	134	.978

8

Cincinnati Reds (1975)

SPARKY ANDERSON, MGR.

BATTING	G by POS	B	AGE	G	AB	R	H	2B	3B	HR	RBI	BB	SO	SB	BA	SA
TONY PEREZ	1B132	R	33	137	511	74	144	28	3	20	109	54	101	1	.282	.466
JOE MORGAN	2B142	L	31	146	498	107	163	27	6	17	94	132	52	67	.327	.508
DAVE CONCEPCION	SS130, 3B6	R	27	140	507	62	139	23	1	5	49	39	51	33	.274	.353
PETE ROSE	3B137, OF35	B	34	162	662	112	210	47	4	7	74	89	50	0	.317	.432
KEN GRIFFEY	OF119	L	25	132	463	95	141	15	9	4	46	67	67	16	.305	.402
CESAR GERONIMO	OF148	L	27	148	501	69	129	25	5	6	53	48	97	13	.257	.363
GEORGE FOSTER	OF125, 1B1	R	26	134	463	71	139	24	4	23	78	40	73	2	.300	.518
JOHNNY BENCH	C121, OF19,1B9	R	27	142	530	83	150	39	1	28	110	65	108	11	.283	.519
MERV RETTENMUND	OF61, 3B1	R	32	93	188	24	45	6	1	2	19	35	22	5	.239	.314
DOUG FLYNN	3B40, 2B30, SS17	R	24	89	127	17	34	7	0	1	20	11	13	3	.268	.346
DAN DRIESSEN	1B41, OF29	L	23	88	210	38	59	8	1	7	38	35	30	10	.281	.429
DARREL CHANEY	SS34, 2B23, 3B13	L	27	71	160	18	35	6	0	2	26	14	38	3	.219	.294
TERRY CROWLEY	OF4,1B4	L	28	66	71	8	19	6	0	1	11	7	6	0	.268	.394
BILL PLUMMER	C63	R	28	65	159	17	29	7	0	1	19	24	28	1	.182	.245
ED ARMBRISTER	OF19	R	26	59	65	9	12	1	0	0	2	5	19	3	.185	.200
JOHN VUKOVICH	3B31	R	27	31	38	4	8	3	0	0	2	4	5	0	.211	.289
DON WERNER	C7	R	22	7	8	0	1	0	0	0	0	0	0	0	.125	.125

PITCHING	T	AGE	W	L	PCT	SV	G	GS	CG	IP	H	BB	SO	ShO	ERA
DON GULLETT (BG)	L	24	15	4	.789	0	22	22	8	160	127	56	98	3	2.42
GARY NOLAN	R	27	15	9	.625	0	32	32	5	211	202	29	74	1	3.16
JACK BILLINGHAM	R	32	15	10	.600	0	33	32	5	208	222	76	79	0	4.11
FRED NORMAN	L	32	12	4	.750	0	34	26	2	188	163	84	119	0	3.73
PAT DARCY	R	25	11	5	.688	1	27	22	1	131	134	59	46	0	3.57
CLAY KIRBY	R	27	10	6	.625	0	26	19	1	111	113	54	48	0	4.70
PEDRO BORBON	R	28	9	5	.643	5	67	0	0	125	145	21	29	0	2.95
CLAY CARROLL	R	34	7	5	.583	7	56	2	0	96	93	32	44	0	2.63
WILL MCENANEY	L	23	5	2	.714	15	70	0	0	91	92	23	48	0	2.47
RAWLY EASTWICK	R	24	5	3	.625	22	58	0	0	90	77	25	61	0	2.60
TOM CARROLL	R	22	4	1	.800	0	12	7	0	47	52	26	14	0	4.98
TOM HALL	L	27	0	0	–	0	2	0	0	2	2	2	3	0	0.00

National League (1975)

							Batting						Pitching						Fielding		
	W	L	PCT	GB	R	OR	2B	3B	HR	BA	SA	SB	CG	BB	SO	ShO	SV	ERA	E	DP	FA
WEST																					
CIN	108	54	.667		840	586	278	37	124	.271	.401	168	22	487	663	8	50	3.37	102	173	.984
LA	88	74	.543	20	648	534	217	31	118	.248	.365	138	51	448	894	18	21	2.92	127	106	.979
SF	80	81	.497	27.5	659	671	235	45	84	.259	.365	99	37	612	856	9	24	3.74	146	164	.976
SD	71	91	.438	37	552	683	215	22	78	.244	.335	85	40	521	713	12	20	3.51	188	163	.971
ATL	67	94	.416	40.5	583	739	179	28	107	.244	.346	55	32	519	669	4	25	3.93	175	147	.972
HOU	64	97	.398	43.5	664	711	218	54	84	.254	.359	133	39	679	839	6	25	4.05	137	166	.979

9

Baltimore Orioles (1970)

Earl Weaver, Mgr.

BATTING	G by POS	B	AGE	G	AB	R	H	2B	3B	HR	RBI	BB	SO	SB	BA	SA
BOOG POWELL	1B145	L	28	154	526	82	156	28	0	35	114	104	80	1	.297	.549
DAVE JOHNSON	2B149, SS2	R	27	149	530	68	149	27	1	10	53	66	68	2	.281	.392
MARK BELANGER	SS143	R	26	145	459	53	100	6	5	1	36	52	65	13	.218	.259
BROOKS ROBINSON	3B156	R	33	158	608	84	168	31	4	18	94	53	53	1	.276	.429
FRANK ROBINSON	OF210, 1B7	R	34	132	471	88	144	24	1	25	78	69	70	2	.306	.520
PAUL BLAIR	(BC) OF128, 3B1	R	26	133	480	79	128	24	2	18	65	56	93	24	.267	.438
DON BUFORD	OF130, 2B3, 3B3	B	33	144	504	99	137	15	2	17	66	109	55	16	.272	.411
ELLIE HENDRICKS	C95	L	29	106	322	32	78	9	0	12	41	33	44	1	.242	.382
MARV RETTENMUND	OF93	R	27	106	338	60	109	17	2	18	58	38	59	13	.322	.544
TERRY CROWLEY	OF27, 1B23	L	23	83	152	25	39	5	0	5	20	35	26	2	.257	.388
ANDY ETCHEBARREN	C76	R	27	78	230	19	56	10	1	4	28	21	41	4	.243	.348
CHICO SALMON	SS33, 2B12, 3B11, 1B2	R	29	63	172	19	43	4	0	7	22	8	30	2	.250	.395
CURT MOTTON	OF21	R	29	52	84	16	19	3	1	3	19	18	20	1	.226	.393
DAVE MAY	OF9	L	26	25	31	6	6	0	1	1	6	4	4	0	.194	.355
CLAY DAIRYMPLE (BN)	C11	L	33	13	32	4	7	1	0	1	3	7	4	0	.219	.344
BOBBY GRICH	SS20, 2B9, 3B1	R	21	30	95	11	20	1	3	0	8	9	21	1	.211	.284
DON BAYLOR	OF6	R	21	8	17	4	4	0	0	0	4	2	3	1	.235	.235
JOHNNY OATES	C4	L	24	5	18	2	5	0	1	0	2	2	0	0	.278	.389
BOBBY FLOYD	SS2, 2B1	R	26	3	2	0	0	0	0	0	0	0	2	0	.000	.000
ROGER FREED	1B3, OF1	R	24	4	13	0	2	0	0	0	1	3	4	0	.154	.154

PITCHING	T	AGE	W	L	PCT	SV	G	GS	CG	IP	H	BB	SO	ShO	ERA
MIKE CUELLAR	L	33	24	8	.750	0	40	40	21	298	273	69	190	4	3.47
DAVE MCNALLY	L	27	24	9	.727	0	40	40	16	296	277	78	185	1	3.22
JIM PALMER	R	24	20	10	.667	0	39	39	17	305	263	100	199	5	2.71
DICK HALL	R	39	10	5	.667	3	32	0	0	61	51	6	30	0	3.10
PETE RICHERT	L	30	7	2	.778	13	50	0	0	55	36	24	66	0	1.96
EDDIE WATT	R	28	7	7	.500	12	53	0	0	55	44	29	33	0	3.27
JIM HARDIN	R	26	6	5	.545	1	36	19	3	145	150	26	78	2	3.54
TOM PHOEBUS	R	25	5	5	.500	0	27	21	3	135	106	62	72	0	3.07
MOE DRABOWSKY	R	34	4	2	.667	1	21	0	0	33	30	15	21	0	3.82
MARCELINO LOPEZ	L	26	1	1	.500	0	25	3	0	61	47	37	49	0	2.07
FRED BEENE	R	27	0	0	.000	0	4	0	0	6	8	5	4	0	6.00
DAVE LEONHARD	R	28	0	0	.000	1	23	0	0	28	32	18	14	0	5.14

American League (1970)

							Batting						Pitching						Fielding		
	W	L	PCT	GB	R	OR	2B	3B	HR	BA	SA	SB	CG	BB	SO	ShO	SV	ERA	E	DP	FA
EAST																					
BAL	108	54	.667		792	574	213	25	179	.257	.401	84	60	469	941	12	31	3.15	117	148	.981
NY	93	69	.574	15	680	612	208	41	111	.251	.365	105	36	451	777	6	49	3.25	130	146	.980
BOS	87	75	.537	21	786	722	252	28	203	.262	.428	50	38	594	1003	8	44	3.90	156	131	.974
DET	79	83	.488	29	666	731	207	38	148	.238	.374	29	33	623	1045	9	39	4.09	133	142	.978
CLE	76	86	.469	32	649	675	197	23	183	.249	.394	25	34	689	1076	8	35	3.91	133	168	.979
WAS	70	92	.432	38	626	689	184	28	138	.238	.358	72	20	611	823	11	40	3.80	116	173	.982

10

New York Yankees (1936)

JOE MCCARTHY, MGR.

BATTING	G by POS	B	AGE	G	AB	R	H	2B	3B	HR	RBI	BB	SO	SB	BA	SA
LOU GEHRIG	1B155	L	33	155	579	167	205	37	7	49	152	130	46	3	.354	.696
TONY LAZZERI	2B148, SS2	R	32	150	537	82	154	29	6	14	109	97	65	8	.287	.441
FRANKIE CROSETTI	SS151	R	25	151	632	137	182	35	7	15	78	90	83	18	.288	.437
RED ROLFE	3B133	L	27	135	568	116	181	39	15	10	70	68	38	3	.319	.493
GEORGE SELKIRK	OF135	L	28	137	493	93	152	28	9	18	107	94	60	13	.308	.511
JAKE POWELL	OF84	R	27	87	324	62	99	13	3	7	48	33	30	16	.306	.429
JOE DIMAGGIO	OF138	R	21	138	637	132	206	44	15	29	125	24	39	4	.323	.576
BILL DICKEY	C107	L	29	112	423	99	153	26	8	22	107	46	16	0	.362	.617
ROY JOHNSON	OF33	L	33	63	147	21	39	8	2	1	19	21	14	3	.265	.367
RED RUFFING	P33	R	32	53	127	14	37	5	0	5	22	11	12	0	.291	.449
MYRIL HOAG(YJ)	OF39	R	28	45	156	23	47	9	4	3	34	7	16	3	.301	.468
JOE GLENN	C44	R	27	44	129	21	35	7	0	1	20	20	10	1	.271	.349
BEN CHAPMAN	OF36	R	27	36	139	19	37	14	3	1	21	15	20	1	.266	.432
JACK SALTZGAVER	3B16, 2B6, 1B4	L	31	34	90	14	19	5	0	1	13	13	18	0	.211	.300
MONTE PEARSON	P33	R	26	33	91	12	23	4	0	1	20	8	13	0	.253	.330
ART JORGENS	C30	R	31	31	66	5	18	3	1	0	5	2	3	0	.273	.348
DON HEFFNER	3B8, 2B5, SS3	R	25	19	48	7	11	2	1	0	6	6	5	0	.229	.313
BOB SEEDS	OF9, 3B3	R	29	13	42	12	11	1	0	4	10	5	3	3	.262	.571
DIXIE WALKER	OF5	L	25	6	20	3	7	0	2	1	5	1	3	1	.350	.700

PITCHING	T	AGE	W	L	PCT	SV	G	GS	CG	IP	H	BB	SO	ShO	ERA
RED RUFFING	R	32	20	12	.625	0	33	33	25	271	274	90	102	3	3.85
MONTE PEARSON	R	26	19	7	.731	1	33	31	15	223	191	135	118	1	3.71
BUMP HADLEY	R	31	14	4	.778	1	31	17	8	174	194	89	74	1	4.34
LEFTY GOMEZ	L	27	13	7	.650	0	31	30	10	189	184	122	105	0	4.38
JOHNNY BROACA	R	26	12	7	.632	3	37	27	12	206	235	66	84	1	4.24
PAT MALONE	R	33	12	4	.750	9	35	9	5	135	144	60	72	0	3.80
JOHNNY MURPHY (JJ)	R	27	9	3	.750	5	27	5	2	88	90	36	34	0	3.38
JUMBO BROWN	R	29	1	4	.200	1	20	3	0	64	93	29	19	0	5.91
TED KLEINHANS	L	37	1	1	.500	1	19	0	0	29	36	23	10	0	5.90
KEMP WICKER	L	29	1	2	.333	0	7	0	0	20	31	11	5	0	7.65
STEVE SUNDRA	R	26	0	0	.000	0	1	0	0	1	2	2	1	0	0.00

American League (1936)

							Batting						Pitching						Fielding		
	W	L	PCT	GB	R	OR	2B	3B	HR	BA	SA	SB	CG	BB	SO	ShO	SV	ERA	E	DP	FA
NY	102	51	.667		1065	731	315	83	182	.300	.483	76	77	663	624	6	21	4.17	163	148	.973
DET	83	71	.539	19.5	921	871	326	55	94	.300	.431	72	76	562	526	13	13	5.00	153	159	.975
CHI	81	70	.536	20	920	873	282	56	60	.292	.397	66	80	578	414	5	8	5.06	168	174	.973
WAS	82	71	.536	20	889	799	293	84	62	.295	.414	103	78	588	462	8	14	4.58	182	163	.970
CLE	80	74	.519	22.5	921	862	357	82	123	.304	.461	66	80	607	619	6	12	4.83	178	154	.971
BOS	74	80	.481	28.5	775	764	288	62	86	.276	.400	54	78	552	584	11	9	4.39	165	139	.972
STL	57	95	.375	44.5	804	1064	299	66	79	.279	.403	62	54	609	399	3	13	6.24	188	143	.969
PHI	53	100	.346	49	714	1045	240	60	72	.269	.376	59	68	696	405	3	12	6.08	209	152	.965
					7009	7009	2400	548	758	.289	.421	558	591	4855	4033	55	102	5.04	1406	1232	.971

11

New York Yankees (1937)

JOE McCARTHY, MGR.

BATTING	G by POS	B	AGE	G	AB	R	H	2B	3B	HR	RBI	BB	SO	SB	BA	SA
LOU GEHRIG	1B157	L	34	157	569	138	200	37	9	37	159	127	49	4	.351	.643
TONY LAZZERI	2B125	R	33	126	446	56	109	21	3	14	70	71	76	7	.244	.399
FRANKIE CROSETTI	SS147	R	26	149	611	127	143	29	5	11	49	86	105	13	.234	.352
RED ROLFE	3B154	L	28	154	648	143	179	34	10	4	62	90	53	4	.276	.378
MYRIL HOAG	OF99	R	29	106	362	48	109	19	8	3	46	33	33	4	.301	.423
JOE DIMAGGIO	OF150	R	22	151	621	151	215	35	15	46	167	64	37	3	.346	.673
JAKE POWELL (IL)	OF94	R	28	97	365	54	96	22	3	3	45	25	36	7	.263	.364
BILL DICKEY	C137	L	30	140	530	87	176	35	2	29	133	73	22	3	.332	.570
GEORGE SELKIRK (BC)	OF69	L	29	78	256	49	84	13	5	18	68	34	24	8	.328	.629
TOMMY HENRICH (JJ)	OF59	L	24	67	206	39	66	14	5	8	42	35	17	4	.320	.553
DON HEFFNER	2B38, SS13, 3B3, 1B1, OF1	R	26	60	201	23	50	6	5	0	21	19	19	1	.249	.328
RED RUFFING	P31	R	33	54	129	11	26	3	0	1	10	13	24	0	.202	.248
JOE GLENN	C24	R	28	25	53	6	15	2	2	0	4	10	11	0	.283	.396
JACK SALTZGAVER	1B4	L	32	17	11	6	2	0	0	0	0	3	4	0	.182	.182
ART JORGENS	C11	R	32	13	23	3	3	1	0	0	3	2	5	0	.130	.174
ROY JOHNSON	OF12	L	34	12	51	5	15	3	0	0	6	3	2	1	.294	.353
BABE DAHLGREN		R	25	1	1	0	0	0	0	0	0	0	0	0	.000	.000

PITCHING	T	AGE	W	L	PCT	SV	G	GS	CG	IP	H	BB	SO	ShO	ERA
LEFTY GOMEZ	L	28	21	11	.656	0	34	34	25	278	233	93	194	6	2.33
RED RUFFING	R	33	20	7	.741	0	31	31	22	256	242	68	131	4	2.99
JOHNNY MURPHY	R	28	13	4	.765	10	39	4	0	110	121	50	36	0	4.17
BUMP HADLEY	R	32	11	8	.579	0	29	25	6	178	199	83	70	0	5.31
MONTE PEARSON	R	27	9	3	.750	1	22	20	7	145	145	64	71	1	3.17
KEMP WICKER	L	30	7	3	.700	0	16	10	6	88	107	26	14	1	4.40
SPUD CHANDLER	R	29	7	4	.636	0	12	10	6	82	79	20	31	2	2.85
FRANK MAKOSKY	R	25	5	2	.714	3	26	1	1	58	64	24	27	0	4.97
PAT MALONE	R	34	4	4	.500	6	28	9	3	92	109	35	49	0	5.48
IVY ANDREWS	R	30	3	2	.600	1	11	5	3	49	49	17	17	1	3.12
JOE VANCE	R	31	1	0	1.000	0	2	2	0	15	11	9	3	0	3.00
JOHNNY BROACA (JT)	R	27	1	4	.200	0	7	6	3	44	58	17	9	0	4.70

American League (1937)

							Batting						Pitching						Fielding		
	W	L	PCT	GB	R	OR	2B	3B	HR	BA	SA	SB	CG	BB	SO	ShO	SV	ERA	E	DP	FA
NY	102	52	.662		979	671	282	73	174	.283	.456	60	82	506	652	15	21	3.65	170	134	.972
DET	89	65	.578	13	935	841	309	62	150	.292	.452	89	70	635	485	6	11	4.87	147	149	.976
CHI	86	68	.558	16	780	730	280	76	67	.280	.400	70	70	532	533	15	21	4.17	174	173	.971
CLE	83	71	.539	19	817	768	304	76	103	.280	.423	76	64	563	630	4	15	4.39	159	153	.974
BOS	80	72	.526	21	821	775	269	64	100	.281	.411	79	74	597	682	6	14	4.48	177	139	.970
WAS	73	80	.477	28.5	757	841	245	84	47	.279	.379	61	75	676	535	5	14	4.58	170	181	.972
PHI	54	97	.358	46.5	699	854	278	60	94	.267	.397	95	65	613	469	6	9	4.85	198	150	.967
STL	46	108	.299	56	715	1023	327	44	71	.285	.399	30	55	653	468	2	8	6.00	173	166	.972
					6503	6503	2294	539	806	.281	.415	560	555	4775	4454	59	113	4.62	1368	1245	.972

12

Philadelphia A's (1930)

CONNIE MACK, MGR.

BATTING	G by POS	B	AGE	G	AB	R	H	2B	3B	HR	RBI	BB	SO	SB	BA	SA
JIMMIE FOXX	1B153	R	22	153	562	127	188	33	13	37	156	93	66	7	.335	.637
MAX BISHOP	2B127	L	30	130	441	117	111	27	6	10	38	128	60	3	.252	.408
JOE BOLEY	SS120	R	33	121	420	41	116	22	2	4	55	32	26	0	.276	.367
JIMMY DYKES	3B123, OF1	R	33	125	435	69	131	28	4	6	73	74	53	3	.301	.425
BING MILLER	OF154	R	35	154	585	89	177	38	7	9	100	47	22	13	.303	.438
MULE HAAS	OF131	L	26	132	532	91	159	33	7	2	68	43	33	2	.299	.398
AL SIMMONS	OF136	R	28	138	554	152	211	41	16	36	165	39	34	9	.381	.708
MICKEY COCHRANE	C130	L	27	130	487	110	174	42	5	10	85	55	18	5	.357	.526
ERIC MCNAIR	SS31, 3B29, 2B5, OF1	R	21	78	237	27	63	12	2	0	34	9	19	5	.266	.333
DIB WILLIAMS	2B39, SS19, 3B1	R	20	67	191	24	50	10	3	3	22	15	19	2	.262	.393
WALLY SCHANG	C36	B	40	45	92	16	16	4	1	1	9	17	15	0	.174	.272
DOC CRAMER	OF21, SS1	L	24	30	82	12	19	1	1	0	6	2	8	0	.232	.268
HOMER SUMMA	OF15	L	31	25	54	10	15	2	1	1	5	4	1	0	.278	.407
SPENCE HARRIS	OF13	L	29	22	49	4	9	1	0	0	5	5	2	0	.184	.204
CY PERKINS	C19, 1B1	R	34	20	38	1	6	2	0	0	4	2	3	0	.158	.211
JIM MOORE	OF13	R	27	15	50	10	19	3	0	2	12	2	4	1	.380	.560
PINKY HIGGINS	3B5, 2B2, SS1	R	21	14	24	1	6	2	0	0	0	4	5	0	.250	.333
JIM KEESEY	1B3	R	27	11	12	2	3	1	0	0	2	1	2	0	.250	.333
EDDIE COLLINS		L	43	3	2	1	1	0	0	0	0	0	0	0	.500	.500

PITCHING	T	AGE	W	L	PCT	SV	G	GS	CG	IP	H	BB	SO	ShO	ERA
LEFTY GROVE	L	30	28	5	.848	9	50	32	22	291	273	60	209	2	2.54
GEORGE EARNSHAW	R	30	22	13	.629	2	49	39	20	296	299	139	193	3	4.44
RUBE WALBERG	L	33	13	12	.520	1	38	30	12	205	207	85	100	2	4.70
BILL SHORES	R	26	12	4	.750	0	31	19	7	159	169	70	48	1	4.19
EDDIE ROMMEL	R	32	9	4	.692	3	35	9	5	130	142	27	35	0	4.29
ROY MAHAFFEY	R	27	9	5	.643	0	33	16	6	153	186	53	38	0	5.00
JACK QUINN	R	46	9	7	.563	6	35	7	0	90	109	22	28	0	4.40
GLENN LIEBHARDT	R	19	0	1	.000	0	5	0	0	9	14	8	2	0	11.00
HOWARD EHMKE	R	36	0	1	.000	0	3	1	0	10	22	2	4	0	11.70
CHARLIE PERKINS	L	24	0	0	.000	0	8	1	0	24	25	15	15	0	6.37
AL MAHON	L	19	0	0	.000	0	3	0	0	4	11	7	0	0	24.75

American League (1930)

					Batting							Pitching						Fielding		
	W	L	PCT	GB	R	OR	2B	3B	HR	BA	SA	SB	CG	BB	SO	ShO	SV	ERA	E	DP	FA
PHI	102	52	.662		951	751	319	74	125	.294	.452	48	72	488	672	8	21	4.28	145	121	.975
WAS	94	60	.610	8	892	689	300	98	57	.302	.426	101	78	504	524	4	14	3.96	159	150	.974
NY	86	68	.558	16	1062	898	298	110	152	.309	.488	91	65	524	572	6	15	4.88	207	132	.965
CLE	81	73	.526	21	890	915	358	59	72	.304	.431	51	69	528	441	4	14	4.88	237	156	.962
DET	75	79	.487	27	783	833	298	90	82	.284	.421	98	68	570	574	3	17	4.70	192	156	.967
STL	64	90	.416	38	751	886	289	67	75	.268	.391	93	68	449	470	5	10	5.07	188	152	.970
CHI	62	92	.403	40	729	884	255	90	63	.276	.391	74	67	407	471	2	10	4.71	235	136	.962
BOS	52	102	.338	50	612	814	257	68	47	.264	.365	42	78	488	356	4	5	4.70	196	161	.968
					6670	6670	2374	656	673	.288	.421	598	565	3958	4080	36	106	4.65	1559	1264	.968

13

New York Yankees (1941)

JOE McCARTHY, MGR.

BATTING	G by POS	B	AGE	G	AB	R	H	2B	3B	HR	RBI	BB	SO	SB	BA	SA
JOHNNY STURM	1B124	L	25	124	524	58	125	17	3	3	36	37	50	3	.239	.300
JOE GORDON	2B131, 1B30	R	26	156	588	104	162	26	7	24	87	72	80	10	.276	.466
PHIL RIZZUTO	SS128	R	23	133	515	65	158	20	9	3	46	27	36	14	.307	.398
RED ROLFE	3B134	L	32	136	561	106	148	22	5	8	42	57	38	3	.264	.364
TOMMY HENRICH	OF139	L	28	144	538	106	149	27	5	31	85	81	40	3	.277	.519
JOE DIMAGGIO	OF139	R	26	139	541	122	193	43	11	30	125	76	13	4	.357	.643
CHARLIE KELLER	OF137	L	24	140	507	102	151	24	10	33	122	102	65	6	.298	.580
BILL DICKEY	C104	L	34	109	348	35	99	15	5	7	71	45	17	2	.284	.417
GEORGE SELKIRK	OF47	L	33	70	164	30	36	5	0	6	25	28	30	1	.220	.360
BUDDY ROSAR	C60	R	26	67	209	25	60	17	2	1	36	22	10	0	.287	.402
JERRY PRIDDY	2B31, 3B14, 1B10	R	21	56	174	18	37	7	0	1	26	18	16	4	.213	.270
FRANKIE CROSETTI	SS32, 3B13	R	30	50	148	13	33	2	2	1	22	18	14	0	.223	.284
RED RUFFING	P23	R	37	38	89	10	27	8	1	2	22	4	12	0	.303	.483
FRENCHY BORDAGARAY	OF19	R	29	36	73	10	19	1	0	0	4	6	8	1	.260	.274
KEN SILVESTRI (IL)	C13	B	25	17	40	6	10	5	0	1	4	7	6	0	.250	.450
JOHNNY LINDELL		R	24	1	1	0	0	0	0	0	0	0	0	0	.000	.000

PITCHING	T	AGE	W	L	PCT	SV	G	GS	CG	IP	H	BB	SO	ShO	ERA
LEFTY GOMEZ	L	32	15	5	.750	0	23	23	8	156	151	103	76	2	3.75
RED RUFFING	R	37	15	6	.714	0	23	23	13	186	177	54	60	2	3.53
MARIUS RUSSO	L	26	14	10	.583	1	28	27	17	210	195	87	105	3	3.09
SPUD CHANDLER	R	33	10	4	.714	4	28	20	11	164	146	60	60	4	3.18
ATLEY DONALD	R	30	9	5	.643	0	22	20	10	159	141	69	71	0	3.57
ERNIE BONHAM	R	27	9	6	.600	2	23	14	7	127	118	31	43	1	2.98
MARV BREUER	R	27	9	7	.563	2	26	18	7	141	131	49	77	1	4.09
JOHNNY MURPHY	R	32	8	3	.727	15	35	0	0	77	68	40	29	0	1.99
NORM BRANCH	R	26	5	1	.833	2	27	0	0	47	37	26	28	0	2.87
STEVE PEEK	R	26	4	2	.667	0	17	8	2	80	85	39	18	0	5.06
CHARLEY STANCEU	R	25	3	3	.500	0	22	2	0	48	58	35	21	0	5.60
GEORGE WASHBURN	R	26	0	1	.000	0	1	1	0	2	2	5	1	0	13.50

American League (1941)

							Batting							Pitching						Fielding		
	W	L	PCT	GB	R	OR	2B	3B	HR	BA	SA	SB	CG	BB	SO	ShO	SV	ERA	E	DP	FA
NY	101	53	.656		830	631	243	60	151	.269	.419	51	75	598	589	13	6	3.53	165	196	.973
BOS	84	70	.545	17	865	750	304	55	124	.283	.430	67	70	611	574	8	11	4.19	172	139	.972
CHI	77	77	.500	24	638	649	245	47	47	.255	.343	91	106	521	564	14	4	3.52	180	145	.971
CLE	75	79	.487	26	677	668	249	84	103	.256	.393	63	68	660	617	10	19	3.90	142	158	.976
DET	75	79	.487	26	686	743	247	55	81	.263	.375	43	52	645	697	8	16	4.18	186	129	.969
STL	70	84	.455	31	765	823	281	58	91	.266	.390	50	65	549	454	7	10	4.72	151	156	.975
WAS	70	84	.455	31	728	798	257	80	52	.272	.376	79	69	603	544	8	7	4.35	187	169	.969
PHI	64	90	.416	37	713	840	240	69	85	.268	.387	27	64	557	386	3	18	4.83	200	150	.967
					5902	5902	2066	508	734	.266	.389	471	569	4744	4425	71	111	4.15	1383	1242	.972

14

St. Louis Cardinals (1931)

GABBY STREET, MGR.

BATTING	G by POS	B	AGE	G	AB	R	H	2B	3B	HR	RBI	BB	SO	SB	BA	SA
JIM BOTTOMLEY	1B93	L	31	108	382	73	133	34	5	9	75	34	24	3	.348	.534
FRANKIE FRISCH	2B129	B	32	131	518	96	161	24	4	4	82	45	13	28	.311	.396
CHARLIE GELBERT	SS130	R	25	131	447	61	129	29	5	1	62	54	31	7	.289	.383
SPARKY ADAMS	3B138, SS6	R	36	143	608	97	178	46	5	1	40	42	24	16	.293	.390
GEORGE WATKINS	OF129	L	31	131	503	93	145	30	13	13	51	31	66	15	.288	.477
PEPPER MARTIN	OF110	R	27	123	413	68	124	32	8	7	75	30	40	16	.300	.467
CHICK HAFEY	OF118	R	28	122	450	94	157	35	8	16	95	39	43	11	.3489	.569
JIMMIE WILSON	C110	R	30	115	383	45	105	20	2	0	51	28	15	5	.274	.337
RIPPER COLLINS	1B68, OF3	B	27	89	279	34	84	20	10	4	59	18	24	1	.301	.487
ERNIE ORSATTI	OF45, 1B1	L	28	70	158	27	46	16	6	0	19	14	16	1	.291	.468
GUS MANCUSO	C56	R	25	67	187	13	49	16	1	1	23	18	13	2	.262	.374
ANDY HIGH	3B23, 2B19	L	33	63	131	20	35	6	1	0	19	24	4	0	.267	.328
JAKE FLOWERS	SS22, 2B20, 3B1	R	29	45	137	19	34	11	1	2	19	9	6	7	.248	.387
WALLY ROETTGER	OF42	R	28	45	151	16	43	12	2	0	17	9	14	0	.285	.391
TAYLOR DOUTHIT	OF36	R	30	36	133	21	44	11	2	1	21	11	9	1	.331	.466
RAY BLADES	OF20	R	34	35	67	10	19	4	0	1	5	10	7	1	.284	.388
MIKE GONZALEZ	C12	R	40	15	19	1	2	0	0	0	3	0	3	0	.105	.105
JOE BENES	SS6, 2B2, 3B1	R	30	10	12	1	2	0	0	0	0	2	1	0	.167	.167
JOEL HUNT	OF1	R	25	4	1	2	0	0	0	0	0	0	1	0	.000	.000
RAY CUNNINGHAM	3B3	R	23	3	4	0	0	0	0	0	1	0	0	0	.000	.000
EDDIE DELKER	3B1	R	24	1	2	0	1	1	0	0	2	0	0	0	.500	1.000
GABBY STREET	C1	R	48	1	1	0	0	0	0	0	0	0	0	0	.000	.000

PITCHING	T	AGE	W	L	PCT	SV	G	GS	CG	IP	H	BB	SO	ShO	ERA
WILD BILL HALLAHAN	L	28	19	9	.679	4	37	30	16	249	242	112	159	3	3.29
PAUL DERRINGER	R	24	18	8	.692	2	35	23	15	212	225	65	134	4	3.35
BURLEIGH GRIMES	R	37	17	9	.654	0	29	28	17	212	240	59	67	3	3.65
JESSE HAINES	R	37	12	3	.800	0	19	17	8	122	134	28	27	2	3.02
SYL JOHNSON	R	30	11	9	.550	2	32	24	12	186	186	29	82	2	3.00
FLINT RHEM	R	30	11	10	.524	1	33	26	10	207	214	60	72	2	3.57
JIM LINDSEY	R	33	6	4	.600	7	35	2	1	75	77	45	32	1	2.76
ALLYN STOUT	R	26	6	0	1.000	3	30	3	1	73	87	34	40	0	4.19
TONY KAUFMANN	R	30	1	1	.500	1	15	1	0	49	65	17	13	0	6.06

National League (1931)

					Batting							Pitching						Fielding		
	W	L	PCT	GB	R	OR	2B	3B	HR	BA	SA	SB	CG	BB	SO	ShO	SV	ERA	E	DP	FA
STL	101	53	.656		815	614	353	74	60	.286	.411	114	80	449	626	17	20	3.45	160	169	.974
NY	87	65	.572	13	768	599	251	64	101	.289	.416	83	90	421	571	17	12	3.30	159	126	.974
CHI	84	70	.545	17	828	710	340	67	83	.289	.422	49	80	524	541	8	8	3.97	169	141	.973
BKN	79	73	.520	21	681	673	240	77	71	.276	.390	45	64	351	546	9	18	3.84	187	154	.969
PIT	75	79	.487	26	636	691	243	70	41	.266	.360	59	89	442	345	9	5	3.66	194	167	.968
PHI	66	88	.429	35	684	828	299	52	81	.279	.400	42	60	511	499	4	16	4.58	210	149	.966
BOS	64	90	.416	37	533	680	221	59	34	.258	.341	46	78	406	419	12	9	3.90	170	141	.973
CIN	58	96	.377	43	592	742	241	70	21	.269	.352	24	70	399	317	4	6	4.22	165	194	.973
					5537	5537	2188	533	492	.277	.387	462	611	3503	3864	80	94	3.86	1414	1241	.971

15

New York Yankees (1928)

MILLER HUGGINS, MGR.

BATTING	G by POS	B	AGE	G	AB	R	H	2B	3B	HR	RBI	BB	SO	SB	BA	SA
LOU GEHRIG	1B154	L	25	154	562	139	210	47	13	27	142	95	69	4	.374	.648
TONY LAZZERI (SJ)	2B110	R	24	116	404	62	134	30	11	10	82	43	50	15	.332	.535
MARK KOENIG	SS125	L	25	132	533	89	170	19	10	4	63	32	19	3	.319	.415
JOE DUGAN	3B91	R	31	94	312	33	86	15	0	6	34	16	15	1	.276	.381
BABE RUTH	OF154	L	33	154	536	163	173	29	8	54	142	135	87	4	.323	.709
EARLE COMBS	OF149	L	29	149	626	118	194	33	21	7	56	77	33	10	.310	.463
BOB MEUSEL (NJ)	OF131	R	31	131	518	77	154	45	5	11	113	39	56	6	.297	.467
JOHNNY GRABOWSKI	C75	R	28	75	202	21	48	7	1	1	21	10	21	0	.238	.297
LEO DUROCHER	2B66, SS29	B	22	102	296	46	80	8	6	0	31	22	52	1	.270	.338
GENE ROBERTSON	3B70, 2B3	L	28	83	251	29	73	9	0	1	36	14	6	2	.291	.339
CEDRIC DURST	OF33, 1B3	L	31	74	135	18	34	2	1	2	10	7	9	1	.252	.326
PAT COLLINS	C70	R	31	70	136	18	30	5	0	6	14	35	16	0	.221	.390
BEN PASCHAL	OF25	R	32	65	79	12	25	6	1	1	15	8	11	1	.316	.456
BENNY BENGOUGH (HJ)	C58	R	29	58	161	12	43	3	1	0	9	7	8	0	.267	.298
MIKE GAZELLA	3B16, 2B4, SS3	R	31	32	56	11	13	0	0	0	2	6	7	2	.232	.232
BILL DICKEY	C10	L	21	10	15	1	3	1	1	0	2	0	2	0	.200	.400
GEORGE BURNS	1B2	R	35	4	4	1	2	0	0	0	0	0	1	0	.500	.500

PITCHING	T	AGE	W	L	PCT	SV	G	GS	CG	IP	H	BB	SO	ShO	ERA
GEORGE PIPGRAS	R	28	24	13	.649	3	46	38	22	301	314	103	139	4	3.38
WAITE HOYT	R	28	23	7	.767	8	42	31	19	273	279	60	67	3	3.36
HERB PENNOCK (IL)	L	34	17	6	.739	3	28	24	18	211	215	40	53	5	2.56
HANK JOHNSON	R	22	14	9	.609	0	31	22	10	199	188	104	110	1	4.30
AL SHEALY	R	28	8	6	.571	2	23	12	3	96	124	42	39	0	5.06
STAN COVELESKI	R	39	5	1	.833	0	12	8	2	58	72	20	5	0	5.74
WILCY MOORE	R	31	4	4	.500	2	35	2	0	60	71	31	18	0	4.20
TOM ZACHARY	L	32	3	3	.500	1	7	6	3	46	54	15	7	0	3.91
FRED HEIMACH	L	27	2	3	.400	0	13	9	5	68	66	16	25	0	3.31
MYLES THOMAS	R	30	1	0	1.000	0	12	1	0	32	33	9	10	0	3.38
ARCHIE CAMPBELL	R	24	0	1	.000	2	13	1	0	24	30	11	9	0	5.25
ROSY RYAN	R	30	0	0	.000	0	3	0	0	6	17	1	5	0	16.50
URBAN SHOCKER (DD)	R	37	0	0	.000	0	1	0	0	2	3	0	0	0	0.00

American League (1928)

							Batting						Pitching						Fielding		
	W	L	PCT	GB	R	OR	2B	3B	HR	BA	SA	SB	CG	BB	SO	ShO	SV	ERA	E	DP	FA
NY	101	53	.656		894	685	269	79	133	.296	.450	51	83	452	487	13	21	3.74	194	136	.968
PHI	98	55	.641	2.5	829	615	323	75	89	.295	.436	59	81	424	607	15	16	3.36	181	124	.970
STL	82	72	.532	19	772	742	276	76	63	.274	.393	76	80	454	456	6	15	4.17	189	146	.969
WAS	75	79	.487	26	718	705	277	93	40	.284	.393	110	77	466	462	15	10	3.88	178	146	.972
CHI	72	82	.468	29	656	725	231	77	24	.270	.358	139	88	501	418	6	11	3.98	186	149	.970
DET	68	86	.442	33	744	804	265	97	62	.279	.401	113	65	567	451	5	16	4.32	218	140	.965
CLE	62	92	.403	39	674	830	299	61	34	.285	.382	50	71	511	416	4	15	4.47	221	187	.965
BOS	57	96	.373	43.5	589	770	260	62	38	.264	.361	99	70	452	407	5	9	4.39	178	139	.971
					5876	5876	2200	620	483	.281	.397	697	615	3827	3704	69	113	4.04	1545	1167	.969

16

New York Yankees (1953)

CASEY STENGEL, MGR.

BATTING	G by POS	B	AGE	G	AB	R	H	2B	3B	HR	RBI	BB	SO	SB	BA	SA
JOE COLLINS	1B113, OF4	L	30	127	387	72	104	11	2	17	44	59	36	2	.269	.439
BILLY MARTIN	2B146, SS18	R	25	149	587	72	151	24	6	15	75	43	56	6	.257	.395
PHIL RIZZUTO	SS133	R	35	134	413	54	112	21	3	2	54	71	39	4	.271	.351
GIL MCDOUGALD	3B136, 2B26	R	25	141	541	82	154	27	7	10	83	60	65	3	.285	.416
HANK BAUER	OF126	R	30	133	437	77	133	20	6	10	57	59	45	2	.304	.446
MICKEY MANTLE	OF121, SS1	B	21	127	461	105	136	24	3	21	92	79	90	8	.295	.497
GENE WOODLING	OF119	L	30	125	395	64	121	26	4	10	58	82	29	2	.306	.468
YOGI BERRA	C133	L	28	137	503	80	149	23	5	27	108	50	32	0	.296	.523
IRV NOREN	OF96	L	28	109	345	55	92	12	6	6	46	42	39	3	.267	.388
JOHNNY MIZE	1B15	L	40	81	104	6	26	3	0	4	27	12	17	0	.250	.394
DON BOLLWEG	1B43	L	32	70	155	24	46	6	4	6	24	21	31	1	.297	.503
BILL RENNA	OF40	R	28	61	121	19	38	6	3	2	13	13	31	0	.314	.463
ANDY CAREY	3B40, SS2, 2B1	R	21	51	81	14	26	5	0	4	8	9	12	2	.321	.531
WILLIE MIRANDA	SS45	B	27	48	58	12	13	0	0	1	5	5	10	1	.224	.276
CHARLIE SILVERA	C39, 3B1	R	28	42	82	11	23	3	1	0	12	9	5	0	.280	.341
GUS TRIANDOS	1B12, C5	R	22	18	51	5	8	2	0	1	6	3	9	0	.157	.255
RALPH HOUK	C8	R	33	8	9	2	2	0	0	0	1	0	1	0	.222	.222
JERRY COLEMAN (MS)	2B7, SS1	R	28	8	10	1	2	0	0	0	0	0	2	0	.200	.200

PITCHING	T	AGE	W	L	PCT	SV	G	GS	CG	IP	H	BB	SO	ShO	ERA
WHITEY FORD	L	24	18	6	.750	0	32	30	11	207	187	110	110	3	3.00
ED LOPAT	L	35	16	4	.800	0	25	24	9	178	169	32	50	3	2.43
JOHNNY SAIN	R	35	14	7	.667	9	40	19	10	189	189	45	84	1	3.00
VIC RASCHI	R	34	13	6	.684	1	28	26	7	181	150	55	76	4	3.33
ALLIE REYNOLDS	R	38	13	7	.650	13	41	15	5	145	140	61	86	1	3.41
JIM MCDONALD	R	26	9	7	.563	0	27	18	6	130	128	39	43	2	3.81
BOB KUZAVA	L	30	6	5	.545	4	33	6	2	92	92	34	48	2	3.33
TOM GORMAN	R	28	4	5	.444	6	40	1	0	77	65	32	38	0	3.39
EWELL BLACKWELL (SA)	R	30	2	0	1.000	1	8	4	0	20	17	13	11	0	3.60
BILL MILLER	L	25	2	1	.667	1	13	3	0	34	46	19	17	0	4.76
RAY SCARBOROUGH	R	35	2	2	.500	2	25	1	0	55	52	26	20	0	3.27
STEVE KRALY	L	24	0	2	.000	1	5	3	0	25	19	16	8	0	3.24
ART SCHALLOCK	L	29	0	0	.000	1	7	1	0	21	30	15	13	0	3.00
JOHNNY SCHMITZ	L	32	0	0	.000	0	3	0	0	4	2	3	0	0	2.25

American League (1953)

	W	L	PCT	GB	R	OR	Batting 2B	3B	HR	BA	SA	SB	Pitching CG	BB	SO	ShO	SV	ERA	Fielding E	DP	FA
NY	99	52	.656		801	547	226	52	139	.273	.417	34	50	500	604	16	39	3.20	126	182	.979
CLE	92	62	.597	8.5	770	627	201	29	160	.270	.410	33	81	519	586	11	15	3.64	127	197	.979
CHI	89	65	.578	11.5	716	592	226	53	74	.258	.364	73	57	583	714	16	33	3.41	125	144	.980
BOS	84	69	.549	16	656	632	255	37	101	.264	.384	33	41	584	642	14	37	3.59	148	173	.975
WAS	76	76	.500	23.5	687	614	230	53	69	.263	.368	65	76	478	515	16	10	3.66	120	173	.979
DET	60	94	.390	40.5	695	923	259	44	108	.266	.387	30	50	585	645	2	16	5.25	135	149	.978
PHI	59	95	.383	41.5	632	799	205	38	116	.256	.372	41	51	594	566	6	11	4.67	137	161	.977
STL	54	100	.351	46.5	555	778	214	25	112	.249	.363	17	28	626	639	7	24	4.48	152	165	.974
					5512	5512	1816	331	879	.262	.383	326	434	4469	4911	88	185	4.00	1070	1344	.978

17

Cincinnati Reds (1940)

BILL MCKECHNIE, MGR.

BATTING	G by POS	B	AGE	G	AB	R	H	2B	3B	HR	RBI	BB	SO	SB	BA	SA
FRANK MCCORMICK	1B155	R	29	155	618	93	191	44	3	19	127	52	26	2	.309	.482
LONNY FREY	2B150	L	29	150	563	102	150	23	6	8	54	80	48	22	.266	.371
BILLY MYERS	SS88	R	29	90	282	33	57	14	2	5	30	30	56	0	.202	.319
BILL WERBER	3B143	R	32	143	584	105	162	35	5	12	48	68	40	16	.277	.416
IVAL GOODMAN	OF135	L	31	136	519	78	134	20	6	12	63	60	54	9	.258	.389
HARRY CRAFT	OF109, 1B2	R	25	115	422	47	103	18	5	6	48	17	46	2	.244	.353
MIKE MCCORMICK	OF107	R	23	110	417	48	125	20	0	1	30	13	36	8	.300	.355
ERNIE LOMBARDI	C101	R	32	109	376	50	120	22	0	14	74	31	14	0	.319	.489
EDDIE JOOST	SS78, 2B7, 3B4	R	24	88	278	24	60	7	2	1	24	32	40	4	.216	.266
MORRIE ARNOVICH	OF60	R	29	62	211	17	60	10	2	0	21	13	10	1	.284	.351
WILLARD HERSHBERGER (DD)	C37	R	30	48	123	6	38	4	2	0	26	6	6	0	.309	.374
LEW RIGGS	3B11	L	30	41	72	8	21	7	1	1	9	2	4	0	.292	.458
LEW GAMBLE	OF10	L	30	38	42	12	6	1	0	0	0	0	1	0	.143	.167
JIMMY RIPPLE	OF30	L	30	32	101	15	31	10	0	4	20	13	5	1	.307	.525
JOHNNY RIZZO	OF30	R	27	31	110	17	31	6	0	4	17	14	14	1	.282	.445
BILL BAKER	C24	R	29	27	69	5	15	1	1	0	7	4	8	2	.217	.261
JIMMIE WILSON	C16	R	39	16	37	2	9	2	0	0	3	2	1	1	.243	.297
MIKE DEJAN	OF2	L	25	12	16	1	3	0	1	0	2	3	3	0	.188	.313
DICK WEST	C7	R	24	7	28	4	11	2	0	1	6	0	2	1	.393	.571
WALLY BERGER		R	34	2	2	0	0	0	0	0	0	0	1	0	.000	.000
VINCE DIMAGGIO	OF1	R	27	2	4	2	1	0	0	0	0	1	0	0	.250	.250

PITCHING	T	AGE	W	L	PCT	SV	G	GS	CG	IP	H	BB	SO	ShO	ERA
BUCKY WALTERS	R	31	22	10	.688	0	36	36	29	305	241	92	115	3	2.48
PAUL DERRINGER	R	33	20	12	.625	0	37	37	26	297	280	48	115	3	3.06
JUNIOR THOMPSON	R	23	16	9	.640	0	33	31	17	225	197	96	103	3	3.32
JIM TURNER	R	36	14	7	.667	0	24	23	11	187	187	32	53	0	2.89
JOE BEGGS	R	29	12	3	.800	7	37	1	0	77	68	21	25	0	1.99
WHITEY MOORE	R	28	8	8	.500	1	25	15	5	117	100	56	60	1	3.62
JOHNNY VANDER MEER	L	25	3	1	.750	1	10	7	2	48	38	41	41	0	3.75
JOHNNY HUTCHINGS	R	24	2	1	.667	0	19	4	0	54	53	18	18	0	3.50
MILT SHOFFNER	L	34	1	0	1.000	0	20	0	0	54	56	18	17	0	5.67
ELMER RIDDLE	R	25	1	2	.333	2	15	1	1	34	30	17	9	0	1.85
RED BARRETT	R	25	1	0	1.000	0	3	0	0	3	5	1	0	0	6.00
WITT GUISE	L	31	0	0	.000	0	2	0	0	8	8	5	1	0	1.13

National League (1940)

							Batting							Pitching						Fielding		
	W	L	PCT	GB	R	OR	2B	3B	HR	BA	SA	SB	CG	BB	SO	ShO	SV	ERA	E	DP	FA
CIN	100	53	.654		707	528	264	38	89	.266	.379	72	91	445	557	10	11	3.05	117	158	.981
BKN	88	65	.575	12	697	621	256	70	93	.260	.383	56	65	393	634	17	14	3.50	183	110	.970
STL	84	69	.549	16	747	699	266	61	119	.275	.411	97	71	488	550	10	14	3.83	174	134	.971
PIT	78	76	.506	22.5	809	783	276	68	76	.276	.394	69	49	492	491	8	24	4.36	217	160	.966
CHI	75	79	.487	25.5	681	636	272	48	86	.267	.384	63	69	430	564	12	14	3.54	199	143	.968
NY	72	80	.474	27.5	663	659	201	46	91	.267	.374	45	57	473	606	11	18	3.79	139	132	.977
BOS	65	87	.428	34.5	623	745	219	50	59	.256	.349	48	76	573	435	9	12	4.36	184	169	.970
PHI	50	103	.327	50	494	750	180	35	75	.238	.331	25	66	475	485	5	8	4.40	181	136	.970
					5421	5421	1934	416	688	.264	.376	475	544	3769	4322	82	115	3.85	1394	1142	.972

18

New York Yankees (1938)

JOE MCCARTHY, MGR.

BATTING	G by POS	B	AGE	G	AB	R	H	2B	3B	HR	RBI	BB	SO	SB	BA	SA
LOU GEHRIG	1B157	L	35	157	576	115	170	32	6	29	114	107	75	6	.295	.523
JOE GORDON	2B126	R	23	127	458	83	117	24	7	25	97	56	72	11	.255	.502
FRANKIE CROSETTI	SS157	R	27	157	631	113	166	35	3	9	55	106	97	27	.263	.371
REDR OLFE	3B151	L	29	151	631	132	196	36	8	10	80	74	44	13	.311	.441
TOMMY HENRICH	OF130	L	25	131	471	109	127	24	7	22	91	92	32	6	.270	.490
JOE DIMAGGIO	OF145	R	23	145	599	129	194	32	13	32	140	59	21	6	.324	.581
GEORGE SELKIRK	OF95	L	30	99	335	58	85	12	5	10	62	68	52	9	.254	.409
BILL DICKEY	C126	L	31	132	454	84	142	27	4	27	115	75	22	3	.313	.568
MYRIL HOAG	OF70	R	30	85	267	28	74	14	3	0	48	25	31	4	.277	.352
BILL KNICKERBOCKER	2B34, SS3	R	26	46	128	15	32	8	3	1	21	11	10	0	.250	.383
JAKE POWELL	OF43	R	29	45	164	27	42	12	1	2	20	15	20	3	.256	.378
JOE GLENN	C40	R	29	41	123	10	32	7	2	0	25	10	14	1	.260	.350
BABE DAHLGREN	3B8, 1B6	R	26	27	43	8	8	1	0	0	1	1	7	0	.186	.209
ART JORGENS	C8	R	33	9	17	3	4	2	0	0	2	3	3	0	.235	.353

PITCHING	T	AGE	W	L	PCT	SV	G	GS	CG	IP	H	BB	SO	ShO	ERA
RED RUFFING	R	34	21	7	.750	0	31	31	22	247	246	82	127	3	3.32
LEFTY GOMEZ	L	29	18	12	.600	0	32	32	20	239	239	99	129	4	3.35
MONTE PEARSON	R	28	16	7	.696	0	28	27	17	202	198	113	98	1	3.97
SPUD CHANDLER	R	30	14	5	.737	0	23	23	14	172	183	47	36	2	4.03
BUMP HADLEY	R	33	9	8	.529	1	29	17	8	167	165	66	61	1	3.61
JOHNNY MURPHY	R	29	8	2	.800	11	32	2	1	91	90	41	43	0	4.25
STEVE SUNDRA	R	28	6	4	.600	0	25	8	3	94	107	43	33	0	4.79
JOE BEGGS	R	27	3	2	.600	0	14	9	4	58	69	20	8	0	5.43
WES FERRELL	R	30	2	2	.500	0	5	4	1	30	52	18	7	0	8.10
IVY ANDREWS	R	31	1	3	.250	1	19	1	1	48	51	17	13	0	3.00
KEMP WICKER	L	31	1	0	1.000	0	1	0	0	1	0	1	0	0	0.00
ATLEY DONALD	R	27	0	1	.000	0	2	2	0	12	7	14	6	0	5.25
LEE STINE	R	24	0	0	.000	0	4	0	0	9	9	1	4	0	1.00
JOE VANCE	R	32	0	0	.000	0	3	1	0	11	20	4	2	0	7.36

American League (1938)

							Batting						Pitching						Fielding		
	W	L	PCT	GB	R	OR	2B	3B	HR	BA	SA	SB	CG	BB	SO	ShO	SV	ERA	E	DP	FA
NY	99	53	.651		966	710	283	63	174	.274	.446	91	91	566	567	10	13	3.91	169	169	.973
BOS	88	61	.591	9.5	902	751	298	56	98	.299	.434	55	67	528	484	10	15	4.46	190	172	.968
CLE	86	66	.566	13	847	782	300	89	113	.281	.434	83	68	681	717	5	17	4.60	151	145	.974
DET	84	70	.545	16	862	795	219	52	137	.272	.411	76	75	608	435	2	11	4.79	147	172	.976
WAS	75	76	.497	23.5	814	873	278	72	85	.293	.416	65	59	655	515	6	11	4.94	180	179	.970
CHI	65	83	.439	32	709	752	239	55	67	.277	.383	56	83	550	432	5	9	4.36	196	155	.967
STL	55	97	.362	44	755	962	273	36	92	.281	.397	51	71	737	632	3	7	5.80	145	163	.975
PHI	53	99	.349	46	726	956	243	62	98	.270	.396	65	56	599	473	4	12	5.48	206	119	.965
					6581	6581	2133	485	864	.281	.415	542	570	4924	4255	45	95	4.79	1384	1274	.971

19

New York Yankees (1923)

MILLER HUGGINS, MGR.

BATTING	G by POS	B	AGE	G	AB	R	H	2B	3B	HR	RBI	BB	SO	SB	BA	SA
WALLY PIPP	1B144	L	30	144	569	79	173	19	8	6	108	36	28	6	.304	.397
AARON WARD	2B152	R	26	152	567	79	161	26	11	10	82	56	65	8	.284	.422
EVERETT SCOTT	SS152	R	30	152	533	48	131	16	4	6	60	13	19	1	.246	.325
JOE DUGAN	3B146	R	26	146	644	111	182	30	7	7	67	25	41	4	.283	.384
BABE RUTH	OF148, 1B4	L	28	152	522	151	205	45	13	41	131	170	93	17	.393	.764
WHITEY WITT	OF144	L	27	146	596	113	187	18	10	6	56	67	42	2	.314	.408
BOB MEUSEL	OF121	R	26	132	460	59	144	29	10	9	91	31	52	13	.313	.478
WALLY SCHANG	(GJ) C81	B	33	84	272	39	75	8	2	2	29	27	17	3	.276	.342
FRED HOFMANN	C70	R	29	72	238	24	69	10	4	3	26	18	27	2	.290	.403
ELMER SMITH	OF47	L	30	70	183	30	56	6	2	7	35	21	21	3	.306	.475
HARVEY HENDRICK	OF12	L	25	37	66	9	18	3	1	3	12	2	8	3	.273	.485
MIKE MCNALLY	SS13, 3B7, 2B5	R	29	30	38	5	8	0	0	0	1	3	4	2	.211	.211
HINKEY HAINES	OF14	R	24	28	25	9	4	2	0	0	3	4	5	3	.160	.240
BENNY BENGOUGH	C19	R	24	19	53	1	7	2	0	0	3	4	2	0	.132	.170
2 ERNIE JOHNSON	SS15, 3B1	L	35	19	38	6	17	1	1	1	8	1	1	0	.447	.605
LOU GEHRIG	1B9	L	20	13	26	6	11	4	1	1	9	2	5	0	.423	.769
MIKE GAZELLA	SS4, 2B2, 3B2	R	26	8	13	2	1	0	0	0	1	2	3	0	.077	.077

PITCHING	T	AGE	W	L	PCT	SV	G	GS	CG	IP	H	BB	SO	ShO	ERA
SAD SAM JONES	R	30	21	8	.724	4	39	27	18	243	239	69	68	3	3.63
HERB PENNOCK	L	29	19	6	.760	3	35	27	21	224	235	68	93	1	3.34
BULLET JOE BUSH	R	30	19	15	.559	0	37	30	23	276	263	117	125	3	3.42
WAITE HOYT	R	23	17	9	.654	1	37	28	19	239	227	66	60	1	3.01
BOB SHAWKEY	R	32	16	11	.593	1	36	31	17	259	232	102	125	1	3.51
CARL MAYS	R	31	5	2	.714	0	23	7	2	81	119	32	16	0	6.22
GEORGE PIPGRAS	R	23	1	3	.250	0	8	2	2	33	34	25	12	0	6.00
OSCAR ROETTGER	R	23	0	0	.000	1	5	0	0	12	16	12	7	0	8.25

American League (1923)

							Batting						Pitching						Fielding		
	W	L	PCT	GB	R	OR	2B	3B	HR	BA	SA	SB	CG	BB	SO	ShO	SV	ERA	E	DP	FA
NY	98	54	.645		823	622	231	79	105	.291	.422	69	102	491	506	9	10	3.66	144	131	.977
DET	83	71	.539	16	831	741	270	69	41	.300	.401	87	61	459	447	9	12	4.09	200	103	.968
CLE	82	71	.536	16.5	888	746	301	75	59	.301	.420	79	76	466	407	10	11	3.91	226	143	.964
WAS	75	78	.490	23.5	720	747	224	93	26	.274	.367	102	70	559	474	8	16	3.99	216	182	.966
STL	74	78	.487	24	688	720	248	62	82	.281	.398	64	83	528	488	10	10	3.93	177	145	.971
PHI	69	83	.454	29	661	761	229	65	52	.271	.370	72	65	550	400	6	12	4.08	221	127	.965
CHI	69	85	.448	30	692	741	254	57	42	.279	.373	191	74	534	467	5	11	4.03	184	138	.971
BOS	61	91	.401	37	584	809	253	54	34	.261	.351	77	78	520	412	3	11	4.20	232	126	.963
					5887	5887	2010	554	441	.282	.388	741	609	4107	3601	60	93	3.99	1600	1095	.968

20

Detroit Tigers (1984)

SPARKY ANDERSON, MGR.

BATTING	G by POS	B	AGE	G	AB	R	H	2B	3B	HR	RBI	BB	SO	SB	BA	SA
DAVE BERGMAN	1B114, OF2	L	31	120	271	42	74	8	5	7	44	33	40	3	.273	.417
LOU WHITAKER	2B142	L	27	143	558	90	161	25	1	13	56	62	63	6	.289	.407
ALAN TRAMMELL	SS114, DH23	R	26	139	555	85	174	34	5	14	69	60	63	19	.314	.468
HOWARD JOHNSON	3B106, SS9, DH4, 1B1, OF1	B	23	116	355	43	88	14	1	12	50	40	67	10	.248	.394
KIRK GIBSON	OF139, DH6	L	27	149	531	92	150	23	10	27	91	63	103	29	.282	.516
CHET LEMON	OF140, DH1	R	29	141	509	77	146	34	6	20	76	51	83	5	.287	.495
LARRY HERNDON	OF117, DH4	R	30	125	407	52	114	18	5	7	43	32	63	6	.280	.400
LANCE PARRISH	C127, DH22	R	28	147	578	75	137	16	2	33	98	41	120	2	.237	.443
DARRELL EVANS	DH62, 1B47, 3B19	L	37	131	401	60	93	11	1	16	63	77	70	2	.232	.384
TOM BROOKENS	3B68, SS28, 2B26, DH1	R	30	113	224	32	55	11	4	5	26	19	33	6	.246	.397
BARBARO GARBEY	1B65, 3B20, DH17, OF10, 2B3	R	27	110	327	45	94	17	1	5	52	17	35	6	.287	.391
JOHNNY GRUBB	OF36, DH33	L	35	86	176	25	47	5	0	8	17	36	36	1	.267	.432
RUSTY KUNTZ	OF67, DH10	R	29	84	140	32	40	12	0	2	22	25	28	2	.286	.414
RUPPERT JONES	OF73, DH2	L	29	79	215	26	61	12	1	12	37	21	47	2	.284	.516
MARTY CASTILLO	3B33, C36, DH1	R	27	70	141	16	33	5	2	4	17	10	33	1	.234	.383
DOUG BAKER	SS39, 2B5, DH1	B	23	43	108	15	20	4	1	0	12	7	22	3	.185	.241
DWIGHT LOWRY	C31	L	26	32	45	8	11	2	0	2	7	3	11	0	.244	.422
ROD ALLEN	DH11, OF2	R	24	15	27	6	8	1	0	0	3	2	8	1	.296	.333
SCOTT EARL	2B14	R	23	14	35	3	4	0	1	0	1	0	9	1	.114	.171
NELSON SIMMONS	OF5, DH4	B	21	9	30	4	13	2	0	0	3	2	5	1	.433	.500
MIKE LAGA	1B4, DH4	L	24	9	11	1	6	0	0	0	1	1	2	0	.545	.545

PITCHING	T	AGE	W	L	PCT	SV	G	GS	CG	IP	H	BB	SO	ShO	ERA
JACK MORRIS	R	29	19	11	.633	0	35	35	9	240	221	87	148	1	3.60
DAN PETRY	R	25	18	8	.692	0	35	35	7	233	231	66	144	2	3.24
MILT WILCOX	R	34	17	8	.680	0	33	33	0	194	183	66	119	0	4.00
JUAN BERENQUER	R	29	11	10	.524	0	31	27	2	168	146	79	118	1	3.48
AURELIO LOPEZ	R	35	10	1	.909	14	71	0	0	138	109	52	94	0	2.94
WILLIE HERNANDEZ	L	28	9	3	.750	32	80	0	0	140	96	36	112	0	1.92
DAVE ROZEMA	R	26	7	6	.538	0	29	16	0	101	110	18	48	0	3.74
DOUG BAIT	R	34	5	3	.625	4	47	1	0	94	82	36	57	0	3.75
GLENN ABBOTT	R	33	3	4	.429	0	13	8	1	44	62	8	8	0	5.93
RANDY O'NEAL	R	23	2	1	.667	0	4	3	0	19	16	6	12	0	3.38
SID MONGE	L	33	1	0	1.000	0	19	0	0	36	40	12	19	0	4.25
BILL SCHERRER	L	26	1	0	1.000	0	18	0	0	19	14	8	16	0	1.89
ROGER MASON	R	25	1	1	.500	1	5	2	0	22	23	10	15	0	4.50
CARL WILLIS	R	23	0	2	.000	0	10	2	0	16	25	5	4	0	7.31

American League (1984)

	W	L	PCT	GB	R	OR	Batting						Pitching						Fielding		
							2B	3B	HR	BA	SA	SB	CG	BB	SO	ShO	SV	ERA	E	DP	FA
EAST																					
DET	104	58	.642		829	643	254	46	187	.271	.432	106	19	489	914	8	51	3.49	127	162	.979
TOR	89	73	.549	15	750	696	275	68	143	.273	.421	193	34	528	875	10	33	3.86	123	166	.980
NY	87	75	.537	17	758	679	276	32	130	.276	.405	62	15	518	992	12	43	3.78	142	177	.977
BOS	86	76	.531	18	810	764	259	45	181	.283	.441	37	40	517	927	12	32	4.18	143	127	.977
BAL	85	77	.525	19	681	667	234	23	160	.252	.391	51	48	512	713	13	32	3.72	123	166	.981
CLE	75	87	.463	29	761	766	222	39	123	.265	.384	126	21	545	803	7	35	4.25	146	163	.977
MIL	67	94	.416	36.5	641	734	232	36	96	.262	.370	52	13	480	785	7	41	4.06	136	156	.978

21

Brooklyn Dodgers (1955)

WALT ALSTON, MGR.

BATTING	G by POS	B	AGE	G	AB	R	H	2B	3B	HR	RBI	BB	SO	SB	BA	SA
GIL HODGES	1B139, OF16	R	31	150	546	75	158	24	5	27	102	80	91	2	.289	.500
JIM GILLIAM	2B99, OF46	B	26	147	538	110	134	20	8	7	40	70	37	15	.249	.355
PEE WEE REESE	SS142	R	36	145	553	99	156	29	4	10	61	78	60	8	.282	.403
JACKIE ROBINSON	3B84, OF10, 2B1, 1B1	R	36	105	317	51	81	6	2	8	36	61	18	12	.256	.363
CARL FURILLO	OF140	R	33	140	523	83	164	24	3	26	95	43	43	4	.314	.520
DUKE SNIDER	OF146	L	28	148	538	126	166	34	6	42	136	104	87	9	.309	.628
SANDY AMOROS	OF109	L	25	119	388	59	96	16	7	10	51	55	45	10	.247	.402
ROY CAMPANELLA	C121	R	33	123	446	81	142	20	1	32	107	56	41	2	.318	.583
DON HOAK	3B78	R	27	94	279	50	67	13	3	5	19	46	50	9	.240	.362
DON ZIMMER	2B62, SS21, 3B8	R	24	88	280	38	67	10	1	15	50	19	66	5	.239	.443
DON NEWCOMBE	P34	L	29	57	117	18	42	9	1	7	23	6	18	1	.359	.632
RUBE WALKER	C35	L	29	48	103	6	26	5	0	2	13	15	11	1	.252	.359
GEORGE SHUBA	OF9	L	30	44	51	8	14	2	0	1	8	11	10	0	.275	.373
FRANK KELLERT	1B22	R	30	39	80	12	26	4	2	4	19	9	10	0	.325	.575
DIXIE HOWELL	C13	R	36	16	42	2	11	4	0	0	5	1	7	0	.262	.357
WALT MORYN	OF7	L	29	11	19	3	5	1	0	1	3	5	4	0	.263	.474
BOB BORKOWSKI	OF9	R	29	9	19	2	2	0	0	0	0	1	6	0	.105	.105
BERT HAMRIC		L	27	2	1	0	0	0	0	0	0	0	1	0	.000	.000

PITCHING	T	AGE	W	L	PCT	SV	G	GS	CG	IP	H	BB	SO	ShO	ERA
DON NEWCOMBE	R	29	20	5	.800	0	34	31	17	234	222	38	143	1	3.19
CLEM LABINE	R	28	13	5	.722	11	60	8	1	144	121	55	67	0	3.25
CARL ERSKINE	R	28	11	8	.579	1	31	29	7	195	185	64	84	2	3.78
BILLY LOES	R	25	10	4	.714	0	22	19	6	128	116	46	85	0	3.59
JOHNNY PODRES	L	22	9	10	.474	0	27	24	5	159	160	57	114	2	3.96
DON BESSENT	R	24	8	1	.889	3	24	2	1	63	51	21	29	0	2.71
KARL SPOONER (SA)	L	24	8	6	.571	2	29	14	2	99	79	41	78	1	3.64
RUSS MEYER (XJ)	R	31	6	2	.750	0	18	11	2	73	86	31	26	1	5.42
ROGER CRAIG	R	24	5	3	.625	2	21	10	3	91	81	43	48	0	2.77
ED ROEBUCK	R	23	5	6	.455	12	47	0	0	84	96	24	33	0	4.71
SANDY KOUFAX (NJ)	L	19	2	2	.500	0	12	5	2	42	33	28	30	2	3.00
JOE BLACK	R	31	1	0	1.000	0	6	0	0	15	15	5	9	0	3.00
CHUCK TEMPLETON	L	23	0	1	.000	0	4	0	0	5	5	5	3	0	10.80
JIM HUGHES	R	32	0	2	.000	6	24	0	0	43	41	19	20	0	4.19
TOM LASORDA	L	27	0	0	.000	0	4	1	0	4	5	6	4	0	13.50

National League (1955)

							Batting						Pitching						Fielding		
	W	L	PCT	GB	R	OR	2B	3B	HR	BA	SA	SB	CG	BB	SO	ShO	SV	ERA	E	DP	FA
BKN	98	55	.641		857	650	230	44	201	.271	.448	79	46	483	773	11	37	3.68	133	156	.978
MIL	85	69	.552	13.5	743	668	219	55	182	.261	.427	42	61	591	654	5	12	3.85	152	155	.975
NY	80	74	.519	18.5	702	673	173	34	169	.260	.402	38	52	560	721	6	14	3.77	142	165	.976
PHI	77	77	.500	21.5	675	666	214	50	132	.255	.395	44	58	477	657	11	21	3.93	110	117	.981
CIN	75	79	.487	23.5	761	684	216	28	181	.270	.425	51	38	443	576	12	22	3.95	139	169	.977
CHI	72	81	.471	26	626	713	187	55	164	.247	.398	37	47	601	686	10	23	4.17	147	147	.975
STL	68	86	.442	30.5	654	757	228	36	143	.261	.400	64	42	549	730	10	15	4.56	146	152	.975
PIT	60	94	.390	38.5	560	767	210	60	91	.244	.361	22	41	536	622	5	16	4.39	166	175	.972
					5578	5578	1667	362	1253	.259	.407	377	385	4240	5419	70	160	4.04	1135	1236	.976

22

New York Yankees (1951)

CASEY STENGEL, MGR.

BATTING	G by POS	B	AGE	G	AB	R	H	2B	3B	HR	RBI	BB	SO	SB	BA	SA
JOHNNY MIZE	1B93	L	38	113	332	37	86	14	1	10	49	36	24	1	.259	.398
JERRY COLEMAN	2B102, SS18	R	26	121	362	48	90	11	2	3	43	31	36	6	.249	.315
PHIL RIZZUTO	SS144	R	33	144	540	87	148	21	6	2	43	58	27	18	.274	.346
BOBBY BROWN	3B90	L	26	103	313	44	84	15	2	6	51	47	18	1	.268	.387
HANK BAUER	OF107	R	28	118	348	53	103	19	3	10	54	42	39	5	.296	.454
JOE DIMAGGIO	OF113	R	36	116	415	72	109	22	4	12	71	61	36	0	.263	.422
GENE WOODLING	OF116	L	28	120	420	65	118	15	8	15	71	62	37	0	.281	.462
YOGI BERRA	C141	L	26	141	547	92	161	19	4	27	88	44	20	5	.294	.492
GIL MCDOUGALD	3B82, 2B55	R	23	131	402	72	123	23	4	14	63	56	54	14	.306	.488
JOE COLLINS	1B114, OF15	L	28	125	262	52	75	8	5	9	48	34	23	9	.286	.458
MICKEY MANTLE	OF86	B	19	96	341	61	91	11	5	13	65	43	74	8	.267	.443
JACKIE JENSEN	OF48	R	24	56	168	30	50	8	1	8	25	18	18	8	.298	.500
BILLY MARTIN	2B23, SS6, 3B2, OF1	R	23	51	58	10	15	1	2	0	2	4	9	0	.259	.345
JOHNNY HOPP	1B25	L	34	46	63	10	13	1	0	2	4	9	11	2	.206	.317
CLIFF MAPES	OF34	L	29	45	51	6	11	3	1	2	8	4	14	0	.216	.431
CHARLIE SILVERA	C18	R	26	18	51	5	14	3	0	1	7	5	3	0	.275	.392
BILLY JOHNSON	3B13	R	32	15	40	5	12	3	0	0	4	7	0	0	.300	.375
BOB CERV	OF9	R	25	12	28	4	6	1	0	0	2	4	6	0	.214	.250

PITCHING	T	AGE	W	L	PCT	SV	G	GS	CG	IP	H	BB	SO	ShO	ERA
ED LOPAT	L	33	21	9	.700	0	31	31	20	235	209	71	93	4	2.91
VIC RASCHI	R	32	21	10	.677	0	35	34	15	258	233	103	164	4	3.28
ALLIE REYNOLDS	R	36	17	8	.680	7	40	26	16	221	171	100	126	7	3.05
TOM MORGAN	R	21	9	3	.750	2	27	16	4	125	119	36	57	2	3.67
BOB KUZAVA	L	28	8	4	.667	5	23	8	4	82	76	27	50	1	2.41
JOE OSTROWSKI	L	34	6	4	.600	5	34	3	2	95	103	18	30	0	3.51
SPEC SHEA	R	30	5	5	.500	0	25	11	2	96	112	50	38	2	4.31
ART SCHALLOCK	L	27	3	1	.750	0	11	6	1	46	50	20	19	0	3.91
TOMMY BYRNE	L	31	2	1	.667	0	9	3	0	21	16	36	14	0	6.86
JOHNNY SAIN	R	33	2	1	.667	1	7	4	1	37	41	8	21	0	4.14
BOBBY HOGUE	R	30	1	0	1.000	0	7	0	0	7	4	3	2	0	0.00
TOM FERRICK	R	36	1	1	.500	1	9	0	0	12	21	7	3	0	7.50
STUBBY OVERMIRE	L	32	1	1	.500	0	15	4	1	45	50	18	14	0	4.60
JACK KRAMER	R	33	1	3	.250	0	19	3	0	41	46	21	15	0	4.61
BOB MUNCRIEF	R	35	0	0	.000	0	2	0	0	3	5	4	2	0	9.00
ERNIE NEVEL	R	31	0	0	.000	1	1	0	0	4	1	1	1	0	0.00
BOB PORTERFIELD	R	27	0	0	.000	0	2	0	0	3	5	3	2	0	15.00
BOB WIESLER (MS)	L	20	0	2	.000	0	4	3	0	9	13	11	3	0	14.00
FRED SANFORD	R	31	0	3	.000	0	11	2	0	27	15	25	10	0	3.67

American League (1951)

							Batting						Pitching						Fielding		
	W	L	PCT	GB	R	OR	2B	3B	HR	BA	SA	SB	CG	BB	SO	ShO	SV	ERA	E	DP	FA
NY	98	56	.636		798	621	208	48	140	.269	.408	78	66	562	664	24	22	3.56	144	190	.975
CLE	93	61	.604	5	696	594	208	35	140	.256	.389	52	76	577	642	10	19	3.38	134	151	.978
BOS	87	67	.565	11	804	725	233	32	127	.266	.392	20	46	599	658	7	24	4.14	141	184	.977
CHI	81	73	.526	17	714	644	229	64	86	.270	.385	99	74	549	572	11	14	3.50	151	176	.975
DET	73	81	.474	25	685	741	231	35	104	.265	.380	37	51	602	597	8	17	4.29	163	166	.973
PHI	70	84	.455	28	736	745	262	43	102	.262	.386	48	52	569	437	7	22	4.47	136	204	.978
WAS	62	92	.403	36	672	764	242	45	54	.263	.355	45	58	630	475	6	13	4.49	160	148	.973
STL	52	102	.338	46	611	882	223	47	86	.247	.357	35	56	801	550	5	9	5.17	172	179	.971
					5716	5716	1836	349	839	.262	.381	414	479	4889	4595	78	140	4.12	1201	1398	.975

23

New York Yankees (1950)

Casey Stengel, Mgr.

BATTING	G by POS	B	AGE	G	AB	R	H	2B	3B	HR	RBI	BB	SO	SB	BA	SA
JOHNNY MIZE	1B72	L	37	90	274	43	76	12	0	25	72	29	24	0	.277	.595
JERRY COLEMAN	2B152, SS6	R	25	153	522	69	150	19	6	6	69	67	38	3	.287	.381
PHIL RIZZUTO	SS155	R	32	155	617	125	200	36	7	7	66	91	38	12	.324	.439
BILLY JOHNSON	3B100, 1B5	R	31	108	327	44	85	16	2	6	40	42	30	1	.260	.376
HANK BAUER	OF110	R	27	113	415	72	133	16	2	13	70	33	41	2	.320	.463
JOE DIMAGGIO	OF137, 1B1	R	35	139	525	114	158	33	10	32	122	80	33	0	.301	.585
GENE WOODLING	OF118	L	27	122	449	81	127	20	10	6	60	69	31	5	.283	.412
YOGI BERRA	C148	L	25	151	597	116	192	30	6	28	124	55	12	4	.322	.533
CLIFF MAPES	OF102	L	28	108	356	60	88	14	6	12	61	47	61	1	.247	.421
JOE COLLINS	1B99, OF2	L	27	108	205	47	48	8	3	8	28	31	34	5	.234	.420
BOBBY BROWN	3B82	L	25	95	277	33	74	4	2	4	37	39	18	3	.267	.339
TOMMY HENRICH	(KJ) 1B34	L	37	73	151	20	41	6	8	6	34	27	6	0	.272	.536
JACKIE JENSEN	OF23	R	23	45	70	13	12	2	2	1	5	7	8	4	.171	.300
BILLY MARTIN	2B22, 3B1	R	22	34	36	10	9	1	0	1	8	3	3	0	.250	.361
JOHNNY HOPP	1B12, OF6	L	33	19	27	9	9	2	1	1	8	9	1	0	.333	.593
CHARLIE SILVERA	C15	R	25	18	25	2	4	0	0	0	1	1	2	0	.160	.160
JIM DELSING		L	24	12	10	2	4	0	0	0	2	2	0	0	.400	.400
RALPH HOUK	C9	R	30	10	9	0	1	1	0	0	1	0	2	0	.111	.222
JOHNNY LINDELL	OF6	R	33	7	21	2	4	0	0	0	2	4	2	0	.190	.190
SNUFFY STIRNWEISS	2B4, 3B1	R	31	7	2	0	0	0	0	0	0	0	0	0	.000	.000
DICK WAKEFIELD		L	29	3	2	0	1	0	0	0	1	1	1	0	.500	.500
HANK WORKMAN	1B1	L	24	2	5	1	1	0	0	0	0	0	1	0	.200	.200
GUS NIARHOS		R	29	1	0	0	0	0	0	0	0	0	0	0	.000	.000

PITCHING	T	AGE	W	L	PCT	SV	G	GS	CG	IP	H	BB	SO	ShO	ERA
VIC RASCHI	R	31	21	8	.724	1	33	32	17	257	232	116	155	2	3.99
ED LOPAT	L	32	18	8	.692	1	35	32	15	236	244	65	72	3	3.47
ALLIE REYNOLDS	R	35	16	12	.571	2	35	29	14	241	215	138	160	2	3.73
TOMMY BYRNE	L	30	15	9	.625	0	31	31	10	203	188	160	118	2	4.74
WHITEY FORD	L	21	9	1	.900	1	20	12	7	112	87	52	59	2	2.81
TOM FERRICK	R	35	8	4	.667	9	30	0	0	57	49	22	20	0	3.63
FRED SANFORD	R	30	5	4	.556	0	26	12	2	113	103	79	54	0	4.54
JOE PAGE	L	32	3	7	.300	13	37	0	0	55	66	31	33	0	5.07
JOE OSTROWSKI	L	33	1	1	.500	3	21	4	1	44	50	15	15	0	5.11
BOB PORTERFIELD (AJ-BJ)	R	26	1	1	.500	1	10	2	0	20	28	8	9	0	8.55
DON JOHNSON	R	23	1	0	1.000	0	8	0	0	18	35	12	9	0	10.00
DUANE PILLETTE	R	27	0	0	.000	0	4	0	0	7	9	3	4	0	1.29
ERNIE NEVEL	R	30	0	1	.000	0	3	1	0	6	10	6	3	0	10.50
LEW BURDETTE	R	23	0	0	.000	0	2	0	0	1	3	0	0	0	9.00
DAVE MADISON	R	29	0	0	.000	0	1	0	0	3	3	1	1	0	6.00

American League (1950)

							Batting						Pitching						Fielding		
	W	L	PCT	GB	R	OR	2B	3B	HR	BA	SA	SB	CG	BB	SO	ShO	SV	ERA	E	DP	FA
NY	98	56	.636		914	691	234	70	159	.282	.441	41	66	708	712	12	31	4.15	119	188	.980
DET	95	59	.617	3	837	713	285	50	114	.282	.417	23	72	553	576	9	20	4.12	120	194	.981
BOS	94	60	.610	4	1027	804	287	61	161	.302	.464	32	66	748	630	6	28	4.88	111	181	.981
CLE	92	62	.597	6	806	654	222	46	164	.269	.422	40	69	647	674	11	16	3.74	129	160	.978
WAS	67	87	.435	31	690	813	190	53	76	.260	.360	42	59	648	486	7	18	4.66	167	181	.972
CHI	60	94	.390	38	625	749	172	47	93	.260	.364	19	62	734	566	7	9	4.41	140	181	.977
STL	58	96	.377	40	684	916	235	43	106	.246	.370	39	56	651	448	7	14	5.20	196	155	.967
PHI	52	102	.338	46	670	913	204	53	100	.261	.378	42	50	729	466	3	18	5.49	155	208	.974
					6253	6253	1829	423	973	.271	.402	278	500	5418	4558	62	154	4.58	1137	1448	.976

24

Cleveland Indians (1920)

TRIS SPEAKER, MGR.

BATTING	G by POS	B	AGE	G	AB	R	H	2B	3B	HR	RBI	BB	SO	SB	BA	SA
DOC JOHNSTON	1B147	L	32	147	535	68	156	24	10	2	71	28	32	13	.292	.385
BILL WAMBSGANSS	2B153	R	26	153	565	83	138	16	11	1	55	54	26	9	.244	.317
RAY CHAPMAN (KB)	SS111	R	29	111	435	97	132	27	8	3	49	52	38	13	.303	.423
LARRY GARDNER	3B154	L	34	154	597	72	185	31	11	3	118	53	25	3	.310	.414
ELMER SMITH	OF129	L	27	129	456	82	144	37	10	12	103	53	35	5	.316	.520
TRIS SPEAKER	OF149	L	32	150	552	137	214	50	11	8	107	97	13	10	.388	.562
CHARLIE JAMIESON	OF98, 1B4	L	27	108	370	69	118	17	7	1	40	41	26	2	.319	.411
STEVE O'NEILL	C148	R	28	149	489	63	157	39	5	3	55	69	39	3	.321	.440
JACK GRANEY	OF47	L	34	62	152	31	45	11	1	0	13	27	21	4	.296	.382
SMOKEY JOE WOOD	OF54, P1	R	30	61	137	25	37	11	2	1	30	25	16	1	.270	.401
JOE EVANS	OF43, SS6	R	25	56	172	32	60	9	9	0	23	15	3	6	.349	.506
GEORGE BURNS	1B12	R	27	44	56	7	15	4	1	0	13	4	3	1	.268	.375
LES NUNAMAKER	C17, 1B6	R	31	34	54	10	18	3	3	0	14	4	5	1	.333	.500
HARRY LUNTE	SS21, 2B3	R	27	23	71	6	14	0	0	0	7	5	6	0	.197	.197
JOE SEWELL	SS22	L	21	22	70	14	23	4	1	0	12	9	4	1	.329	.414
PINCH THOMAS	C7	L	32	9	9	2	3	1	0	0	0	3	1	0	.333	.444
JOE HARRIS (DO) 29																

PITCHING	T	AGE	W	L	PCT	SV	G	GS	CG	IP	H	BB	SO	ShO	ERA
JIM BAGBY	R	30	31	12	.721	0	48	39	30	340	338	79	73	3	2.89
STAN COVELESKI	R	31	24	14	.632	2	41	37	26	315	284	65	133	3	2.48
RAY CALDWELL	R	32	20	10	.667	0	34	33	20	238	286	63	80	0	3.86
GUY MORTON	R	27	8	6	.571	1	29	17	5	137	140	57	72	1	4.47
DUSTER MAILS	L	24	7	0	1.000	0	9	8	6	63	54	18	25	2	1.85
GEORGE UHLE	R	21	4	5	.444	1	27	6	2	85	98	29	27	0	5.18
ELMER MYERS	R	26	2	4	.333	1	16	7	2	71	93	23	16	0	4.82
DICK NIEHAUS	L	27	1	2	.333	2	19	3	0	40	42	16	12	0	3.60
BOB CLARK	R	22	1	2	.333	0	11	2	2	42	59	13	8	1	3.43
JOE BOEHLING	L	29	0	1	.000	0	3	2	0	13	16	10	4	0	4.85
TONY FAETH	R	26	0	0	.000	0	13	0	0	25	31	20	14	0	4.32
TIM MURCHISON	L	23	0	0	.000	0	2	0	0	5	3	4	0	0	0.00
GEORGE ELLISON	R	23	0	0	.000	0	1	0	0	1	0	2	1	0	0.00
SMOKEY JOE WOOD	R	30	0	0	.000	0	1	0	0	2	4	2	1	0	22.50

American League (1920)

							Batting						Pitching						Fielding		
	W	L	PCT	GB	R	OR	2B	3B	HR	BA	SA	SB	CG	BB	SO	ShO	SV	ERA	E	DP	FA
CLE	98	56	.636		857	642	300	95	35	.303	.417	73	93	401	466	10	7	3.41	184	124	.971
CHI	96	58	.623	2	794	666	267	92	37	.294	.400	111	112	405	440	8	10	3.59	198	142	.968
NY	95	59	.617	3	839	629	268	71	115	.280	.426	64	88	420	480	16	11	3.31	194	129	.969
STL	76	77	.497	21.5	797	766	279	83	50	.308	.419	118	84	578	444	9	14	4.03	233	119	.963
BOS	72	81	.471	25.5	651	699	216	71	22	.269	.350	98	91	461	481	11	6	3.82	183	131	.972
WAS	68	84	.447	29	723	802	233	81	36	.291	.386	160	80	520	418	10	10	4.17	232	95	.963
DET	61	93	.396	37	651	832	228	72	30	.270	.359	76	76	561	483	7	7	4.04	230	95	.964
PHI	48	106	.312	50	555	831	219	49	44	.252	.338	50	81	461	423	5	2	3.93	265	126	.960
					5867	5867	2010	614	369	.283	.387	750	705	3807	3635	76	67	3.79	1719	961	.966

25

Detroit Tigers (1968)

MAYO SMITH, MGR.

BATTING	G by POS	B	AGE	G	AB	R	H	2B	3B	HR	RBI	BB	SO	SB	BA	SA
NORM CASH	1B117	L	33	127	411	50	108	15	1	25	63	39	70	1	.263	.487
DICK MCAULIFFE	2B148, SS5	L	28	151	570	95	142	24	10	16	56	82	99	8	.249	.411
RAY DYLER	SS111	R	29	111	215	13	29	6	1	1	12	20	59	0	.135	.186
DON WERT	3B150	R	29	150	536	44	107	15	1	12	37	37	79	0	.200	.299
JIM NORTHRUP	OF151	L	28	154	580	76	153	29	7	21	90	50	87	4	.264	.447
MICKEY STANLEY	OF130, 1B15, SS9, 2B1	R	25	153	583	88	151	16	6	11	60	42	57	4	.259	.364
WILLIE HORTON	OF139	R	25	143	512	68	146	20	2	36	85	49	110	0	.285	.543
BILL FREEHAN	C138, 1B21, OF1	R	26	155	540	73	142	24	2	25	84	65	64	0	.263	.454
AL KALINE	OF74, 1B22	R	33	102	327	49	94	14	1	10	53	55	39	6	.287	.428
DICK TRACEWSKI	SS51, 3B16, 2B14	R	33	90	212	30	33	3	1	4	15	24	51	3	.156	.236
TOM MATCHICK	SS59, 2B13, 1B6	L	24	80	227	18	46	6	2	3	14	10	46	0	.203	.286
GATES BROWN	OF17, 1B1	L	29	67	92	15	34	7	2	6	15	12	4	0	.370	.685
JIM PRICE	C42	R	26	64	132	12	23	4	0	3	13	13	14	0	.174	.273
WAYNE COMER	OF27, C1	R	24	48	48	8	6	0	1	1	3	2	7	0	.125	.229
EARL WILSON	P34	R	33	40	88	9	20	0	1	7	17	2	35	0	.227	.489
EDDIE MATHEWS	(XJ) 3B6, 1B6	L	36	31	52	4	11	0	0	3	8	5	12	0	.212	.385
DAVE CAMPBELL	2B5	R	26	9	8	1	1	0	0	1	2	1	3	0	.125	.500
LENNY GREEN	OF2	L	34	6	4	0	1	0	0	0	0	1	0	0	.250	.250
BOB CHRISTIAN	1B1, OF1	R	22	3	3	0	1	1	0	0	0	0	0	0	.333	.667

PITCHING	T	AGE	W	L	PCT	SV	G	GS	CG	IP	H	BB	SO	ShO	ERA
DENNY MCLAIN	R	24	31	6	.838	0	41	41	28	336	241	63	280	6	1.96
MICKEY LOLICH	L	27	17	9	.654	1	39	32	8	220	178	65	197	4	3.19
EARL WILSON	R	33	13	12	.520	0	34	33	10	224	192	65	168	3	2.85
JOE SPARMA	R	26	10	10	.500	0	34	31	7	182	169	77	110	1	3.71
JOHN HILLER	L	25	9	6	.600	2	39	12	4	128	92	51	78	1	2.39
FRED LASHER	R	26	5	1	.833	5	34	0	0	49	37	22	32	0	3.31
PAT DOBSON	R	26	5	8	.385	7	47	10	2	125	89	48	93	1	2.66
JON WARDEN	L	22	4	1	.800	3	28	0	0	37	30	15	25	0	3.65
DON MCMAHON	R	38	3	1	.750	1	20	0	0	36	22	10	33	0	2.00
DENNIS RIBANT	R	26	2	2	.500	1	14	0	0	24	20	10	7	0	2.25
DARYL PATTERSON	R	24	2	3	.400	7	38	1	0	68	53	27	49	0	2.12
LES CAIN	L	20	1	0	1.000	0	8	4	0	24	25	20	13	0	3.00
JOHN WYATT	R	33	1	0	1.000	2	22	0	0	30	26	11	25	0	2.40
ROY FACE	R	40	0	0	.000	0	2	0	0	1	2	1	1	0	0.00
JIM ROOKER	L	26	0	0	.000	0	2	0	0	5	4	1	4	0	3.60

American League (1968)

							Batting						Pitching						Fielding		
	W	L	PCT	GB	R	OR	2B	3B	HR	BA	SA	SB	CG	BB	SO	ShO	SV	ERA	E	DP	FA
DET	103	59	.636		671	492	190	39	185	.235	.385	26	59	486	1115	19	29	2.71	105	133	.983
BAL	91	71	.562	12	579	497	215	28	133	.225	.352	78	53	502	1044	16	31	2.66	120	131	.981
CLE	86	75	.534	16.5	516	504	210	36	75	.234	.327	115	48	540	1157	23	32	2.66	127	130	.979
BOS	86	76	.532	17	614	611	207	17	125	.236	.352	76	55	523	972	17	31	3.33	128	147	.979
NY	83	79	.512	20	536	531	154	34	109	.214	.318	90	45	424	831	14	27	2.79	139	142	.979
OAK	82	80	.506	21	569	544	192	40	94	.240	.343	147	45	505	997	18	29	2.94	145	136	.977
MIN	79	83	.488	24	562	546	207	41	105	.237	.350	98	46	414	996	14	29	2.89	170	117	.973
CAL	67	95	.414	36	498	615	170	33	83	.227	.318	62	29	519	869	11	31	3.43	140	156	.977
CHI	67	95	.414	36	463	527	169	33	71	.228	.311	90	20	451	834	11	40	2.75	151	152	.977
WAS	65	96	.404	37.5	524	665	160	37	124	.224	.336	29	26	517	826	11	28	3.64	148	144	.976
					5532	5532	1874	338	1104	.230	.339	811	426	4881	9641	154	307	2.98	1373	1388	.978

Bibliography

Allen, Lee. *The Cincinnati Reds*. New York: Putnam, 1948.

Allen, Maury. *Roger Maris: A Man For All Seasons*. New York: Donald I. Fine, 1986.

———. *Where Have You Gone, Joe DiMaggio*. New York: Dutton, 1975.

Anderson, Dave, and Murray Chass, Robert Creamer and Harold Rosenthal. *The Yankees: The Four Fabulous Eras of Baseball's Most Famous Team*. New York: Random House, 1980.

Anderson, Sparky, and Dan Ewald. *Bless You Boys: Diary of the Detroit Tigers' 1984 Season*. Chicago: Contemporary, 1984.

Anderson, Sparky, and Si Burick. *The Main Spark: Sparky Anderson and the Cincinnati Reds*. Garden City, N.Y.: Doubleday, 1978.

Appel, Martin, and Burt Goldblatt. *Baseball's Best: The Hall of Fame Gallery*. New York: McGraw-Hill, 1977.

Campanella, Roy. *It's Good To Be Alive*. Boston: Little, Brown, 1959.

Carmichael, John P. *My Greatest Day in Baseball*. New York: A.S. Barnes, 1945.

Cohen, Richard M., and David S. Neft. *The World Series*. New York: Collier, 1986.

Connor, Anthony J. *Voices From Cooperstown: Baseball's Hall of Famers Tell It Like It Was*. New York: Collier, 1982.

Creamer, Robert W. *Babe: The Legend Comes to Life*. New York: Simon and Schuster, 1974.

———. *Stengel: His Life and Times*. New York: Simon and Schuster, 1984.

Fleming, G.H. *Murderers' Row: The 1927 New York Yankees*. New York: William Morrow, 1985.

Frommer, Harvey. *Baseball's Greatest Managers*. New York: Franklin Watts, 1985.

Gallagher, Mark. *Day by Day in New York Yankees History*. New York: Leisure Press, 1983.

———. *Explosion! Mickey Mantle's Legendary Home Runs*. New York: Arbor House, 1987.

———. *The Yankee Encyclopedia*. New York: Leisure Press, 1982.

Golenbock, Peter. *Bums: An Oral History of the Brooklyn Dodgers*. New York: Putnam, 1984.

———. *Dynasty: The New York Yankees 1949-64*. Englewood Cliffs, N.J.: Prentice-Hall, 1975.

Graham, Frank. *The New York Yankees: An Informal History*. New York: Putnam, 1958.

Hollander, Zander, editor. *The Complete Handbook of Baseball*. New York: Signet/New American Library, 1976, 1985, 1987.

Honig, Donald. *The American League: An Illustrated History*. New York: Crown, 1983

———. *Baseball America: The Heroes of the Game and the Times of Their Glory*. New York: Macmillan, 1985.

———. *Baseball's 10 Greatest Teams*. New York: Macmillan, 1982.

———. *The Man in the Dugout*. Chicago: Follett, 1977.

———. *The National League: An Illustrated History*. New York: Crown, 1983.

———. *The New York Mets: The First Quarter Century*. New York: Crown, 1987.

———. *The New York Yankees: An Illustrated History*. New York: Crown, 1987.

———. *The World Series: An Illustrated History from 1903 to the Present*. New York: Crown, 1986.

James, Bill. *The Bill James Historical Baseball Abstract*. New York: Villard Books, 1986.

Karst, Gene, and Martin J. Jones, Jr. *Who's Who in Professional Baseball*. New Rochelle, N.Y.: Arlington House, 1973.

Kubek, Tony and Terry Pluto. *Sixty-One: The Team/The Record/The Men*. New York: Macmillan, 1987.

Lang, Jack, and Peter Simon. *The New York Mets: Twenty-five Years of Baseball Magic*. New York: Henry Holt, 1987.

Langford, Walter M. *Legends of Baseball: An Oral History of The Game's Golden Age*. South Bend, Ind.: Diamond Communications, 1987.

LeConte, Walter. *The Ultimate New York Yankees Record Book*. New York: Leisure Press, 1984.

Lieb, Fred. *Baseball As I Have Known It* Coward. New York: McCann & Geoghegan, 1977.

———. *Connie Mack: Grand Old Man of Baseball*. New York: Putnam, 1945.

———. *The St. Louis Cardinals: The Story of a Great Baseball Club*. New York: Putnam, 1944.

Lewis, Franklin. *The Cleveland Indians*. New York: Putnam, 1949.

Mack, Connie (Cornelius McsGillicuddy). *My 66 Years in the Big Leagues: The Great Story of America's National Game*. Philadelphia: John C. Winston, 1950.

Madden, Bill. *Daily News Scrapbook History of the New York Mets 1986 Season*. New York News, 1987.

Masterson, Dave, and Timm Boyle. *Baseball's Best: The MVPs*. Chicago: Contemporary, 1985.

Mantle, Mickey, and Herb Gluck. *The Mick*. Garden City, N.Y.: Doubleday, 1985.

Meany, Tom. *Baseball's Greatest Teams*. New York: A.S. Barnes, 1949.

Mosedale, John. *The Greatest Of All: The 1927 New York Yankees*. New York: The Dial Press, 1983.

Musial, Stan, and Bob Broeg. *Stan Musial: "The Man's" Own Story*. New York: Doubleday, 1964.

Neft, David S., and Richard M. Cohen. *The Sports Encyclopedia: Baseball*. Seventh Edition. New York: St. Martin's/Marek, 1987.

Official Baseball Guide. St. Louis: The Sporting News, 1987 and previous years. (Also, for various years: *Spalding Official Base Ball Guide* and *Reach Official Base Ball Guide*).

Reichler, Joseph L., editor. *The Baseball Encyclopedia*. Sixth Edition. New York: Macmillian, 1986.

Reidenbaugh, Lowell. *The Sporting News Selects Baseball's 25 Greatest Pennant Races*. St. Louis: The Sporting News, 1987.

Reidenbaugh, Lowell. *The Sporting News Selects Baseball's 50 Greatest Games*. St. Louis: The Sporting News, 1986.

Ritter, Lawrence S. *The Story of Baseball*. New York: William Morrow, 1983.

Ritter, Lawrence and Donald Honig. *The Image of Their Greatness: An Illustrated History of Baseball from 1900 to the Present*. New York: Crown, 1984.

———. *The 100 Greatest Baseball Players of All Time*. New York: Crown, 1986.

Salant, Nathan. *Superstars, stars, and just plain heroes*. New York: Stein and Day, 1982.

———. *This Date In New York Yankees History*. New York: Stein and Day, 1979.

Smith, Curt. *Voices of The Game: The First Full-Scale Overview of Baseball Broadcasting, 1921 to the Present*. South Bend, Ind.: Diamond Communications, 1987.

Smith, Ken. *Baseball's Hall of Fame*. New York: Grosset & Dunlap, 1979.

Smith, Robert. *Baseball's Hall of Fame*. New York: Bantam, 1973.

Thorn, John, and John B. Holway. *The Pitcher*. New York: Prentice Hall Press, 1987.

Tullius, John. *I'd Rather Be a Yankee: An Oral History of America's Most Loved and Most Hated Baseball Team*. New York: Macmillan, 1986.

Index